SOCIETY AND DEVELOPMENT IN CONTEMPORARY INDIA:

Geographical Perspectives

SOCIETY AND DEVELOPMENT IN CONTEMPORARY INDIA

Geographical Perspectives

Ranjit Tirtha

Professor of Geography
Eastern Michigan University

Drawings by:

Derwin Bell

Department of Geology
University of Michigan

HARLO PRESS   DETROIT, MICH.

Copyright © 1980 by Ranjit Tirtha

Library of Congress Catalog Card No. 80-83157

ISBN 0-8187-0040-8

Available from the author

Ranjit Tirtha

Department of Geography
Eastern Michigan University
Ypsilanti, Michigan 48197

Price: $12.50

Printed by Harlo Press, 50 Victor, Detroit, Michigan 48203

For Abha, Rajiva, Raka and Janak,
Friends and Partners in Life

CONTENTS

Section One
ENVIRONMENTAL AND HISTORICAL BACKGROUND   23

Section Two
SOCIETY AND CULTURE   87

LIST OF FIGURES

11

LIST OF TABLES

PREFACE

Purpose and Scope

As a young professor in India in the early 1960's struggling to develop an introductory course on India's socio-economic geography, I was immediately struck by a virtual absence of a textbook on the subject, excepting, of course, O. H. K. Spate's authoritative and comprehensive *India and Pakistan.* Spate's mammoth study was clearly for the more advanced students.

Since then, I have mulled over the idea of bringing out a concise geography with a non-regional orientation for the beginning college student. Subsequently, the publication of R. L. Singh's *India: A Regional Geography,* B. L. C. Johnson's *South Asia, India: Resources and Development,* and A. Dutt's *India: Resources, Potentialities and Planning* only reinforced my idea. Singh's book is distinctly regional in orientation, others either leave out or inadequately deal with themes that I consider to be essential to any socio-economic geography of contemporary India, namely: cultural-societal groupings, politico-geographical structures and developmental processes. This study is an attempt to focus primarily on these themes while seeking to present a geographical introduction to the contemporary or post-colonial India.

Organization and Special Features

The arrangement of the book is simple, perhaps too traditional. Following the two chapters on the historical and environmental background which forms Section One, the three chapters in Section Two deal with India's demographic structure, and the cultural-political patterns. Sec-

15

tion Three is a geographic analysis of the status of developmental progress achieved in contemporary India. A chapter on settlements and urbanization is included in this section, along with those on the agricultural economies, industrialization, planning, and trade as urbanization process represents an integral element of development.

India includes within its borders a large part of mankind. Its problems and efforts towards economic development are of vital importance to the rest of the world, particularly to the Third World, most of which shared similar colonial experience and problems of development. In its experiments in democracy, and in its struggle for unity, stability and survival, the Indian experience has become a model or a case-study for the Third World. For this reason particular attention is given to the analysis of selected Indian problems, like Family Planning Programs, Five Year Plans, the Green Revolution, Patterns of Religions, Linguistic States, the question of a National Language, the role of English Speech, and International Relations, which have relevance for the developing countries. Other topics like the Caste System and Kashmir Problem peculiar only to India and not directly of consequence to the Third World, are also critically analyzed. It is hoped that this book will be useful to general courses in South Asian Studies, and to lay persons interested in Indian current events in addition to the geography student. It is intended to be not just a geography but a general reader too. Hopefully, it should not only be read but enjoyed as well!

ACKNOWLEDGMENTS

Consciously or unconsciously this book has been derived from many sources, and influenced by several persons. Each chapter has been scrutinized by at least two authorities, usually more. Their review and advice immeasurably improved its quality as it progressed from an outline stage to that of a final version. Whatever deficiencies or errors remain, I alone am to blame.

First of all, I am particularly indebted to Professors Joseph Schwartzberg, John Brush, Norton Ginsburg, James McDonald and V. Nath. Each page bears the imprint of their advice. Professors Schwartzberg and Brush critically and exhaustively reviewed several chapters. Professor McDonald, my department colleague, deserves my special gratitude for his meticulous editorial help. Without his assistance I would have fallen into pitfalls usually encountered by a luckless new writer in an alien tongue. Dr. Nath's suggestions on Planning, Settlements and Industrialization provided insights which could only be claimed by a geographer who has had a long-standing first-hand experience in India's development process. The help of these authorities saved me from many errors and brought to my attention sources which I am sure I would have overlooked. Professor Ginsburg provided invaluable moral support throughout the book's transition from the first draft to its finished copy.

Secondly, I would like to put on record my appreciation of the Eastern Michigan University and particularly of my colleague and Chairman Professor Elwood Kureth for granting me occasional released time and sabbatical leave to work on the book. Finally, sincere thanks are due to the following for their manifold help at different stages of the book's growth: Professors Pradyumna Karan, Robert Ward, R. S. Ganapathy, Zaki Munshi, Dean Donald Drummond, and Dr. Om Sharma. Shirley Cabral and Rebekah Wale provided valuable secretarial help. To Susan Kleemann, a graduate student in geography, I owe special thanks for her ungrudging help ranging from the screening of errors to discussions on India's economy. My thanks are also due to Mr. Derwin Bell who prepared the illustrations and maps of a quality that will outlast the text that accompanies them. I am sure that I have omitted names, not because of any lack of appreciation on my part, but due to my imperfect memory. My special gratefulness to my family and children who had to undergo two years' of suffering as I plodded along toward a final draft and made heavy and unjustified demands on their time for innumerable little things connected with the smooth passage of the book. My father has always been a source of inspiration for writing. This publication marks the fulfillment of his wish made several years ago.

I also wish to express my gratefulness to Mr. L. W. Mueller, President of Harlo Press, for his continual advice and support in bringing out this book efficiently and quickly through the press.

Ranjit Tirtha

Summer, 1980

A WORD TO THE READERS

Maps are kept to a minimum. These are carefully designed to function as necessary adjuncts to the text as well as to whet reader's appetite to use a standard Altas like the *School Atlas* by the Government of India or *Goode's Atlas*. For an ambitious student, *A Historical Atlas of South Asia* edited by Joseph E. Schwartzberg is particularly recommended for its wealth of scholarship and extensive cartographic record of India's socio-economic and political history.

Spellings usually conform to the *School Atlas* mentioned above or the publications of the Census of India. Distances, weights, measures, volumes generally follow the international metric systems. Unless otherwise indicated chloropleth maps represent data by districts. The use of footnotes has been eschewed.

SOCIETY AND DEVELOPMENT IN CONTEMPORARY INDIA:

Geographical Perspectives

SECTION ONE

Environmental
and
Historical Background

CHAPTER 1

SPATIAL
AND PHYSICAL FRAMEWORK

The triangular peninsula jutting into the Indian Ocean with its apex pointing southward from the continent of Asia, delineated in the north by the steeply rising Himalaya Mountains, and in the east and west by its flanking off-shoots, has been historically known as the Indian subcontinent. Within the limits thus marked off by these physical features are included the countries of Pakistan, Bangladesh, Nepal, Bhutan, Sri Lanka, and India. The cultural and political fortunes of these countries have been so intertwined as to define the area in terms of an Indian Culture Realm.

In area and size, India is the largest of these political constituents and the most centrally located and is apparently destined to play a major role on the subcontinent (Figure 1.1). The Indian mainland (excepting the island groups of Andaman-Nicobars, and Lakshadweep, in the Bay of Bengal and the Arabian Sea) lies between 8° and 37° North, and 68°-97° East, the Tropic of Cancer roughly dividing the landmass into two unequal parts. To its north the Himalayan kingdoms of Nepal and Bhutan are sandwiched between the Tibetan Region of the People's Republic of China and the plains of North India. The small Himalayan principality of Sikkim which lies between Nepal and Bhutan was incorporated into India in 1975. In the northwest, India shares a sensitive and occasionally volatile boundary with Pakistan, created across the Indus Basin as a consequence of the partitioning of the subcontinent in 1947. The former principality of Jammu and Kashmir has been disputed between India and Pakistan since their births. It has been *de facto* partitioned between the two since 1950. In the north-

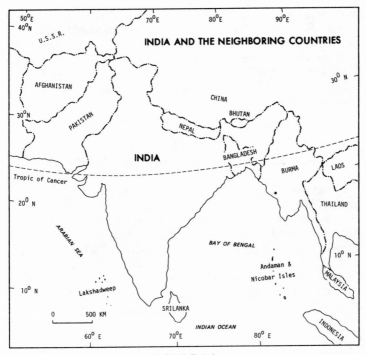

FIGURE 1.1

east, beyond the eastern offshoots of the Himalaya, lies Burma. Bangladesh, which broke off from Pakistan in 1972 as an independent nation, is almost an enclave within India, landlocked between Indian territory except to the south where it is accessible through the Bay of Bengal. Sri Lanka lies just off India's southern tip in the Indian Ocean. Over 20,000 square miles of disputed territory lies along India's 9,425 mile land-border shared with China in the north and northeast. This mountainous and inhospitable territory has been the scene of Sino-Indian hostilities.

The coastline of over 3,500 miles along the Arabian Sea in the west and Bay of Bengal in the east, the two arms of the Indian Ocean, has only sporadically remained active in trade or communications. Despite vigorous trans-oceanic connections established by Indian kings in Southeast Asia and the implanting of Indian art, architecture, religions, and social traditions in these colonies, Indian coasts effectively insulated the Indian culture "realm" from the outside world. Since the Indian Ocean has remained a natural defensive base for the subcontinent, any power-play in it, such as the consolidation of the U.S. naval base at Diego Garcia or the Soviet movements off the coast of East Africa, is looked upon with apprehensive disfavor by the Indian administration.

INDIA
A GEOGRAPHICAL/HISTORICAL EXPRESSION

Virtually isolated from the two mainstreams of Asian history, the civilization of China and the Islamic world of the Middle East, the Indian culture essentially represents a third stream of Asian history. Originating with the Aryanization of the Indo-Ganga basin as early as 1500-2000 B.C., and largely based on the subsequent development of Hindu thought, early Indian civilization was broadened by the incorporation of religious, artistic, political, and social mores of invaders from the west, and gradually evolved throughout ancient, medieval and modern times into a distinctive Indian culture.

Ancient Greeks used the term "Indoi" for the people living near the Indos (Indus) River, adopted apparently from the Sindhu of the ancient Sanskrit texts. The land of the Indois represented the Indian subcontinent, all the area lying east of the Suleiman Range. The later Muslim versions became "Hindu" for the people, and "Hindustan" for the area, more specifically for the territory of Muslim consolidation in north India. The southern peninsular part was *Dakshinapatha* (literally, the south) or Deccan in ancient Hindu writings. The entire subcontinent was styled as *Bharata Varsha* by ancient Hindu writers, the land of the legendary King Bharata, stretching from Kashmir in the north to the southernmost tip, and Afghanistan in the west to Assam in the east. The concept of Bharata Varsha, or a pan-India, has remained eversince an ideal among India's rulers.

"India" as a geographic expression has its base in the territorial layout of the subcontinent, and the distribution of physical features within it. Effectively contained within the physical parameters, the subcontinent has been insulated from the historic forces emanating from China and the Middle East. Isolation from the north has been more complete. Except for localized trade between India and Tibet, and the diffusion of Mahayana Buddhism, the India-China exchange was minimal over the high, inaccessible, snow-clad passes and difficult terrain. Even Buddhism travelled to China centuries after its origin in India and diffusion to other lands. The two civilizations matured independently and exclusively, the Himalayan barriers or oceans separating the two. In fact, the Indians and the Chinese both remained oriented largely inward, exclusive, with little interest in commerce. Contacts over the rain-swept, malarial, disease-ridden forests of the Assam hills in the northeast segment of the Himalaya, and its eastern offshoots separating the subcontinent from Burma were also slight. Buddhism diffused to Burma and southeast Asia by sea.

Isolation has been less restrictive on the western and northwestern side. Lying to the east of the plateaus of Afghanistan and Iran, several of the mountains, the Suleiman, the Hindu Kush and the Kirthar are, although rocky, bare and harsh in appearance, breached by several accessible passes. A succession of invasions flowed through these passes (the Khyber and the Bolan being more notable), starting from the distant Aryans in 1500 B.C. to the Mughals in the 15th century. In the course of time, the invaders became Indianized, absorbed much of the social systems, and transmitted some of theirs to the existing Indian mores. Beyond these ranges, and in part to the south, lie the inhospitable and dry lands of the tribal groups.

Trans-oceanic contacts between India and other places have been, however, notable, especially with the Mediterranean World and southeast Asia. As early as the 1st century A.D. flourishing trade in Indian spices, ivory, silks, and precious stones existed between South Indian ports of Malabar and the Roman ports. Even prior to that, commercial contacts between the Indus Valley Civilization and the Sumerians in 2500 B.C. had been established. In the 11th and 12th centuries, Hindu kings, traders, priests and Buddhist missionaries went to Indonesia, Burma, Cambodia, Thailand and Malaya. Large Hindu empires were set up. Indian social and political institutions, legal systems, art forms and architectural monuments still persist there in varying forms. The temple town of Angkor Vat in Kampuchea Republic (Cambodia) and Borabudor in Java are eloquent testimonies to the times of the Indian colonization in southeast Asia. During the 15th and 16th centuries European powers encroached upon Indian territories through the ocean routes. The culmination of European colonial expansion was the consolidation of a vast British empire over the subcontinent in the later 17th century. The geographical and cultural expression "India" was indeed perpetuated by the establishment of a long history of a single administration, political systems and economic linkage under the British. Prior to that, inter-oceanic relations between India and the outside were brief, scarce, and inconsequential.

The lack of an integrated and continuing pan-Indian administration during the long and chequered history of the subcontinent is reflected in its regional diversities of language, religion, and race. Despite the obvious contradictions and diversities, an undercurrent of Indian civilization kept social and political life as a functioning identity for all historic times. Even after the emergence of the three major countries of Pakistan, Bangladesh and India in the aftermath of the post-colonial period, the historical and geographical expression "India" for the subcontinent clearly defined as it is by physical and human forces, remains largely valid. The three major countries of south Asia have shared a common historical, artistic and linguistic heritage and face common problems in the future. Common boundaries, cultural associations and economic links would continue to intertwine their futures.

PHYSICAL FRAMEWORK

The arrangement of relief features of the subcontinent is relatively simple, if grand, in design (Figure 1.2). The southern peninsular part, occupied mostly by the Deccan Plateau, is an old, stable block of subdued relief sloping gently toward the east coast. It is flanked on both the eastern and western sides by mountain ranges. In the northern parameters of the subcontinent lie the long, sweeping mountain chain of the Himalaya with its western and eastern off-

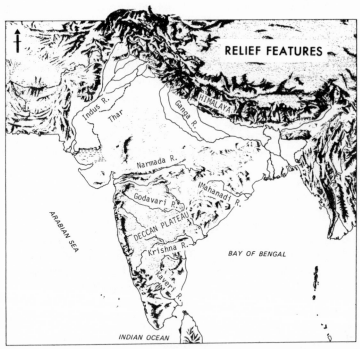

FIGURE 1.2

shoots, and containing several ranges of young folded, deeply dissected and unstable structures attaining the world's
highest elevations. Between the two lies the vast alluvial
plains of the Indo-Ganga river basins, which, according to
geologists, resulted from the in-filling of the structural
trough (a long, deep depression) between the peninsular
block of Deccan to the south, and the northern mountain
ranges of the Himalaya. Within this rather simplistic tripar-
tite division exist diversities in structure, drainage, soil conditions, topography and geologic history.

According to the most accepted geological theory, the
Deccan tableland was once a part of an ancient supercontinent, Gondwanaland, which included the present-day continents of Africa, Australia, Antartica and parts of Brazil in
South America as well. Its subsequent fracturing and movement, and the formation of mountains and other relief

features are attributed to continental drift or movements of the plates which composed the ancient supercontinent. Such forced are even now going on. To the north of Gondwanaland was another vast plate of ancient Angaraland. Between these two ancient supercontinents existed a huge geosynclinal depression, into which were poured sediments by rivers of the two flanking supercontinents. The colossal infilling of the sediment in the depression disturbed the gravity equilibrium of the crust or the plates of the continents, creating forces of mountain building. The northern plate advanced toward Gondwanaland, and the sediments of the intervening trough or "geosyncline" were buckled up to form the present-day Himalaya. As the Himalaya was rising under the impact of the advancing plate from the north, erosional processes were removing sediments for deposition in the marine gulfs separating the northern plate from the southern one. The present-day Indo-Ganga Plains resulted from the deposition and infilling by the sediments in the geosyncline subsequent to the erosional history of the mountains. These processes are still continuing, and the deposits from the Himalaya are being accumulated in the Indo-Ganga plains. As the plains are being depressed by the sediments produced by the continued erosion of the Himalaya, the lightened Himalaya is rising to maintain, in geologic terminology, an isostatic equilibrium. The present-day Deccan Plateau is the ruptured segment of the Gondwanaland plate.

The Himalaya Mountain System

The Himalaya forms a part of an extensive and complex mountain system, the hub of which lies in Central Asia in the Pamir Knot. From Pamir it swings in an unbroken arc of several parallel ranges for over 1500 miles, rising abruptly almost like a wall flanking the northern, western, and eastern borders of the Indian subcontinent. Its central and the highest range, the Great Himalaya, contains 40 peaks which rise to altitudes between 25,000 and 29,000 feet.

These ranges, together with the high-altitude Tibetan Plateau further north, have exercised profound climatic and cultural influences on the subcontinent. The mountains act as an effective barrier blocking the inflow of cold, dry air masses in north India during winter. During summer it

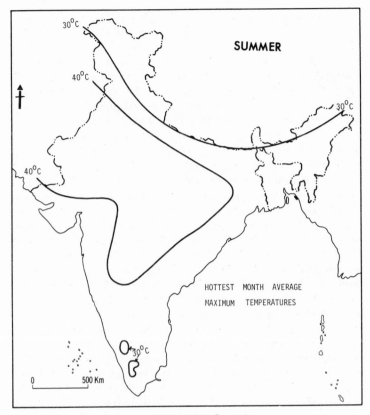

FIGURE 1.3

deflects the moist monsoon winds along its southern flanks, and causes the moist winds to precipitate in the North Indian Plains and the Brahmaputra Valley. The Himalaya also causes the jet-stream circulation of the upper atmosphere to assume a main course south of it in winter, and helps the passage of a series of cyclonic storms (Figure 1.4). The various meteorological factors, the passage of jet streams in summer, the monsoonal precipitation in summer, coupled with the high altitudes of the Himalayan ranges, all contribute to the accumulation of large amounts of snow and the formation of permanent ice fields and glaciers in the Great Himalayan ranges. The Himalaya thus becomes the feeding ground of major perennial rivers which are extensively utilized for year-round irrigation in the subcontinent.

In structure and relief, the Himalaya offers a sharp contrast to the Deccan Plateau. Its topography is youthful, rugged and dissected, containing V-shaped valleys in highly folded and faulted structures resulting from their uplifts and compressions and the youthful erosional processes prevailing on their surfaces whereas relief of the Deccan Plateau is slight and the rock-structures stable and old. The unusually high elevations of the Himalaya have resulted from the mountain building forces during Tertiary times in geologic history (about 60-65 million years ago). The intense folds and compression of rocks suggest a buckling up and uplifting of enormous sedimentary strata once these were deposited in a geosynclinal depression or *Tethys*. The material was compressed in the form of rockwaves when Angaraland, the plate of the northern supercontinent moved toward Gondwanaland. Marine fossils embedded in the Himalaya at 14,000 to 17,000 feet altitudes indicate the existence of such an ancient Tethys ocean, separating the two ancient supercontinents, at the location of the present day Himalaya. The movement of the Angaraland, and subsequent compression and buckling of the sediments previously deposited by rivers from the supercontinents into the Tethys, as indicated earlier, resulted in the Himalaya. The trendlines as reflected in rock structures and surface features of the Himalaya run parallel to the margins of the north Indian plains, and suggest that the kinetic forces producing the Himalaya were transverse in direction, i.e., came from the north. Subsequent geologic history has been explained by the gravity studies. It has been argued that the forces of isostatic equilibrium were generated by the removal of sediment from the mountain range, and the infilling of the Tethys. The Himalaya is still active in places and suggests the relative youthfulness of the Himalaya.

The Himalaya is arranged in parallel ranges. The ranges of the Main or Great Himalaya lie immediately to the south of the Tibetan Plateau and contain the highest elevations (several peaks over 25,000 feet in altitude). The Inner or Lesser Himalaya lies to its south is about 50 miles in length and contains series of overthrust folds and jagged relief with several interconnected ridges, rising to 10,000 to 15,000 feet. The Outer Himalaya consists of low-lying ranges of altitudes ranging between 2,000 and 3,000 feet at the foothills of the previous two. In the western segment of the Outer Himalaya such hills are known as Siwalik hills, which essentially form a zone of low basins and depressions or "dunes." Their origin has been ascribed to the recent warping and faulting of the unconsolidated gravely materials of the southern parts of the Himalaya.

Often the Himalaya has been divided in longitudinal sections, from west to east, the Kashmir Himalaya, the Punjab Himalaya, Kumaon Himalaya, the Central or Nepal Himalaya, Sikkim Himalaya, Bhutan Himalaya, and the Assam Himalaya. These sectional divisions are purely locational and exhibit the general pattern of the parallel ranges. At various places within the ranges erosional and structural valleys are found. Good examples of these valleys are: in Kashmir, the Vale of Kashmir, and in the Central Himalaya, the Kathmandu Valley. The Vale of Kashmir is a synclinal depression covered by a broad floor of young deposits, the center of which is a flood-plain of Jhelum River. To the south the valley is enclosed by a mountain range Pir Panjal, blocking the valley's accessibility to India. To the north of the valley lies the Great Himalayan chains of Zaskar, Ladakh and Karakoram, often attaining elevations of over 20,000 feet. Like most Himalayan structures, these are youthful, and are deeply dissected and folded. In the northwest corner of the continent these converge toward the Pamir Knot.

The Himalaya contains only a few passes separating the subcontinent from the Tibetan Plateau, most lying at high altitudes of 12,000 and 13,000 feet, passable only during a brief period of summer, and are difficult to transverse. Their climatic and cultural influence was to seal off the subcontinent from the north.

The western flanks of the Himalaya are along the Afghanistan-Pakistan frontier. The two major arc systems are the Suleiman and Kirthar ranges. Their northeast-southwest trend-line, with convexity eastward suggests that a compressional force acted from the west when these mountains were being formed. Although similar in structure to the Himalaya, these are low in relief and elevation, rising at their highest to 11,000 feet. Historically, the several easily traversable passes in these bare and rocky ranges have frequently been used by invaders from the west. The eastern flanks of the Himalaya lie close to the India-Burma border, and often form a succession of tangled, arcuate north-south ranges, such as the Patkai and Naga mountains. Rarely rising over 7,000 feet in altitude, the highest peak being 12,500 feet, the mountains are clothed with dense forests, which, coupled with difficult terrain, have acted as an effective physical and cultural barrier between India and Burma.

The Indo-Ganga Plains

The vast plains of northern India, Pakistan and Bangladesh form a major topographic and physiographic division of the subcontinent's landscapes, the other two being the Himalaya Mountain system and the Deccan Plateau. These lowlands include the basins of the two major river systems of northern India, the Ganga and the Indus, together with their numerous tributaries. Occupying only one-fifth of the area, but supporting half the population of southern Asia, the plains have historically been the nerve-center of their political, cultural and economic activities.

In sheer scale, the plains are truly immense, covering a crescent-shaped area of over 400,000 square miles, 1,900 miles long and 100-200 miles wide, stretching from the Indus Delta in the west through the Plains of Pakistan and Ganga Plains in northern India to the Ganga-Brahmaputra Delta in Bangladesh. Though smaller than the structural plains of North America, the Indo-Ganga Plains form the largest stretch of alluvial plain in the world.

Geologically, the plains belong to the Tertiary period, the youngest element in the structure of the subcontinent. The vast plains were built by deposits in a depression, the Tethys or geosynclinal sea, lying between the Himalaya in the north and the peninsular block of Deccan Plateau in the south. Gradually the Tethys was filled up by the sediments brought by streams from the northern and southern blocks on either side of the geosynclinal depression, burying the hard rocks of the peninsular Deccan block except in a few places, such as Aravalli hills in Rajasthan State, the Ridge near Delhi, and the Shillong mountains in Assam State. While the process of sediment in-filling was going on, the peninsular block to the south was forced downward by tectonic pressures exerted by the northern block. The sediments deposited are among the deepest in the alluvial plains of the world, reaching as much as 6,500 feet. The depths vary, from over 5,000 feet in the Ganga Delta to 1,500-2,000 feet in the basin of the Indus River. The alluvium (fine sediments) is so deep that for miles one may not find a small stone on the surface in the lower Ganga basin. The Ganga delta is still sinking under the continuing sedimentation.

Topographically, these vast plains are flat for hundreds of miles, forming a long, nearly straight horizon. The flat, even monotony of the plains is relieved only by minor local modifications in relief, introduced by river bluffs, hollows, and at places, by badlands formed by gully erosion. Notable examples of badland relief formed by gully erosion are in the lower Chambal basin. Relief gradients are so gentle that the water-parting between the basins of the Ganga and Indus rivers, lying about 100 miles northwest of Delhi, is only 900 feet in elevation above sea level, although it is located 900 miles from the Arabian Sea and over 1,000 miles from the Bay of Bengal. From this water-divide, the Ganga plain slopes gently to the southeast to the sea with a gradient of 11-12 inches per mile, and the gradient of the Indus plain which slopes southwestward from the water-divide is only a little greater.

The Indo-Ganga topography consists, in general, of a succession of floodplains and the slightly higher ground of 100 to 200 feet of local relief in the interfluves (known as *doabs*) lying away from the rivers. These bluffs are not given to periodic flooding and are composed of older alluvium (*kankar*) and may contain gravels, sand and coarser materials. The newer alluvium (*bhangar*) lies in the immediate vicinity of the river courses, natural levees and the adjoining territory. Gentle gradients help promote river meanders, the occasional shifting of river courses, and the creation of meander scars and ox-bow marshes. As the rivers gently meander through their journey towards the deltas, they have become braided into several channels forming large aggradational plains. The Indus and its tributaries are aligned approximately north-southward. The Ganga and its tributaries run parallel to the water-divide between the two river basins, but swing to the east toward the Bay of Bengal. The southern tributaries of the Ganga river run southwest to northeast. In general, the rivers have cut into their right banks due to the rotation of the earth, leaving these higher in elevation than the left banks. It is thus easier to build irrigation channels from the left banks.

The Ganga receives its greatest volume from its northern snow fed Himalayan tributaries. Its volume is progressively increased as it proceeds towards the delta in area of increasing rainfall. In contrast, the Indus River traverses an area of decreasing rainfall, receiving little flow from the west. Its Himalayan tributaries lie mostly north of latitude 28° N. In its lower journey it passes through semi-arid territory. Most of the Indus alluvium is deposited early, leaving the lower basin comparatively less fertile.

At the foot of the Himalaya in the Ganga basin lies an irregular zone of low, piedmont alluvial fans, an area of marshy underground seepage, known as the *Tarai*. This malarial marshland has long been a neglected area. The work of draining and mosquito control is still in its infancy in this potentially fertile and cultivable area.

East of the lower Indus Basin lies the Rajastan or *Thar* desert, cutting across the Indo-Pakistani border. Much of its surface is covered by a veneer of loose soil, interrupted by rocky projections and wind-blown sandy ridges. Underlying this veneer, hard, crystalline rocks similar to those of the Deccan Plateau are found. The Aravalli range belongs to this category. A prehistoric river channel, the Ghaggar, passes through the desert. It can be traced for 600 miles from the Punjab in India to Sind in Pakistan. The Ghaggar basin once drained into the Rann of Kutch, and probably formed a part of the Indus Basin. The Rann is now a salty marshland inundated seasonally during the summer monsoon season.

The partitioning of the subcontinent in 1947 created physical and human problems, both in the Ganga-Brahmaputra Delta as well as the Middle Indus Basin. The main problem hinged around the division of the waters between the new countries. In the Punjab or the traditional land of the five tributaries of the Indus River, political partitioning created problems of water irrigation. During the British occupation a series of irrigation canals were contructed, capitalizing on the constant slope slantwise across the interfluves. After partition, Pakistan was left at the mercy of India for the flow of waters which originated from area controlled by India. The Indus Waters Agreement in 1960 resolved the problem by specific allocations.

The Deccan Plateau

The peninsular part of the subcontinent is mostly a raised tableland of old, stable structure, known generally as the Deccan Plateau. The western and northwestern parts of the plateau extend up to Kutch in Gujarat and the Aravalli Range in Rajastan. Its northern limits run parallel to and 50 miles south of the course of Ganga-Yamuna rivers. Several outliers of the plateau rise above the sediments of the Indo-Ganga plains, e.g., Delhi Ridge, Kirana Hills (in Pakistan) and Shillong Hills. Almost the entire peninsula south of the line formed by the Vindhya-Satpura-Mahadeo hills is termed the Deccan Plateau.

The tableland is, in fact, made up of several plateaus of subdued relief, with elevations ranging between 1000 and 3000 feet above sea level, flanked on the west and east sides by the coastal ranges. In the south, where the two coastal ranges appear to merge, are two high granitic massifs, the Nilgiri Hills and the Caradamon Hills, rising to elevations of about 8500 feet. The western flanking ranges, the Western Ghats or the Sahyadri Mountains rise as a bold escarpment of 4000 to 5000 feet above the western coast, leaving a very narrow coastal plain. Toward the interior, the Western Ghats assume a hill-like appearance. The ranges flanking the eastern side of the Deccan Plateau are the Eastern Ghats and are not as rugged, or high, or as continuous as the Western Ghats. These are merely discontinuous hills with elevations between 2000-2500 feet. In their northern section, the Eastern Ghats and the adjoining interior plateau area contain several minerals, notably iron ore, manganese and mica.

Geologically, the Deccan Plateau is the oldest part of the subcontinent, a "shield" of old, stable rocks. Gneisses and schists dating from Pre-Cambrian times (500-2000 million years ago), cover half of its area. The structures are similar to the Laurentian uplands of Canada, and plateaus of South Africa and western Australia. Other common rock formations of the Deccan Plateau are as old as 200-500 million years.

Surface configuration consists of undulating hills with

rounded, broad, low summits of peneplanes and residual blocks. The general slope, influenced in part by fracturing and tilting, is toward the east. The major rivers, Godavari, Krishna and Kaveri start within 50 miles of the Arabian Sea and flow eastward for distances of 300 to 600 miles across the tableland to the Bay of Bengal. The rivers flow in broad, shallow valleys, their grading disturbed by gaps and enclosed escarpments. Entirely dependent on rainfall, these are nearly dry in the hot weather, and are of little value for irrigation. The north central section of the Deccan Plateau is tilted northward, resulting perhaps from the tectonic pressures of the ancient northern supercontinent, and the drainage is toward the Ganga Basin (Rivers Son and Chambal) of the North Indian Plains.

The northwestern part of the Deccan Plateau, about 250,000 square miles, is covered by thick horizontal beds of lavas, the Deccan Trap. The average thickness is 2000 to 5000 feet. It is thought that in times of Tertiary crustal instability associated with the formation of the Himalaya, a succession of lava flows spread over the area, solidifying into the Trap. The lava formations have been eroded and give the impression of a mesa-like topography. In the northern limits of the Deccan Plateau, the two mountain ranges, the Vindhya and the Satpura, rise in sharp escarpments. The Satpura is a structurally uplifted area, a horst, whereas the river Tapti flows in a structural trough or graben; both run parallel to the Narmada river, and drain westward to the Arabian sea, unlike most rivers of the Deccan Plateau. The Narmada Tapti waterways have been the historic routeways from the Bay of Cambay on the western coast to Varanasi in Ganga plains. The Aravalli mountains in the Rajasthan desert approximately define the northwestern limits of the Deccan Plateau. The Aravalli is a worn-out stump of the ancient mountains and rises to 5,600 feet at its highest altitude.

The peninsula has almost continuous coastal plains on its margins, developed from the alluvial fans deposited by the rivers of the plateau. The eastern plains are broader, especially where the deltas have been built by the east flowing rivers, and progression of the deltaic plains is still continuing. The west coast is narrower, except around the gulf of Cambay, and at its extreme southern tip in Kerala. The water-divide between the Arabian Sea and Bay of Bengal drainage is close to the Arabian Sea, with few, shorter west-coast rivers, leaving little scope for their depositional action. A large amount of India's mineral wealth is found in the Deccan Plateau. The richest area is in its northeastern section, the Chota Nagpur region. Several coalfields lie in the down-faulted sedimentary rocks of Chota Nagpur region in South Bihar. Other mineral-rich areas of the Deccan Plateau are in Mahanadi Valley and north Andhra Pradesh. In addition, mica, iron ore, manganese, and gold are obtained in several parts of Deccan in Orissa, Madhya Pradesh, Andhra Pradesh, Karnataka, and eastern Maharashtra. Most mineral deposits are associated with the metamorphosed Cambrian rocks.

CLIMATIC CHARACTERISTICS

A most distinguishing characteristic of South Asia's climate is the prevalence of monsoonal (from the Arabic word *mausim* meaning "season"), or seasonal wind system, the alternating dry cold continental winds in winter and water-laden tropical, oceanic winds in summer. This term is applicable to most, but not all, parts of the subcontinent. This idealized perception of the monsoon climate best applies to the areas of northern and western India and Pakistan. In the extreme south, in Kerala, tropical rain-forest climate prevails, whereas along the southern parts of the eastern coast, the retreating monsoon bring rainfall in winter after picking up moisture over the Bay of Bengal. In the northwestern parts of the subcontinent, in Pakistan and the Punjab plains, western disturbances bring winter rainfall. These exceptions apart, the monsoonal winds have almost a universal effect, and are of great human significance. Most summer weather crops (*kharif*) depend on rainfall associated with the monsoon winds. Any major deviation from the seasonal rhythm, a late arrival or an early retreat of the monsoons, resulting in a deficiency of rain, can well spell foodgrain shortages or even famine.

In general, the monsoon may be described as similar but on a larger, continental scale, the land-and-sea breeze mechanism. It consists of annual reversal of seasonal wind systems, between cool, dry land-winds in winter and warm, rain-bearing winds in summer. Traditional hypotheses ascribe their origin to the development of a distinct thermal low-pressure system over the Indus plains during summer, effectively separated from the Central Asian counterpart by the Himalaya and the Tibetan Plateau. This results in a gigantic monsoonal indraught of the moist winds of the Arabian Sea and the Bay of Bengal during summer. This Indus low-pressure system induces the indraught of the moist-laden summer winds which bring rainfall to the western coast and the Western Ghats. The Deccan remains comparatively dry as it lies in the rainshadow of the Western Ghats. Another monsoon current curves up the Ganga plains, progressively losing moisture during its travel toward the Indus plains. The greatest impact of the Bay of Bengal "current" is in Brahmaputra Valley of Assam and the Ganga-Brahmaputra delta. The Himalaya acts as a barrier and the current is diverted leftward to the Ganga plains. In the Himalaya, this tropical, maritime air is present up to elevations of 15,000 feet. Beyond that, most of the moisture has already fallen. The Tibetan plateau is dry as it lies in the Himalayan rainshadow area. In winter, the subcontinent presents a reversed situation. The high pressure system of the subcontinent induces the flow of cool, subsiding, dry air from the northwest across the Indo-Ganga plains. This phenomenon takes place south of the Himalaya, which now effectively blocks the cold, continental air originating from the Siberian high pressure cell.

This simplistic concept of the monsoon winds as related to the development of "low" and "high" pressure cells south of the Himalaya during the summer and winter seasons, giving rise to the seasonal wind systems and associated climatic features, fails to explain several of the characteristics of the Indian monsoons. The traditional model which emphasizes purely thermal factors, which are responsible for the development of surface pressure conditions, does not fully explain the characteristic vagaries connected with the timing and incidence of summer rainfall, its "bursts," and "lull," and "breaks." Furthermore, the traditional models are inadequate in explaining the distribution and behavior of depressions which bring wide-ranging rains to the plains of Pakistan and north India. Recent advances in the study of the dynamics of the upper atmosphere and its relationship with surface air circulation have yielded fruitful explanations of the behavior of the Indian monsoons. Tropical regional meteorology of the subcontinent has now been analyzed within the global framework, and the role of the Himalaya and its association with air waves and currents at various altitudes has been better understood. While a review of the recent theories concerning the mechanism of Indian monsoon is outside the scope of our treatment, it may be pointed out that the Himalaya has effectively controlled the passage routes of the upperstream jet circulation, and has divided the jet stream into two seasonal off-shoots; a northern route is established in summer, and one south of Himalaya in winter. The latter affects principally the flow of easterly surface depressions across the north Indian and Pakistani plains in winter. The main findings of recent research are incorporated in the descriptions of the seasons below.

A convenient climatic division of the calendar in areas where monsoon have their greatest impact is: (a) the rainy season of southwest summer monsoons, (b) the winter season of northwest dry winds, and (c) the intervening hot season between winter and arrival of the summer monsoons.

The Hot Season
From March to May, during the northward movement of the sun's vertical noon rays, and the increasing length of days causes a belt of the most intense solar radiation to move progressively northward over the tropical areas of South Asia, advancing by June into the extra-tropical zone. Temperatures mount as the season advances first in the tropical zone, and then beyond it in the extra-tropical areas. For example, in March the highest daytime temperatures of over 40° C are recorded in central Deccan, Maharashtra and central Andhra Pradesh. In April, highest daytime temperatures (43.5° C) are experienced in Madhya Pradesh, and in May these are 48° C in Rajasthan and Sind (Pakistan), and about 45° to 47° C in most of the Indo-Ganga plains. In north India, and away from the coast, the diurnal ranges also increase. The highest temperatures are recorded in the Thar desert, on the Indus Plains, and occasionally in the middle Ganga plains. In June, Deccan also

records high temperatures (37° C daily maximum) although somewhat lower than the Indo-Ganga plains (41° C or over as daily maximum). The only areas with daily maximum temperatures below 37° C are the coastal plains and the higher altitudes of the mountains. During these summer months afternoons are unbearably hot, and almost all human activity is suspended until the sunset. Men and beast take shelter indoors. This description applies to most parts of India except the high mountains and coastal areas.

Meteorologically, this is the season of continental dry, stable hot winds from the northwest, which permit the intense heating of the land before the summer solstice (June 22). The sun gradually moves northward toward the Tropic of Cancer (until June 22) causing a reduction in the dynamic power of the cold polar airmass which held sway during winter. Until May a dynamic anticyclone centered in Afghanistan-Iran continues to affect the climate of the northwestern part of the subcontinent. Summer (hottest month) average maximum temperatures are shown in Figure 1.3.

Throughout these months the Himalaya acts as a topographic barrier to the low-altitude air and the jet-stream which has moved north of it. As the season advances, a thermal low is being gradually established at the surface over the northwestern part of the subcontinent, while the jet-stream swings south of the Himalaya.

In the remaining sections of the subcontinent, especially the eastern part (Assam, Bangladesh) the jet-stream path produces dynamic depressions, conducive to precipitation; 250-500 mm of rain falls between March and May.

In response to the high-pressure systems developed in this season and the path of the jet streams, a long trajectory of western continental air of 20,000 to 23,000 feet altitude is deflected southward over tropical India. In its southward journey this low-level air passes over the Bay of Bengal and the Arabian sea and becomes humidified. Such modified continental air is on-shore in Malabar, Sri Lanka and Coastal Tamil Nadu. It is heated enough to rise and come in contact with the dry air aloft, bringing convectional rainfall to the eastern and southern coastal areas of Deccan. Popular notion ascribes this rainfall to the retreating monsoons coming from the northwest, picking up moisture in the Bay of Bengal and bringing rainfall.

The Rainy Season of the Southwest Monsoon

From May to June, heating on the land produces a low-pressure system in the overlying atmosphere with rapidly ascending air and winds inward toward the low-pressure area. Such a low pressure area or belt is developed in the northwestern part of the subcontinent (Lower Indus Basin, western Thar Desert) and may be viewed within the broader framework of the well-established equatorial low-pressure belt which is stationed between latitude 5° and 10° north by the end of May, but shifts to 25° north by about June 15 following the northward movement of the sun. It is made more intense in the lower Indus Basin by the high degree of solar insolation. Maritime air quickly moves into the peninsular India and Bengal toward the low-pressure system of northwest India from the Arabian Sea and Bay of Bengal. This change in the development of pressure systems and consequently the direction of winds is further facilitated by the northward movement of the intertropical front. Winds are southward over the Arabian Sea and Bay of Bengal. The southeast trade winds of the southern hemisphere cross the equator responding to the northward migration of the inter-tropical front and change their direction to southwest as monsoon winds.

This traditional explanation of the thermal causation of the summer monsoons fails to account for the "pulsations" of the monsoon, its "breaks" and "bursts." Pierre Pedelaborde has recently proposed a more reasoned explanation of the pulsation phenomena which is based on our increased knowledge of upper-air movements. While not discarding thermal factors, the new theory emphasizes the significance of the roles of jet stream in the upper air and of the Himalaya-Tibet as the topographic barrier in explaining the erratic behavior of the timing and incidence of Indian monsoons. According to this "upper air and perturbation hypothesis," the Himalaya, the Tibetan Plateau, and several high altitude mountains like the Kunlun, the Pamir Knot, the Hindu Kush, are able to alter the flow of jet stream which normally travels between latitudes of 20°-40° North at altitudes of 15,000-25,000 feet. The jet stream is bifurcated; the summer branch lies north of the Tibetan highlands, connected as it is with the northward movement of the surface winds but traveling northward to Central

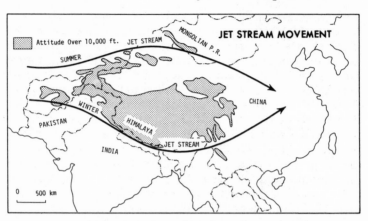

FIGURE 1.4

Asia, whereas the southern branch stays south of the Himalaya during the winter (Figure 1.4).

By the second week of June, the jet stream moves entirely north of the subcontinent into Central Asia. This causes the indraught of free equatorial air to the north and northwest of the continent leading to the formation of dynamic depressions which had already been established by thermal factors. The situation, therefore, aggravates the triggering of the "burst" of the monsoon, allowing as it does the in-flow of equatorial air deep into India. The "pulsations" of the monsoons are attributed to the dynamic waves originating from interaction of the upper air jet stream and the surface air which develop in the intertropical front, rather than a juxtaposition of a frontal surface between two contrasting surface air masses.

The summer monsoon winds arrive in two major southwest streams; one from the Arabian Sea brings large amounts of precipitation to the windward plains along the western coast and Sri Lanka; and a second from the Bay of Bengal stream brings heavy rainfall to Bengal, Bangladesh and the Brahmaputra Valley and its adjoining mountains. The moist air stream that strikes the western coast is forced to rise abruptly by the Western Ghats and produces heavy orographic rainfall. At elevations of 2000 to 3000 feet in the Western Ghats and Assam hills rainfall is over 3000 mm during these months. Cherrapunji in Assam hills (elevation 4300 feet) surrounded on three sides by high mountains, receives the greatest impact of the summer monsoon, experiencing a world record rainfall of about 7600 mm during these five months out of a total annual precipitation of 10,400 mm. Although much precipitation results from convectional downpours, the warm, flooded landscape also provides a base for moisture intake by air through evaporation.

Most of the Deccan Plateau lies in the "rain shadow" of the southwest air stream of the Arabian Sea. Most moisture is shed until the crest of the Western Ghats is reached. To the east of the crest in the interior air is subsiding and dry. East of the Western Ghats, peninsular India remains, in general, dry, excepting the extreme southern tip and parts of the eastern coast.

The Arabian Sea current does not bring rainfall in the Thar Desert. The only topographic barrier, the Aravalli Mountains are aligned paralled to the monsoons. Only a portion of high altitudes and its southern tip capture some precipitation.

A part of the Bay of Bengal monsoon stream strikes the Himalaya after crossing the Ganga delta, is uplifted and sheds copious precipitation. High altitudes of the Himalaya also divert the moist stream westward into the Ganga plains of north India. This diversion, or channeling effect carries rainfall farther west. As the monsoon stream moves westward in the Ganga plains, it continues to shed moisture, becoming increasingly dry. Most places in the middle Ganga plains receive between 650-1300 mm of rainfall during the rainy season. By the time it reaches the Indus Basin it has lost most of its moisture, although some precipitation occurs in the Kashmir mountains. Thar Desert in Rajasthan and Pakistan remains practically dry as it is too far westward in the journey of Bay of Bengal stream of the monsoons. Rainfall, in general, is less than 375 mm between June to October. Despite the establishment of an intense surface "low" over the Thar Desert and the Lower Indus Basin, the absence of relief barriers to the inflow of the southwestern monsoon contributes to scanty rainfall.

The amount of summer rainfall, therefore, varies in the different parts of the subcontinent, depending as it does on their locations with reference to distance from the coast or from the Himalaya, their altitudes, the direction of the monsoon winds and whether the locations lie on the windward or leeward side of mountains (Figure 1.5).

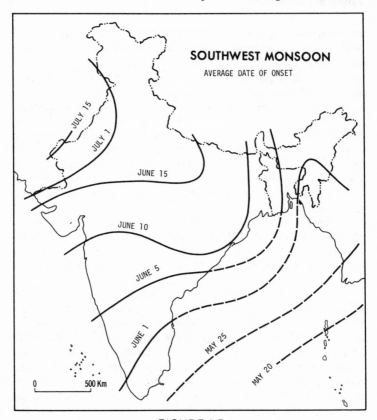

FIGURE 1.5

Compounding this irregular distribution of the incidence of summer monsoons is its proverbial irregular timing, mention of which has been made earlier, and the prevalence of tropical cyclones of the Bay of Bengal which bring, on the average, about a dozen tropical storms annually to Ganga-Brahmaputra delta region. These storms have repeatedly caused large scale destruction. A recent storm (November 1970) carrying winds of over 150 miles per hour and 20 foot waves, killed over 200,000 persons in Bangladesh in addition to completely annihilating settlements in a large area. A few tropical storms also affect the coastal areas in Tamil Nadu and Andhra Pradesh.

By early September the monsoons lose vigor and begin to

retreat from the Ganga plains as the polar dynamics of the northern hemisphere begin to reassert themselves. The prevailing winds are now westerly. By October the monsoon has "retreated" (a term incorrectly applied) from the Ganga Brahmaputra Delta, i.e., the westerly winds have been established. The inter-tropical front has moved southward. The "retreating" monsoons bring rainfall, however, to the coasts of Tamil Nadu and Sri Lanka.

The Cool Season

By mid-October the southerly branch of the jet stream is established to the south of the Himalaya. Northern hemispheric polar air is controlling the upper air dynamics. From November to March, continental, dry air masses dominate the entire northern plains of India and Pakistan. Insolation during winter is reduced and the land is cooler; atmospheric pressure is thus higher than over the adjacent seas. A high pressure cell is developed at the latitude of 15°-20° north and between longitude 70°-80° east. The establishment of this anitcyclonic high pressure cell is further reinforced by the resumption of the jet stream. In response to the development of the pressure system winter-monsoon winds blow from west to east in the Indo-Ganga plains, and recurve in a northeasterly direction over the peninsular parts. Cool, dry air at the surface and stable, dry air aloft produce cloudless, sunny winter in the subcontinent. The mean January temperature is about 21° C in southern India and 15.5° C in the north Indian and Pakistan plains. North of latitude 28° N., January mean temperature falls below 15° C and light frosts occur in the plains. In the Himalaya, temperatures decrease sharply with altitude. Figure 1.6 gives the winter (January) coolest month average temperatures.

Exceptions to the general rule of .cool, dry weather are the Tamil Nadu coast and the Punjab plains. Rainfall in Tamil Nadu is related to the seasonal shift of prevailing winds, the north-east trades or the so-called "retreating" monsoons which pick up moisture in the Bay of Bengal and bring precipitation to the coast of Tamil Nadu. The northern part of the coast along the Bay of Bengal remains comparatively dry in this season as it lies parallel to the direction of winds, and presents little topographic irregularity to capture moisture.

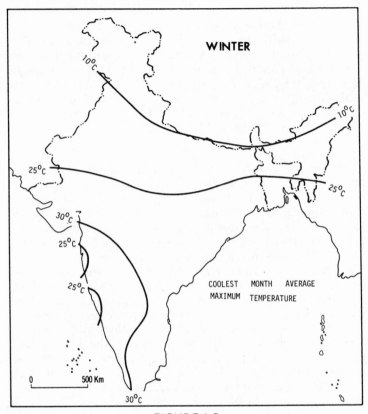

FIGURE 1.6

The Tamil Nadu region exhibits a different rainfall region than anywhere else in India. The pattern consists of a dry season between January through June, followed by a summer of light monsoon rains, and succeeded by a major rainy season between October and December.

As noted earlier the northwestern part of the subcontinent, the Punjab plains and the upper Indus basin receive winter rainfall caused by the cyclonic depressions which follow the path of the jet stream's quasi-permanent branch from west to east, south of the Himalaya. Mid-latitude cyclones average 4 to 5 a month between December and March, and travel from the Mediterranean Sea through Iran, Afghanistan, Pakistan, Western Kashmir and the

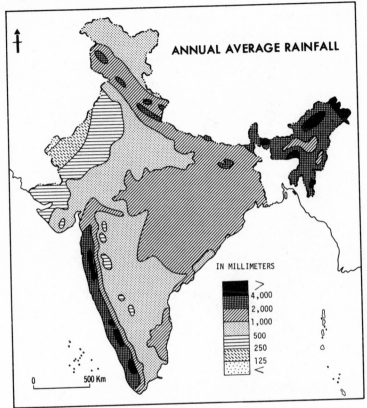

IN MILLIMETERS

> 4,000
2,000
1,000
500
250
125
<

FIGURE 1.7

Himalayan flanks of northwestern India. These bring only light precipitation which is of great value to the winter crops like wheat, cotton and mustard. The cool weather rains account for 125 to 200 mm, about one-half of the annual rainfall in this area. The average annual rainfall distribution in the country is shown in Figure 1.7.

The Climatic Regions

The foregoing review of factors controlling the climates suggests the existence of a wide variety of regional distributions of rainfall regimes, temperature ranges and pressure-wind systems over the subcontinent. It is, therefore, most convenient to study the climate diversities by dividing the

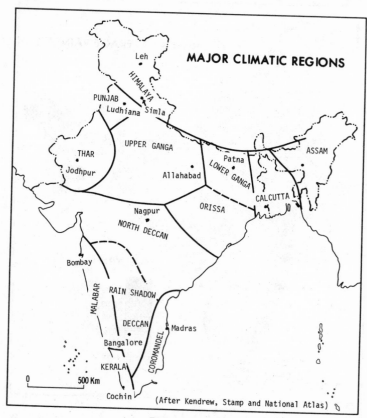

MAJOR CLIMATIC REGIONS

(After Kendrew, Stamp and National Atlas)

FIGURE 1.8

subcontinent into major climatic regions. Among the best known climatic classifications are those of Köppen, Thornthwaite and Kendrew. The following functional classification, a modification of the Köppen and Kendrew-Stamp classifications, clearly shows the distinction between the more "continental" North and the Peninsula. This distinction follows in general the 25° C isotherm for maximum average monthly temperature for winter (Figure 1.6). In the north, the continental part, winters are cooler, fit for the growth of such temperate crops as wheat and barley, although wheat growing also extends farther south in the western Deccan. The continental peninsular thermal division is of special significance in human geography, especially, in its relation to the dietary and health conditions of the people in the two macrodivisions.

The climatic data-tables (Table 1.1) list several stations exemplifying the climatic regions mentioned below, and the figure of Major Climatic Regions gives their locations (Figure 1.8).

1. *The Himalaya Type* follows the Himalayan ranges from Kashmir to Assam. Rainfall is orographically induced and occurs with seasonal variations throughout the year. Rainfall incidence depends on altitude, the alignment of mountain ranges in respect to the direction of the monsoon winds, and the relative distance from the sea. Summers are mild, winters are cold. A typical station is Simla.

2. *Punjab Type* is a typically continental climate. Ranges of temperatures are high. It has some winter rainfall, induced by western depressions, although the rainiest season is in summer from the Bay of Bengal stream of the southwest monsoon. Rainfall is between 500-750 mm annually. The mean January temperature at Ludhiana is below 15° C. This region lies in the Upper Indus Basin, extending eastward to include parts of adjoining Punjab state in India.

3. *Upper Ganga Type* receives moderate rainfall (between 700 to 1000 mm annually), most of which falls during the summer months. Winters are cool, with mean January temperature between 15° and 25° C. The summers are very hot. Daily maximum temperature rises to over 42° C during late May or June. Average daily mean maximum for the same period is 40° to 42° C. Allahabad is a good example.

4. The region of *Lower Ganga Type* is merely a transitional one with milder winters (16°-20° C January mean), heavier annual rainfall and a smaller seasonal range of temperatures than in the Upper Ganga Type. In the southern part (Orissa, Eastern Madhya Pradesh) winters are milder (20°-23° in January). There is little or no winter rainfall.

5. *Calcutta Type* lies in Ganga-Brahmaputra Delta and Central East India. It is an area of high rainfall, over 1500 mm annually. The temperature conditions are similar to the previous two types. Calcutta is an example.

6. *Coromandel Type* prevails along the southern segment of the eastern coast. Winters are warmer than in all

the previous regions, with mean January temperatures over 24° C. Summers are hot, but do not attain the extreme temperature of Upper Ganga Type. Seasonal ranges also are smaller. Months of greatest rainfall are in winter (November and December) received from the retreating monsoons which pick up moisture over the Bay of Bengal. Madras is a typical station of this region.

7. *Kerala Type* lies in the southern segment of the western coast. A region of very heavy rainfall and tropical high temperature with little seasonal variation. January temperatures average above 24° C. Most precipitation (over 3000 mm annually) is received from the vigorous southwest on-shore summer monsoon winds during the months of May through July, although there is no dry month. Cochin is a good example.

8. The Malabar coast, or the northern segment of the western coast resembles the Kerala Type except that it has a distinct dry season. Bombay is a good example of this *Malabar Type*. Most of the precipitation (over 1875 mm annually) is received in the summer months between June and September from the summer monsoons. Winters are as warm as in the Kerala Type.

9. *Deccan Type* prevails in the interior of the Peninsula. The area immediately to the east of the West Ghats is a rainshadow belt and includes southern Maharashtra, Karnataka and Western Andhra Pradesh. It is a dry region with annual rainfall less than 650 mm, received mostly during the summer. Bellary is a good example. Winters are cooler than in the eastern and western coastal regions (Coromandel, Kerala, and Malabar Types), whereas summers are warmer, due to the interior locations. This segment of the Deccan Type may be called the *Rainshadow Subtype* region. To the north and northeast of this subtype is an area of moderate rainfall (ranging between 650 and 1,300 mm annually). Nagpur is a good example. Gujarat, North Maharashtra, southwestern parts of Madhya Pradesh belong to this subtype, which may be called *North Deccan Subtype*.

10. *Assam Type* lies in Assam, Manipur, Arunachal Pradesh, Nagaland, Meghalaya and Mizoram. It is an area of very heavy rainfall (over 2000 mm annually), most of which falls in summer, between May and August, from the northeast monsoons. Tezpur is an example.

TABLE 1.1

CLIMATIC DATA FOR SELECTED STATIONS

(Temperature in degrees C and Rainfall in mm)

Type, Station	Jan	Feb	Mar	Apr	May	June	July	Aug	Sept	Oct	Nov	Dec	Annual
Himalaya													
Simla													
Av. daily max.	8	9	14	18	22	23	21	19	19	17	14	11	
Av. temp.	5	6	11	15	18	20	19	17	17	14	11	8	
Av. rainfall	61	69	61	53	66	175	424	434	160	33	13	28	1,574
Punjab													
Ludhiana													
Av. temp.	13	16	21	27	33	34	31	30	30	26	20	15	
Av. rainfall	35	35	29	11	9	54	191	173	136	35	3	14	725
Upper Ganga													
Allahabad													
Av. daily max.	24	26	33	40	42	40	33	32	33	32	28	24	
Av. temp.	16	19	25	31	35	34	30	29	29	26	20	16	
Av. rainfall	23	15	15	5	15	127	320	254	213	58	8	8	1,032

Type, Station	Jan	Feb	Mar	Apr	May	June	July	Aug	Sept	Oct	Nov	Dec	Annual
Calcutta													
Calcutta													
Av. daily max.	27	29	34	36	36	33	32	32	32	32	29	26	
Av. temp.	20	22	28	30	30	30	29	29	29	28	24	20	
Av. rainfall	10	31	36	43	140	297	325	328	252	5	20	114	1,582
Coromandel													
Madras													
Av. daily max.	29	31	33	35	38	38	36	35	34	32	29	29	
Av. temp.	24	25	28	31	33	33	31	31	30	28	26	25	
Av. rainfall	36	10	8	15	25	48	91	117	119	305	356	140	1,233
Kerala													
Cochin													
Av. daily max.	32	32	33	33	32	29	29	29	29	31	31	32	
Av. temp.	27	28	29	30	29	27	26	27	27	28	28	28	
Av. rainfall	23	20	51	125	297	724	592	353	196	340	170	41	3,106
Malabar													
Bombay													
Av. daily max.	28	28	30	32	33	32	29	29	29	32	32	31	
Av. temp.	24	24	26	28	30	29	27	27	27	28	28	26	
Av. rainfall	10	18	15	15	20	224	371	290	203	56	20	13	2,078

Type, Station	Jan	Feb	Mar	Apr	May	June	July	Aug	Sept	Oct	Nov	Dec	Annual
Deccan Rainshadow													
Nagpur													
Av. daily max.	28	32	37	41	43	37	31	31	32	32	29	27	
Av. temp.	21	24	29	33	36	32	28	28	28	26	23	20	
Av. rainfall	10	18	15	15	20	224	371	290	203	56	20	13	1,251
Assam													
Tezpur													
Av. daily max.	23	24	28	28	31	32	32	32	32	30	27	24	
Av. temp.	17	19	23	24	27	29	29	29	29	26	22	18	
Av. rainfall	13	28	58	158	252	305	366	366	208	107	18	5	1,880
Thar													
Jodhpur													
Av. daily max.	24	27	32	37	41	40	36	34	34	35	31	26	
Av. temp.	17	19	24	29	34	34	32	30	29	27	22	18	
Av. rainfall	3	5	3	3	10	36	102	122	61	8	3	3	364

MAJOR VEGETATION TYPES

Historical evidence indicates that an almost continuous belt of forest-cover was spread over north India at the time of Alexander's invasion in the 4th century B.C. Even during the 10th and 14th centuries, the Ganga plain was covered with vast patches of forest. However, only a few areas at high altitudes or the coastal swamps now remain where plant cover reaches its climatic potentialities. Elsewhere, man's modification of and interference with the "original" plant cover has resulted in its removal or degradation creating serious problems of soil erosion and the growth of stunted jungly vegetation (thickets, bushes and dwarf trees). At present, forests occupy only about 18 percent of the total land of the country.

In general, natural vegetation types follow the distribution of rainfall, higher altitudes being the major exception areas. Based largely on annual rainfall distribution, four broad categories of vegetation are commonly identified. Evergreen Broadleaved forests occupy areas receiving over 2000 mm annual rainfall. Deciduous Broadleaved trees are associated with areas of 1000 to 2000 mm rainfall. Dry Deciduous Broadleaved forests and open Thorny Scrubland occupy areas with 500 to 750 mm annual rainfall. Thorny scrubs and bushes are found in the semideserts and deserts receiving less than 500 mm annual precipitation. Within these four broad categories of vegetation, 16 major vegetation types may be recognized, shown in Figure 1.9 which is modified from the *National Atlas of India*.

Tropical Wet Evergreen forests are typical rain forests with their best strands growing in areas receiving over 2500 mm annual rainfall. In their "natural" form their main area of distribution is an elongated strip along the Western Ghats at altitudes between 1500 and 4500 feet south of Bombay. Parts of Assam, Annamalai Hills, Coorg, and the Andaman-Nicobar Islands in the Indian Ocean are some other areas of concentration. On their drier side, these are bordered by *Tropical Semi Evergreen* forest along the Western Coast from Bombay to Kerala. Elsewhere, this type is found in Assam and Meghalaya. Both these types contain dense forest cover of tall trees rising to about 100 feet. The Semi-Evergreen type contain mixed strands of deciduous trees,

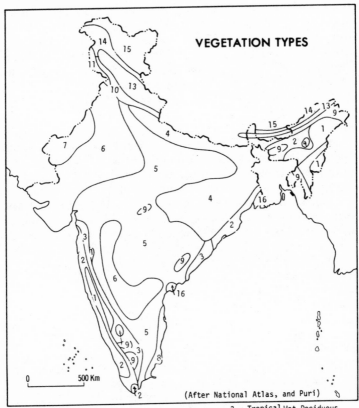

VEGETATION TYPES

(After National Atlas, and Puri)

1. Tropical Evergreen 2. Tropical Semi Evergreen 3. Tropical Wet Deciduous
4. Tropical Moist Deciduous 5. Tropical Dry 6. Tropical Thorn 7. Tropical Desert
8. Tropical Dry Evergreen 9. Subtropical Wet 10. Subtropical Pine 11. Subtropical
Dry 12. Wet Temperate 13. Moist Temperate 14. Dry Temperate 15. Alpine 16. Tidal

FIGURE 1.9

especially toward their drier edges. Most of these forests are
administered by the forestry department of the state governments. Plywood and rattan are the main products. Adjoining these two types in Assam, the Western Ghats, Annamalai Hills, and Coorg lies the *Tropical Moist Deciduous*
type characterized by widely spaced and broad-leafed trees,
like laurel, hollock and ebony, reflecting the seasonal
rhythm of an adequate precipitation of 1000 to 2000 mm
annually. A variation of the moist deciduous vegetation type

covers a large part of Orissa, Chota Nagpur Plateau, South Bihar, eastern Madhya Pradesh (including Dandakaranya) and the submontane Terai areas of Siwaliks along the southern Himalayan fringes in Himachal Pradesh and Uttar Pradesh. *Sal* is a typical tree of these areas, yielding substances used in the manufacture of *lac*.

Toward the drier parts of the Moist Deciduous type lies the *Tropical Dry Deciduous* type which covers large portions of the subcontinent from the Ganga Plains and the states of Madhya Pradesh, Maharashtra in Central India to Tamil Nadu in extreme south. Although *sal* is still an important example of trees of this type, especially toward the moister margins, several other trees gain regional importance. Examples of these trees are: *sandal, shisham,* satinwood and teak. Mysore state is a major producer of teak and sandal trees. Most of these trees are now utilized for commercial uses, the manufacture of furniture and handicraft artifacts.

Tropical Thorn and *Tropical Desert* types are associated with semi-deserts and deserts receiving rainfall less than 500 mm annually. Main areas lie along the Pakistan border and cover most of Rajasthan, south Punjab, Haryana, parts of western Madhya Pradesh, and Gujarat states. The *Great Thar Desert* is a good example of the extremely dry section of these types. In the *Thorn* type broadleaved, deciduous thorny bushes, generally widely-spaced and with heights ranging from 3 to 5 feet, make up most of the vegetation. In true desert conditions their size shrinks and the stunted trees and bushes give way to thorny and very widely-spaced vegetation. *Babul* and *khair* are the chief examples of such trees.

Tropical Dry Evergreen is associated with the coastal region of Tamil Nadu and southern parts of Andhra Pradesh. Rainfall is less than 2000 mm annually, mostly ranging between 1000 and 1500 mm, but characterized by a distinct but short dry period summer. Most of the land has been cleared for agriculture during centuries of human occupance. Areas of the *Subtropical Wet* type are spotty, clinging to high altitudes (between 3000-5000 feet altitude) in Shillong Plateau, Nilgiri Hills, and in the Himalaya. Oak, beech and ash are the main trees. Toward the drier margins but in the same altitudes, lies the *Subtropical Pine* type. Within its distribution is found an admixture of oak and *chir* trees. Most trees are exploited for the production of furniture, railroad sleepers, resin, and paper. *Subtropical Dry* type occurs in a few spotty areas in the Himalaya foothills at elevations between 1500 to 5000 feet. Acacian and scrubby trees form most of the vegetation in this type.

Wet Temperate type occurs in the Nilgiri and Annamalai Hills, at altitudes between 3000 and 5500 feet in areas experiencing rainfall over 1250 mm annually. Magnolias, laurels, rhododendrons are the major trees. *Moist Temperate* type is more northerly in location in respect to the *Wet Temperate* type in the Nilgiri Hills, whereas in the Himalaya it lies at altitudes between 6000 and 10,000 feet. Broadleaved evergreens, as well as conifers, pines, silver fir, and spruce are the major varieties. Undergrowth consists generally of oaks, laurels and bamboos. The *Dry Temperate* variety is largely found in the Inner Himalayas, Kashmir, Sikkim, generally on the leeward side. Conifers like *deodars* and junipers predominate. The *Alpine* type is a very high altitude variety, lying beyond 11,500 feet altitude in the Himalaya. The vegetation consists of a shrubby forest of firs, junipers, birches and rhododendrons. The *Tidal* Forest type consists mainly of mangroves and swamps in the Ganga-Brahmaputra delta. Main trees are hardwood palms used mostly for fuel and boatmaking.

Vegetation Ecology
Systematic deforestation of the woodlands, shifting cultivation, and overgrazing for thousands of years over most of the subcontinent has stripped it of its natural vegetation and turned it into a vast scrubland. Woodland is confined to the riverine strips, the Tarai, village groves (of *tamarind, bunyan,* mangoes), and the coastal areas. The exceptions are the areas in the Himalaya, the Western Ghats, and other hills (as in Assam and the Nilgiris). The Deccan Plateau is dotted with short grasses and scattered trees. Most of north India has been cleared for crop cultivation, only a few tree groves cling to the village settlements.

Estimated to affect 150 million acres, soil erosion has become a major problem. It is especially acute in the Punjab Siwaliks, Chambal Valley, and parts of Assam and Burma borderlands. Shifting cultivation and *jhumming* (slash and burn) activities have been and are widely practiced in the tribal areas of Assam, Arunachal, and Central India. Sheet erosion in most of these areas has produced lowering of watertable and has reduced these areas to a stubby wasteland.

Ancient scriptures have extolled the importance of "natural" vegetation and trees. Medieval literature also abounds in the beauty of groves, trees and forests. Most deforestation probably occurred after the medieval period. During the British rule a few studies and reports pointed out these problems but little effort was devoted to remedy the situation. Since Independence, the government has lent moral support to the "greening" of the country by rhetorical exhortations. Official efforts have largely remained halting, half-hearted and ineffectual. What is needed is a concerted, coordinated, comprehensive, national plan integrated into the national Five Year Plans.

MAJOR SOIL PATTERNS

During the British rule in India, a vast body of fascinating accounts of soils, rich in local names and folklore, and often replete with shrewd observations, had emerged in the district gazetteers and official reports. These accounts, often based on centuries old farming experiences, were generally directed toward the assessment of differential soil-fertility and its land-revenue associations, but did not attempt classification and distribution of soil types in the country.

Since its establishment in 1956 the Soil Survey of India has been engaged in the production of scientific analysis of the soil distribution of a few selected areas of the country. Its final goal is to prepare detailed and accurate soil maps, based on the latest soil classification systems for the entire country. Given the dimensions of the problem and its modest budget, the Survey has been able to produce few such maps.

Recent attempts to divide the country into broad categories of soil types are contained in the *National Atlas of India* (1957), the *Irrigation Atlas of India* (1972) and Spate's *India, Pakistan and Ceylon* (1967). The last two have utilized the 7th approximation Soil Classification developed by the U.S. Department of Agriculture (USDA). Virtually ignoring the role of man in the formation of soil types, traditional soil grouping (zonal, azonal and intrazonal) relied essentially on the genesis and development of soil-profile. The 7th approximation defines soil classes strictly in terms of their morphology and composition as produced by a set of natural and human forces. The classification is determined by quantifiable criteria. The broadest category is that of the soil "orders" which recognizes the major properties of the soil profile, like its color and organic content within the climatic framework. Recognition of human modification in changing the soil and organic content is also considered. "Orders" are divided into 47 "sub orders" which are defined in terms of specific climatic variables (e.g., seasonality of precipitation, etc.). The division of the "sub orders" are divided into 185 soil groups based largely on the color and chemical content of the soils. At the lower level of the classification are the 16,000 soil families, series and types.

Figure 1.10 presents a division of the country into broad soil regions at the level of soil orders. Discussion of these includes wherever possible, tentative speculations regarding the distribution of suborders within the broad regional framework. Five soil orders, Aridosol, Alfisol, Inceptisol, Ultisol, and Vertisol, are identified by their broad regional distributions. The sub order of Entisols contain undifferentiated soil-horizons and occur in deserts and rugged mountains. Aridosols are associated with the semi-desert areas (*Tropical Thorn* vegetation type) of Thar Desert, western Haryana, Southern Punjab and western Rajasthan. Defined by absence of water availability for six months, their soil horizon tends to be pale or gray or reddish in color with little or no humic content. On older land surfaces, such as in Thar Desert and Gujarat, aridosols contain a horizon of clay accumulation (the argillic horizon). Elsewhere, one or more pedogenic horizons containing calcium carbonate accumulation occur, especially in areas of poor drainage or from uncontrolled leaching resulting from irrigation. With the passage of time salts rise up on the surface rendering surface soil toxic or unfit for cultivation. In Punjab and Rajasthan these salts are called *thur*. Their reclamation is a concern for the government and farmers. Prevention of salinization

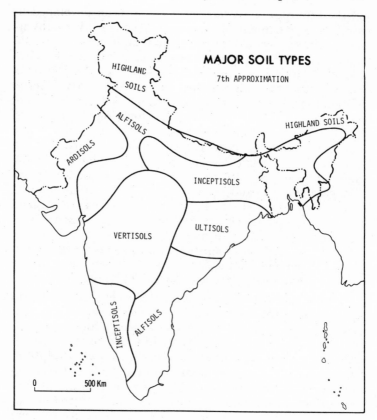

FIGURE 1.10

is achieved by flushing soil salts downwards by a controlled use of water. Another serious concern in such areas is the rise of watertable resulting from constant irrigation which has created serious waterlogging problems. Here again, controlled irrigation and construction of cemented canal channels help alleviation of the problem. Intrinsically, such areas have high mineral content in the surface horizon. Wise farm management, desalinization and anti-waterlogging programs have resulted in high agricultural productivity in the Punjab and Haryana states.

In the true deserts, western Rajasthan (Thar Desert), entisols with immature horizons inhibit any farming. *Psamment* soil sub order of entisols is widely prevalent here.

Alfisols, the soils of middle latitudes, brownish or grayish in color, are distributed in areas receiving medium rainfall (500 to 1000 mm annually). These are usually underlined by alluvium which is rich in mineral bases. The 7th approximation allocates to these the areas of north Punjab, north Haryana, eastern Rajasthan, western Madhya Pradesh (Tropical Dry Deciduous type of Vegetation) and the Chambal Valley; the latter two areas receive a rain of dust from the adjacent deserts which adds mineral-rich bases to the soils. Areas in Punjab and Haryana, however, are underlain by alluvium which is rich in mineral bases. Alfisols also cover large portions of the Deccan peninsula, along the eastern coast in Andhra Pradesh, Tamil Nadu and in eastern Karnataka. Here the soils are reddish in color and belong to the *Ustalf* suborder (which is defined in terms of containing a long dry period over 90 cumulative days). Alfisol soils are good for cultivation of small grains (wheat, millets, pulses) and irrigated crops (cotton). Good farm management, provision of irrigation, machine technology and the utilization of better strains of crops have brought "Green Revolution" to Punjab and Tamil Nadu.

Inceptisols are produced over a wide range of climatic latitudinal and physiographic conditions. Containing immature or poor soil horizon, developed in water-surplus regions, these are best found on relatively young geomorphic surfaces like the alluvial sediments of the floodplains. Inceptisols form important lowland soils of the Ganga-Brahmaputra valleys. Its *aquept* sub order is formed in areas saturated with water obtained during the rainy period. The parent matter is composed of salt and clay deposited by river tributaries during river floods in the delta. The best example is the *aquepts* of Ganga delta region which are formed in an area of continual sedimentation. Soil color is generally gray. The middle and lower Ganga Plains are very productive, composed as these are of the "newer" alluvium, and have been intensively cultivated for centuries. The higher reaches of the interfluves are covered with "older" alluvium containing calcareous concretionary substances *(bhangar)*. Irrigation permits the cultivation of a large variety of dry-season crops, like wheat, cotton, ground nuts, pulses, and sugarcane. Crop yields, low at present, can be improved with the introduction of the "Green Revolution."

Inceptisols of Kerala belong to the *tropept* sub order, which develops in low latitudes under continuously warm to hot climatic conditions with no or a small dry season. Soils are reddish brown in color.

Vertisols belong to a special category and cover a distinctive area in western Deccan Plateau (Maharashtra, West Madhya Pradesh, north Mysore). These are characterized by a high content of clay minerals which shrink greatly when dried out and swell when saturated. The soils form, therefore, wide cracks during the dry season. Remarkably "self-ploughed" by the loosened soil-particles fallen from the ground into the cracks, the soil swallows itself and retains soil-moisture. Such soils are popularly known as "black lava" or the *regur* and are associated with cotton cultivation in western Deccan. Despite their high base the soils, except for the cultivation of crops like cotton and millets during the time of "self-ploughing" (and self moisting period), are of little agricultural value. Ploughs drawn by buffaloes or oxen till the soil with difficulty. Only with sufficient investment in power-driven machinery and soil-treatment for improvement of soil-structure, can *ustert* soil areas hold promise of adding to the food resources of this agriculturally poor region of the country.

Ultisols are produced under forest vegetation with warm alternating dry-moist season. Seasonal leaching, therefore, usually occurs and soil bases are depleted, resulting in the formation of subsurface clay accumulation. "B" horizon is generally red or yellowish brown, due to the concentration of oxides of iron. The *ustult* suborder is formed in areas with warm to hot climate. Chief areas of this suborder are south Bihar, north Orissa, and east Madhya Pradesh. Large territory of the suborder is under forest or shifting cultivation, and is generally low in agricultural productivity. Given adequate farm management and use of modern technology, ultisols can become agriculturally productive.

The soils of the Himalaya mountains are complex. Rugged glaciers, snowfields, and areas of steep relief are mostly denuded of soils. Valley floors of river basins contain recent alluvium *inceptisols*. The agriculturally productive Jhelum Valley in Kashmir belongs to this category. Other soil orders are entisols with little or poor soil horizons. Most of eastern Ladakh belongs to the entisol order.

(The areas of India, Pakistan, Bangladesh, Nepal, Bhutan and Sri Lanka are 3.3 million square kilometers, 796,095 square kilometers, 142,776 square kilometers, 140,798 square kilometers, 47,000 square kilometers, 65,610 square kilometers; and populations in 1979 were estimated at 661 million, 80 million, 87 million, 13.7 million, 1.3 million and 16.5 million respectively.)

CITATIONS AND SELECT BIBLIOGRAPHY

Chatterji, S. P. (ed.), *National Atlas of India.* Calcutta and Dehradun, 1957

Geddes, A., "The Alluvial Morphology of Indo-Gangetic Plain," *Transactions.* I. B. G., Vol. 28, 1960, pp. 262-63

Government of India, *Irrigation Atlas of India.* Dehra Dun, 1972.

Kendrew, W. G., *Climates of the Continents.* Oxford, 1961.

Learmonth, A. T. A., *The Vegetation of the Indian Sub-Continent.* Canberra, 1964.

Pedelaborde, P., *Le Moussons.* Paris, 1958.

Puri, G. S., *Indian Forest Ecology.* New Delhi, 1961.

Shrinivasan, V., "South West Monsoon Rainfall in the Gangetic West Bengal," *Indian Journal of Meteorology and Geophysics.* Vol. II, 1960, pp. 5-18.

Singh, R. L., (ed.), *India: A Regional Geography.* Varanasi, 1971.

Spate, O. H. K., and A. T. A. Learmonth, *India and Pakistan and Ceylon.* 3rd ed., London, 1967.

Schwartzberg, J. E., (ed.), *A Historical Atlas of India.* Chicago, 1978.

Trewartha, G. T., *Earth's Problem Climates.* Madison, 1961.

U.S. Department of Agriculture, *Soil Classification: A Comprehensive System, 7th Approximation.* Washington, 1960.

Wadia, D. N., *Geology of India.* 3rd ed., London, 1961.

CHAPTER 2

RISE OF INDIAN CIVILIZATION
AND THE INDIAN STATE

The Indian civilization, like Mesopotamian, Assyrian, Egyptians, and Chinese civilizations, is ancient. But unlike them it has had a continuous, although not entirely recorded, history dating back to several centuries before the Christian era. The Indian subcontinent which includes present-day Pakistan and Bangladesh has been inhabited since at least the Stone Age (5000-6000 B.C.). Archeological excavations during the last twenty years covering a large area from Baluchistan in Pakistan to Bengal and Sri Lanka have produced evidence of land settlement as early as the 5th millenium B.C. The earliest communities were engaged primarily in hunting, collecting and domesticating cattle, buffalo and sheep. Several of these communities persisted for a long time even after the appearance of the first agriculturalists, pastoralists, and the users of such metals as copper, bronze and iron.

BEGINNINGS OF URBAN CIVILIZATION

Developed first in the Indus Delta area during the third millennium B.C., the Indus Valley Civilization, representing the earliest known civilization in the subcontinent, appears to have spread north and then east during the succeeding centuries. This civilization persisted for 500 to 700 years and covered an area of over one-half million square miles from Baluchistan to the Ghaggar Basin, west of Delhi (Figure 2.1). Remarkably uniform in several cultural traits (agricultural products, inscriptions on seals, figurines and artifacts of proto-religious significance), the Indus Valley

INDUS VALLEY CIVILIZATION

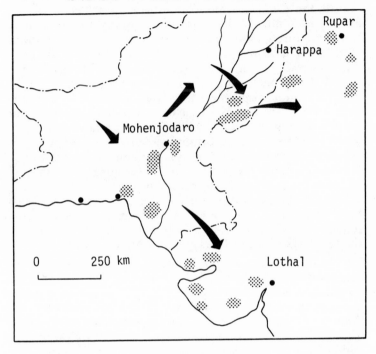

Chief Sites

Outward Drift of the Harappans

FIGURE 2.1

Culture Region was primarily an urban and commercial civilization. Internal communication links were mainly developed along the river. Trading connections with the outside world were established through several ports along the Arabian Sea from the Gulf of Cambay to Baluchistan.

From the geographical standpoint the planning and design of the Indus Valley cities are characteristic: their grid-iron lay-out, north-south axis dimensions of about one and a half mile square area and the existence of a large for-

tified "citadel mound" to the west with the larger city
toward the east. Common building material consisted of
burnt and unburnt brick, with an occasional timber lacing.
Stone was rarely used. A wide variety of house sizes, from a
singleroom dwelling unit to a large house, containing
private wells, cooking and bathing areas and a large compound have been unearthed. A well-organized sewage
system of drains disposing wastes from houses into the main-
street drains served most of the city. A wide variety of stores
and craft shops (potters' kilns, dyers' materials, and metal
works) formed an important section of the city. The
"citadel" contained several public buildings which were used
for administrative purposes as well as for storing food grains.
In Mohenjo-daro, a large centrally located "Great Bath"
which was probably used for ritual group bathing has also
been found. Estimates based on the count of dwelling units
suggest that about 30,000 to 40,000 persons lived in each of
the two large cities of Harappa and Mohenjo-daro.

The cities were supported by a vast agricultural base
of the fertile river basins. Wheat, rice, dates, melons, and
leguminous plants were the principal crops grown. Cattle,
sheep, camels and donkeys were the chief domesticated
animals. Copper, silver and bronze were used to produce
implements, seals and artifacts. Pottery was mass produced.
Indications are that the use of woven fabric of cotton was
common. The larger settlements were interconnected by
river transport and land routes, facilitating inland commerce which involved acquiring raw materials in exchange
for finished products and was dwarfed by a much wider external trade in lead, gold and precious stones with the
Mesopotamian cities. A regular system of weights and
measures was developed for commercial purposes.

Several of the unearthed seals and figurines exhibit the
prevalence of a fairly developed level of artistic and social
activity. Scenes of mythological and religious significance
depicted on a number of seals suggest the existence of inci-
pient forms of religious practices. Faint traces of relationships between the later Hindu god Shiva and the goddess
Durga have been perceived by some authorities. The existence of several burial sites indicated Harappan belief in
man's afterlife. Attempts to decipher the Harappan script
have largely failed, but its unmistakable resemblance to

the Dravidian languages of South India, possibly with Old Tamil, is apparent.

Between 2,500 and 1,700 B.C. the agricultural settlements and the associated urban economic structure of this civilization had taken root in the Indus Basin. As the external commercial contacts developed, the civilization diffused itself to the Ganga Valley and the coastal regions of South India.

For reasons not properly understood, this urban civilization declined quite suddenly by 600 B.C. Geological and ecological factors, such as changes in the river courses, salinization and waterlogging of soils and expansion of the desert and climatic changes making the area physically inhospitable, have been advanced for the nearly complete disappearance of the Indus Valley civilization.

ARYANIZATION OF INDIAN CIVILIZATION

The advent of the Indo-Aryans marks the beginnings of Indian history. Aryanization of India and the subsequent establishment of Hindu tradition starts with them. Little is known about the Indo-Aryans. Linguistic and literary evidence, however, point to their unmistakable links with the Indo-Europeans as well as to the fact that they came from the northwest, the direction of the Iranian Plateau, in successive waves between 1500 and 600 B.C. Early Vedic literature, as well as the contemporary Iranian literature of the Avesta, attest to such migrations, although precise source-regions and timing of these movements are still obscure. Most scholars favor the idea that these migrations originated in Central Asia; literary and linguistic evidence suggests that they were probably a part of great and complex folk movements which brought ancient Persians into Iran and the Greeks into Greece. Such common customs among these widely spread ancient people, such as cremation of the dead, the use of iron, and their dress forms, as well as their institutions as King, Council and Assembly, indicate their common origins.

The Vedic literature (1200-700 B.C.) is our primary source of information regarding the behavior of these migrations: the direction of migratory currents, the gradual diffu-

sion of migrants over the north Indian plains, and the settlement patterns and socio-economic structure of the society.
Additional knowledge is obtained from the two Hindu epics,
the Ramayana and the Mahabharata (500 B.C.). As the
Aryan invaders gradually settled over the North Indian
Plains, they pushed the indigenous people, possibly the early
Dravidians, to the east and the south and assimilted them in
part. Gradually they established a new socio-economic order
and introduced new languages, literatures, philosophies and
ideas of social behavior. The growth of Sanskrit, which is
closely related to the Indo-European linguistic family,
parallels the growth of the Vedic literatures and philosophy
during this momentous period of the Aryanization of India's
history.

The early Aryans were nomadic pastoralists. As they
moved into the North Indian Plains and finally penetrated
into Southern India beyond the Vindhya Hills, they gradually cleared the forests and started establishing agrarian
communities. To some historians the story of the Ramayana
illustrates the historic Aryan penetration of South India.
While Aryans were settling in the north-western parts of the
subcontinent, through a process of their contact and interaction with the relatively underdeveloped aboriginals, society became divided into stratified classes, first along apparently occupational lines, but eventually organized along
strict caste-based rules.

Meanwhile, several philosophical systems regarding
nature, matter and spirit were being evolved and refined. A
vast body of rituals, worship and caste regulations was written in the Upanishads, treatises which form the basis and
culmination of Hindu thought. Doctrines of *maya* (illusion),
karma (moral consequences) and transmigration were expounded. Several deities, such as Vishnu and Shiva, also
emerged, transcending the importance of the early Aryan
deities (e.g. Usha, Indra and Varuna) which represented the
various forms of nature.

During the 6th century B.C., two sects, Buddhism and
Jainism, stood up against the ritualistic and polytheistic
forms of Hinduism; each attempted to offer a satisfactory
solution to the mystery of life and death. Each also struck
against the entrenched caste system of the society. In this
last effort they singularly failed, for the caste system remain-

ed a bedrock of society; yet caste-based forces ultimately toned up the moral fiber of Hinduism by introducing such practices of *Ahimsa* (non-violence) and truthfulness, which, though preached by Hinduism earlier, were henceforth reinforced more vigorously in Hindu society.

THE MAURYAN EMPIRE

The first successful attempt to consolidate the tribal and political units of north India into a single political entity was realized by the Mauryan Kings (325-170 B.C.). A detailed account of the administration and the prevailing socio-economic structure of society can be obtained from the contemporary accounts of Kautilya (who wrote a famous treatise on the administrative role and techniques of the rulers) and Magasthenes, a Chinese pilgrim who stayed in India during the Mauryan times and recorded extensively on the nature of society. The Mauryan government was a centralized bureaucracy pivoted around the king. The imperial system was sustained financially by the income derived from the land taxes, internal commerce and foreign trade. A number of cities flourished in the empire, and were connected by a well-developed system of highways. Artisans formed a major section of the urban populations. Several urban guilds of artisans, bankers and merchants existed and exercised a powerful influence on the city administration. The state maintained a large standing army. Under Ashoka, the greatest of the Mauryan rulers, the empire was subdivided into at least four large provinces, each administered by a royal prince. The provinces were sub-divided into districts. District administration, which became the basis of Mughal and British rule, was essentially inherited from the Mauryans.

Ashoka (c. 274-236 B.C.) was one of the most illustrious kings in India's history. During his rule, the Mauryan empire was extended to cover almost the entire subcontinent. He became a convert to Buddhism and had the central principles of the Buddhist religion inscribed on rock pillar edicts at prominent places within his empire. The designs of these pillars and the insignia used on rock edicts are now used as the symbols of Indian tradition in government documents.

By preaching the idea of *Dhamma,* an attitude of social piety and conscience, he tried to weld the nation into a unified force. Since national conscience was still feeble, his ideals could not survive for long.

In 326 B.C., Alexander of Greece invaded northwestern India through the passes from Afghanistan. He could not advance beyond the River Beas in present-day Punjab and stayed in the country for only a short while. His quick and fleeting stay and sudden departure, left only a few marks on Indian society. After his invasion Greek influence started to percolate slowly into the country. The Gandhara sculpture patronized by the Kushans, who ruled northwest India a few centuries later, bears unmistakable Hellenic influence. The Gandhara sculpture tradition blended the Greek facial features and dress style with the traditional native motifs in the statues of Buddha.

By 150 B.C. the vast Mauryan empire had started to crumble. A number of small states had emerged. The disintegration of the subcontinent into several political units along regional lines became a recurrent pattern in Indian history.

An important development during Mauryan and post-Mauryan times was the development of a commercial economy and the establishment of trade routes both within the country and with the outside world. A flourishing civilization had independently developed earlier in South India which maintained commercial and cultural contacts with Aryan north India during and after Mauryan times. Several land routes joined the Ganga Plains with Taxila (now in Pakistan) and Kabul (in present-day Afghanistan) and, across Iran, with the Black Sea ports. The maritime trade routes from the Indian ports to the Persian Gulf and further westward to the eastern Mediterranean Sea were also firmly established. The Roman Emperor Augustus received two trade missions from India between 25-21 B.C.

After a lapse of several centuries, large sections of the country, at least in north and central India, were united by the Gupta Kings, who attempted to revive the imperial idea of a *Chakravartin* (supreme ruler) of a pan-Indian empire. In addition to its military glories, the Gupta Age (320-540 A.D.) achieved notable successes in artistic and humanistic spheres and is often acclaimed as the Classical or Golden

Age of India. Indian art, literature, architecture and philosophy reached a high level of perfection. Treatises on metallurgy, astronomy and mathematics were written. Several systems of painting, sculpture, music, dance, drama, legal theory and philosophy were perfected. It was a time of intense intellectual and cultural renaissance. The famous Buddhist University of Nalanda was founded. A detailed and lively account of the society and economy during the Gupta Age has been handed down to us by a Chinese Buddhist pilgrim, Fa-hsien who traveled in India from 405 to 411 A.D.

After the collapse of the Gupta Empire around 540 A.D., the country once again returned to a state of disorganization and political fragmentation. Invasions from Central Asia by the Huns and other groups had already started. Several tribes including the Huns, the Shakas and the Scythians migrated to India in large numbers and set up small principalities in northwest India. Gradually, they adopted Indian ways and were assimilated into society. The rise of the Rajput families, who later became the ruling dynasties in Rajasthan, has been attributed to the social changes resulting from the movements and assimilation of these groups into Hindu society during post-Gupta times.

The Southern Peninsula had, through the centuries, developed its own linguistic, philosophic and cultural traditions. Very rarely had the military arm of the north Indian emperors interfered in their political and administrative affairs. Powerful kingdoms like the Pallavas, Chalukyas (and later the Cholas) and Rashtrakutas were the south Indian empires established between the 4th and 10th century A.D. Within these kingdoms, a distinctive Dravidian culture took root. Tamil and associated Dravidian languages had reached a high degree of development.

By the 10th century, north India was again fragmented and several smaller regional kingdoms, associated with several Rajput families and the descendants of the Huns, the Shakas and the Scythians had emerged. Noteworthy among those were the Solankis, Paramars, Chauhans and Tomars. Regional feelings were also expressed in the development of local languages such as Gujarati, Bengali, Rajasthani, and Hindi which began to be used in preference to Sanskrit.

THE EARLY MUSLIM PERIOD

By the 8th century, Islam had been firmly rooted in Arabia and had started to encroach upon the lower Indus Basin. Until the 10th century the Islamic invasions were sporadic and did not take root in the subcontinent. Increasingly, these became more regular and intense, and during the succeeding centuries the petty, warring Hindu principalities could not for long withstand their onslaughts. Islam came to India finally from Central Asia, rather than from Arabia. By the 10th century the Turks had begun penetration from the northwest, from present-day Afghanistan and Pakistan, through the several passes in the area. After repeated attempts, they were successful in consolidating their power in northwest India and eventually in the occupying of the throne at Delhi. Several Turkish dynasties ruled over Delhi Sultanate and expanded their authority over a large portion of the Indo-Ganga Plains. Their rule was generally marked by the rigid enforcement of the Islamic law, increase in the power of the nobility and succession disputes. Invasions from Central Asia continued, often crippling the Delhi Sultanate. Notable among such invasions was the one by Timur, a ruler of a vast empire in Central Asia who struck Delhi in 1398 A.D. with a devastating blow in the wake of which the Delhi empire crumbled and broke into several regional Muslim and Rajput states.

While Hindu India in the north was being preyed upon by Islamic invasions, South India led a separate life. Islam came to South India eventually, however, centuries later. The establishment of the Muslim kingdom of Bahmani (c. 1347-1527 A.D.) represented such a political thrust of Islam into southern India. As a challenge to the Bahmani empire, the vast empire of Vijayanagar (c. 1336-1646 A.D.) became the last bastion of Hinduism against this Islamic thrust from North India. The Vijayanagar empire was notable in many respects. The present day linguistic regions of the Dravidian speech and culture experienced renewed development in it, and its rulers vigorously pursued the development of fine arts and cultural traditions.

An undercurrent of Hindu revival was reasserting itself during the period 1350-1450 A.D., a century of political turmoil for northern India, beneath the rise and fall of dynastic

rules. Basically a religious movement aimed at self-preserva-
tion, Hindu resurgence manifested itself in various aspects
of life, literature, art, philosophy and architecture. Rajasthan and South India were the bastions of Hindu resistance
against the Islamic foreign encroachments. Its final outcome was the evolution of an Indian civilization in which
Muslims became a major element in Indian national life,
although the Hindus remained a dominant constituent in a
plural society.

THE MUGHAL EMPIRE

The establishment of the Mughal rule in north India in
1526 A.D. opened a new and long chapter in Indian history.
Originally natives of Central Asia, the Mughals established a
vast empire encompassing not only the northern part of India, but during its greatest extension, large sections of
Southern India as well. Gradually they inter-married with
the natives and were assimilated into society. They adopted,
in general, less restrictive religious policies than the Turks.
Akbar (c. 1556-1605 A.D.), perhaps the greatest of the
Mughal rulers, vigorously pursued tolerant policies conducive to greater harmony between the various communities. His policies were responsible for achieving greater
political unity, social progress and economic development in
the country. India, once again, became one of the richest
and more powerful countries in the world with which Persia,
Turkey and several European nations sought friendly relations and commercial links.

Akbar expanded the empire by military annexations as
well as by matrimonial alliances with the princely households of the Rajputs. The empire was sub-divided into 15
provinces (*suba*), several districts (*sarkar*), and subdistricts
(*pargana* or *mahal*). The subas were run by efficient,
centrally-appointed governors (*subedars*). The army was
well-trained and organized. The Mughal imperial system
and bureaucracy of courts, revenue department and police
system became the forerunner for the British administrative
machinery. The present-day structure of the Indian and
Pakistani administrations is basically patterned after the
Mughal arrangement.

The Mughal rulers were patrons of art, literature and architecture. They introduced a new court language, Urdu, which arose out of an interaction of Sanskrit (the existing language) and Persian brought by the Mughals and Turks into India. The graceful Indo-Sarcenic style of architecture flourished under their active patronage. They constructed hundreds of beautiful monuments, forts, tombs, mosques, gardens and public buildings reflecting this form of architecture. The Shalimar gardens of Srianagar and Lahore, the famous mausoleum of Taj Mahal and the mosques at Agra, and the abandoned city of Fatehpur Sikri are eloquent examples of Mughal patronage of art.

Aurangzeb (1658-1707 A.D.), the grandson of Akbar, was able to extend the Mughul empire to its greatest extent, covering most of the subcontinent. His fanatically intolerant religious policies toward non-Muslims, however, sowed the seeds of rebellion in several parts of the country; among the Rajputs in Rajasthan, the Jats near Delhi, the Sikhs in the Punjab and the Marathas in western Deccan. Soon regional chiefs began asserting themselves in anti-Mughal revolts. Even during his lifetime his vast empire began to crumble. A large Maratha empire, which was established in the northwest Deccan, became a source of great irritation to Aurangzeb. This Maratha empire (later Confederacy) persisted for over 150 years and finally succumbed to the onslaughts of the Muslim States of Deccan (Hyderabad) and the penetration of the British East India Company. By 1817 A.D., after the Third Maratha War, the British had gained control over most of the Maratha Confederacy.

ESTABLISHMENT OF BRITISH RULE

The Europeans arrived in South Asia in search of profitable trade in spices, metals, brocades and porcelain. They possessed superior maritime techniques which were helpful to them in this quest. Their commercial activity started in the 16th century. The Dutch, the Portuguese, the French and the English each competed for power and economic gains in the subcontinent. After passing through stages of intrigue and rivalry with the other European companies, the British East India Company had emerged victorious as the single most important force in the country by 1750. The company successfully interceded into the internal affairs of the weak rulers of Bengal and swiftly gained a stronghold over the Lower Ganga Valley as well as the strategic ports of Bombay and Madras along the coast. This extension of British rule in north India was facilitated by the political vacuum and civil strife in the area following the collapse of the Mughal empire.

Between 1760 and 1856, British supremacy was consolidated in the Indo-Gangetic Plains and the coastal areas, and was eventually extended to the entire subcontinent. Although most of the country had fallen to British control, within the British-occupied territories lay over 600 units which were internally administered by the native princes. By the treaties of paramountcy their rulers owed allegiance to the British. The British not only controlled the external affairs of these states, but also their internal security. Furthermore, they maintained a tight surveillance over the states through residents representing the Crown, who often meddled in the states' succession disputes and internal affairs. By the establishments of military stations known as the cantonments and by the institution of grants and favors to the rulers, the Crown virtually controlled the princely states and in time of grave political disorder could even take over their internal administration. By the Doctrine of Lapse of 1854, it could, and in several instances did, annex the princely territories to directly administered British India.

By 1856, the British control had achieved its maximum extent in space as it had also crystallized firmly in policy and practice. Historians are often puzzled at the question of the imposition of a completely alien control over a large area containing a rich and unique civilization. Prior to British control, the conquering rulers had become Indianized and merged into the native society. But the new masters remained socially aloof. In fact, they were able to take advantage of the divisiveness of the society, rent by class and caste distinctions. Often one prince was pitched against the other and preferred an unwelcome outsider to defeat by the unwelcome neighbor. There were other factors for the relatively swift British acquisition of supremacy over India. Their technical superiority, military organization and discipline contrasted with the religious cultural background of the natives rooted in inscrutable fate. Furthermore, the British military push was backed by overseas reinforcements through its seapower and reserves of soldiers.

The British did not particularly change the prevailing administrative or revenue systems established during the Mughal period, but gave these a new direction and set a more paternalistic tone. The administration at the sub-district (*sarkar* or *taluka*) and village level went on as before. At the district level the main administrative functions were controlled by Englishmen, at the lower level these continued to be in the hands of the Indians. The military and police departments were, however, tightly controlled by the British.

Among the notable socio-economic changes introduced by the East India Company were the new laws of buying and selling of property, particularly in respect to agricultural lands. This eventually widened significantly the existing class distinctions in the Indian society. The commerical classes were the prime beneficiaries. A large class of land-proprietors grew up who were initially intermediaries between the landed peasantry and the government and acted as revenue collectors. New laws enabled them to confiscate lands from delinquent payers.

A second and perhaps a more far-reaching change in the economic sphere was the introduction of new machine-industries. A direct result of this was the decline of ancient crafts, such as cotton and silk weaving. The British also established a new legal system together with a vast network of courts which were in part based on the Mughal and traditional systems, but proved more efficient. The new civil service and the organization of the army were patterned somewhat on the European model. On the social front, only a few attempts were made to intrude into the existing mores of the society. Notable among the new ordinances were the abolition of the practice of *sati*, the burning of Hindu widows on the funeral pyres of their husbands, the suppression of *thuggi*, and the ritual murders at certain religious ceremonies.

Even more far-reaching than the welfare programs was the introduction of English as a medium of transaction of government affairs at the national and provincial levels; this spurred the growth of English-speaking schools. Indirectly it helped diffuse several western ideas regarding arts, sciences and government through books written in English. The English-medium schools churned out a vast army of clerks, accountants, revenue officers and magistrates for the ponderous bureaucracy of the administration. The cumulative effects of these changes were the growth of landed aristocracy, English education and the growth of military and civil social clubs. All these created even deeper rifts among the already class-ridden society. Slowly but surely, there emerged a small, but powerful, western-educated elite among the Indians. Trained in western education, the children of this elite group, however, slowly began clamoring for the greater participation of Indians in the administration of the country.

The diffusion of the western education system and political ideology was also achieved by the Christian missionary organizations through their vast network of church-affiliated schools. The Christian missionary activity was primarily aimed at conversions among the native population. It was only mildly successful, but it was directly responsible for the furtherance of the western educational systems through its network of excellent schools and hospitals.

CONSOLIDATION OF BRITISH EMPIRE

The first jolt to British rule in India was experienced in 1857 in the form of a military revolt which became a turning point in the administrative functioning of this period. Soon the military revolt turned into a more popular rebellion. The dispossessed princes of the Ganga Plains rallied at the back of the mutineering soldiers. The land-owning class in northern and western India were already seething with hostility as a protest against the land-revenue settlement. The western innovations had militated against the socio-religious cutsoms of the society. The missionary activity was deeply and widely resented. After subduing the revolting armies, the British Parliament transferred power from the East India Company to the Crown and initiated a new social and constitutional policy aimed in particular at a more efficient government management of executive, legislative and legal affairs. Gradually, following the passing of the administration directly into the hands of the British government, the federal administration became an increasingly centralized bureaucracy, run by a tight, efficient but complex hierarchy of Indian Civil Service, which was manned exclusively at first and later prodominantly by the English. India became a British colony.

These changes further led to radical constitutional readjustments. Strict and uniform laws had to be enforced in order to effectively rule a large colony. Spheres yielding greatest economic exploitations with minimum of economic investment for developmental programs were singled out. The existing village, local and regional economic structure based on handicrafts and subsistence economy had to be broken and replaced with new market centers and control of the economy. The development of these market centers and the effective control of the country required a large and efficient professional and clerical class. All of these policies were vigorously pursued after 1858.

By 1920, British imperial power, the *Raj*, had become the largest stretch of British possessions in the world, and India a source of large revenues to the Crown, derived mainly from the vast agricultural production, expanding trade and industrial development. About half of the enormous land-revenues were spent on supporting a huge standing army. Taxes on opium and salt also yielded large revenues. Personal income tax, introduced around 1880, became a big contributor to the official revenues.

The country was divided into provinces (presidencies in the case of Bombay and Madras) which were administered by governors appointed by the Viceroy. The governors were political appointees and were directly responsible to the Secretary of State in England.

The crowning glory of British rule was the construction of a vast network of railroads across the subcontinent after 1858. The railroads accelerated the pace of raw material extraction from the rich agricultural countryside, and speeded up the transition from subsistence food-crop production to a commercial agricultural economy, thus contributing substantially to the economic development of the country. This efficient system of transportation dealt a death-blow to indigenous handicraft industries. Trains rushed vast quantities of cheap manufactured goods from England to the inland towns for distribution to the villages. The craftsmen

were thus forced to return to the soil for a living. Village
after village, known for handicrafts, lost its traditional
markets. Railroads also provided the military with swift
means of movement in case of revolt or emergency.

There were beneficial results too. The government acquired greater access to the countryside to transport foodgrains for relief in case of drought or famine. Furthermore,
rich coalfields of Bihar and Orisssa were developed during
the early twentieth century. The iron and steel company in
Bihar and textile industries in Bombay and Calcutta were
also established. Highways, steamboats, banks, insurance
agencies, printing presses, modern stock exchanges and
telegraph connections all accelerated the process of transformation of the economy and modernization of the production and exchange system.

THE INDEPENDENCE MOVEMENT

Meanwhile, an elite class of English-educated Indians
was gradually emerging which increasingly competed with
the Englishmen for employment in the Indian Civil Service,
legal services and education. The Universities of Bombay,
Calcutta and Madras had also been established around
1857. Many of the Indians, including some who broke away
from the Indian Civil Service, later on became leaders of the
nationalist movements in the country. The Indian National
Congress founded in 1885, became the rallying ground for
many nationalistic-minded youths. In succeeding years, the
Indian National Congress emerged as the principal political
party which started a long and strenuous struggle for greater
participation of Indians in the legislative machinery of the
administration. Later on it changed its objectives to obtaining complete independence of the country from British control.

As the independence movement gathered momentum
during the early twentieth century, nationalists in the Indian National Congress eventually split into Hindu and
Muslim factions. Initial British response to the nationalist
demand was a stiff attitude and several nationalist leaders
including Mahatma Gandhi and Jawaharlal Nehru were im-
prisoned for long terms. At times the nationalist movement

was somewhat clouded by centrifugal forces set in the Congress party, as well as due to the emergence of a new party during the 30's, the Muslim League. The latter pressed adamantly for a separate regional identity ("homeland") for the Muslims. With the emergence of the Muslim League, the Congress, which had all along mobilized a broadly based nationalist support, felt hampered to deal with the British by itself. As talks on independence advanced during the 40's, the Muslim League leadership, spearheaded by Mohammed Ali Jinnah, opted for a separate independent "homeland" for the Muslims, to be named *Pakistan* and to be carved out of the subcontinent. The goal of a united political entity for the country became unfeasible and the Indian National Congress agreed to the partition of the country in order to achieve independence from the British.

The two independent nations were finally created out of the subcontinent in 1947, principally within the geographical framework of the concentrations of the Hindus and Muslims in the subcontinent. The initial years of independence were full of turmoil for both countries. Even before the partitioning of the subcontinent, Hindu-Muslim riots had erupted in areas which underwent division between the countries, notably the Punjab in the west, and Bengal in the east. Over 12 million persons, Hindus and Muslims, left their ancestral homes and migrated to areas of their religious affiliations across the newly-created international borders. Homes and business establishments were abandoned in the flight for life. The new international borders disregarded traditional established networks of railroads, irrigation canals and manufacturing areas. This division posed severe problems of equitable distribution of human and natural resources between the two countries. Refugee rehabilitation for the millions was, however, the immediate problem before any programs of economic development and administrative establishment could be instituted. Fortunately, well-trained Indian and Pakistan officers quickly brought civil order in the two new countries in the aftermath of partition.

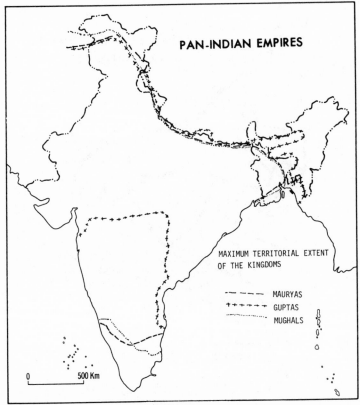

PAN-INDIAN EMPIRES

MAXIMUM TERRITORIAL EXTENT
OF THE KINGDOMS

— — — — MAURYAS
+ + + + + + GUPTAS
.... MUGHALS

0   500 Km

FIGURE 2.2

POLITICAL AND CULTURAL
CORE AREAS

It can be clearly discerned from the preceding overview
of the history of Indian civilization that a recurrent pattern
of territorial instability of political bases and development of
subregionalisms in the subcontinent has been a major theme
in Indian historical geography. The cherished goal of
establishing a pan-Indian empire, an Arya Vrata ruled by a
Chakravartin, was accomplished only a few times, under
Ashoka, Aurangzeb, and more recently, during British rule
(Figure 2.2). Even during these exceptional periods of vast

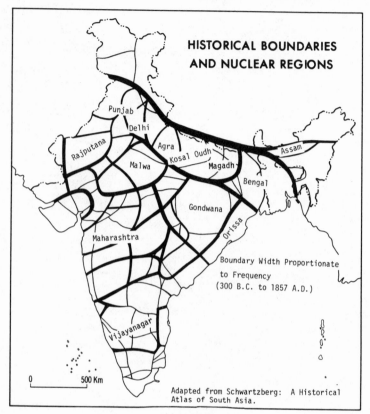

HISTORICAL BOUNDARIES
AND NUCLEAR REGIONS

Punjab
Delhi
Rajputana
Agra
Kosal Oudh
Malwa
Magadh
Assam
Bengal
Gondwana
Maharashtra
Orissa

Boundary Width Proportionate
to Frequency
(300 B.C. to 1857 A.D.)

Vijayanagar

0   500 Km

Adapted from Schwartzberg: A Historical
Atlas of South Asia.

FIGURE 2.3

empires, the southern tip of the country always escaped control of the central all-India authority.

No less striking is the theme of the broad cultural division of the subcontinent into the Aryan North and Dravidian South. Only Hinduism transcended the linguistic and
ethnic regionalism dividing the northern and western plains
of the subcontinent from its non-Aryan component, per-
meated into, and made an enduring stronghold in Dravidian
India. Recurrent political instability and territorial fragmentation of the political units, combined with the Aryan-
Dravidian dichotomy, produced cultural subregionalism or
core-areas based on local political control over ethnic and
linguistic subgroups (Figure 2.3). Even during British rule,

direct administrative control did not extend over the entire country; India was fragmented into a patchwork of over six hundred princely kingdoms of varying sizes, the larger of which were entrenched into the historic core regions, in addition to the British-ruled territory covering two-thirds of the country.

The various core-areas thus developed in rich agricultural lands and were, in general, isolated from each other by physical barriers like mountains, deserts, or forests. Insulated from the mainstream of history for centuries, the areas of refuge and isolation also developed regional cultures, as in the Kashmir Valley and the Assam Valley. Several smaller refuge areas are still occupied by the various tribal groups (Bhils, Gonds, Santhals) often speaking langauges unrelated to the Indo-European or Dravidian families, and still retaining distinctive archaic cultures. Such areas are found in the jungles of Gondwana, the Rajmahal Hills between Bihar and Bengal, the mountains surrounding the Assam Valley, and in the Cardamon Hills in southern India.

The most persistent external boundary of the country has been one to the north and west of the Indo-Ganga Plains, historically separating these plains from Nepal, Tibet, Afghanistan, and Iran. In the Northeast, Assam has also remained for long periods outside India's central authority. The most stable of the internal political boundaries within the subcontinent has been along the Narmada-Chota Nagpur line, separating the Indo-Aryan Gangetic Plains from the Peninsular, with the exception of Maharashra, essentially Dravidian India. Within this broad Indo-Aryan-Dravidian supra-regional framework, either dynastic or core (nuclear) regions crystallized which remained relatively stable, submerging temporarily and recurrently under the national (pan-Indian) authority. Only in modern times did the British superimpose their authority over the entire subcontinent. Figure 2.3 shows historical boundaries and identifies major nuclear regions in the country. Boundary widths are proportionate to their frequency.

CITATIONS AND SELECT BIBLIOGRAPHY

Basham, A. L., (ed.), *A Cultural History of India*. Oxford, 1975.

Chatterjee, A. C., *Short History of India*. New York, 1957.

Dodwell, Ed., *Cambridge Shorter History of India*. Cambridge, 1934.

Gopal, S., *British Policy in India, 1858-1905*. Cambridge, 1965.

Griffith, P. J., *British Impact on India*. London, 1952.

Panikkar, K. M., *Survey of Indian History*. Bombay, 1947.

Panikkar, K. M., *The Determining Periods of Indian History*. Bombay, 1962.

Rawlinson, H. G., *India, A Short Cultural History*. London, 1952.

Singhal, D. P., *India and World Civilization*. Vol. 2, London, 1972.

Spear, P., *A History of India*. Vol. 2, Harmondsworth, 1966.

Schwartzberg, J. E., *A Historical Atlas of South Asia*. Chicago, 1978.

Thapar, R., *A History of India*. Vol. 1, Harmondsworth, 1966.

Watson, F., *A Concise History of India*. New York, 1975.

Wolpert, S., *A New History of India*. New York, 1977.

SECTION TWO
Society and Culture

CHAPTER 3

DEMOGRAPHIC STRUCTURE
AND POPULATION PROBLEMS

India is the second most populous country in the world. Containing over 15 percent of the world's population on only 2.5 percent of its area, India's population of 661 million (estimate for 1979) far exceeds the combined populations of the United States of America and the Soviet Union. No other country of comparable size even approaches its present average population density of about 200 persons per square kilometer (over 500 persons per square mile), a figure well over five times the world's average, and still rapidly rising. Its current annual rate of growth of 1.9 per cent (*World Population Data Sheet, 1979*), though not among the highest in the world, has been steadily increasing; it is nearly twice as high as it was 30 years ago. Translated in absolute terms, the country is adding 12 million persons—almost Australia's total population—to its existing numbers every year. If the current rate of increase remains unrestrained, the country's population will double itself by the turn of the century, surpassing one billion.

Large population increments in the last thirty years have left the country until recently with food shortages and dependence on other countries for foodgrain imports. Although the government is cognizant of these problems and has launched family planning programs, a real breakthrough in this area is not yet in sight. Some gains toward achieving foodgrain self-sufficiency have recently been made, but the results may be temporary. The population explosion and foodgrain inadequacy are among the major problems facing the country. This chapter deals with India's demographic composition and selected aspects of its population problem. Six areas of the population problem have been selected for brief discussion: problems of illiteracy, foodgrain inadequacy and population explosion, manpower and unemployment, programs of human fertility, the problem of public health and disease prevalence, and problems related to urbanization. Problems of urbanization are discussed separately in Chapter 7. Chapter 4 on "Society and Culture" is devoted to the cultural aspects of India's population and the related problems of caste inequalities, linguistic and religious divisions. Chapter 6 also deals with the foodgrain situation.

GROWTH DYNAMICS
AND SPATIAL DIMENSIONS

India has been one of the early centers of population concentration in the world. As far back as two to three millennia B.C. a sophisticated urban civilization flourished in the Indus Basin in the Indian subcontinent. Several sites (Harappa, Mohenjodaro, etc.) in the Indus Basin have revealed the existence of well-planned cities, domestication of agricultural plants and animals, a wide circulation of artifacts prepared of copper, gold, silver, bronze and the development of manufacturing crafts like weaving and metal work. Early Aryans who settled northern India from 3000-7000 years ago also possessed a technology capable of supporting a fairly dense population. During the period of Aryan settlement (Vedic India), over 20 cities flourished in north India (Schwartzberg, Plate III. A.1, 1978). By the 4th century B.C. north Indian plains contained large concentrations of populations. Greek and Indian records of this time indicate that early Aryan civilization of northern India compared favorably with that of medieval Europe in its heyday of civilization. Chandragupta (c. 321-297 B.C.), the first pan-Indian ruler, is believed to have maintained a standing army of 700,000 men. During Ashoka's rule (c. 274-236 B.C.) Indian civilization attained a high level of development in administration, commerce, agricultural techniques and the utilization of metals. Indian population during this time has been estimated at 110-150 million. For about 2000 years following Ashoka's rule population remained nearly stationary. Population gains of peaceful times were cancelled by periods of high mortality resulting from wars, epidemics and famines. The estimates of population at the time of Akbar's rule (c. 1556-1605 A.D.) range between 85-117 million (Nath, Chapter 5).

Rapid gains in population numbers began to occur only after the later part of the 19th century, when natural checks on population growth were diminished by the virtual elimination of several diseases (cholera, plague, malaria), the introduction of better public health standards, the spread of law and order and a consequent reduction in banditry and crime, a reduction in the frequency and severity of famines and consequent increases in life expectancy. The first complete census of the country in 1881 yielded a count of 256 million (including modern Pakistan and Bangladesh), almost twice the population of the 16th century. Since then a comprehensive decennial census has been maintained. Table 3.1 gives the results of the total population count since 1901.

In the first two decades of the 20th century, population growth was slow and sporadic. Since 1921, however, population has shown a continuous trend of accelerating growth. The contrasting patterns, before and since 1921 are apparent, and are related to the mortality situation of the two periods. Before 1921 death rates were estimated at 42-48 per 1,000 persons per year, thus nearly cancelling increases resulting from high birth rates. Since then death rates have declined markedly (Table 3.2) but only after 1950 did birth rates fall below 40 per 1,000 per year. These demographic factors account for the doubling of the rate of increase from 1.0 to 2.0 per cent between 1921-1971. In absolute terms, between 1941 and 1971, 228.7 million people were added to the total population, a figure well over the current total population of the United States. In a single decade of 1961-1971, population registered an increase of 108.2 million!

The average density of population of the country is 515 persons per square mile (200 per sq. km.), one of the highest in the world for countries of equal or larger size. Within the country, however, there is a wide variation in the distribution of population. In Figure 3.1 the regional variations are categorized into five levels, which can be generalized into three broad spatial types: (A) high density (more than 200

TABLE 3.1

GROWTH OF INDIA'S POPULATION, 1901-1971

Census	Population In Millions	Change in Millions	Percent of Change From Preceding Decade
1901	236.3	—	—
1911	252.1	+ 15.8	+ 5.7
1921	251.4	− 0.7	− 0.3
1931	279.0	+ 27.6	+ 11.0
1941	318.7	+ 39.7	+ 14.2
1951	361.1	+ 42.4	+ 13.3
1961	439.2	+ 78.1	+ 21.5
1971	547.4	+ 108.2	+ 24.6

Sources:
1. *Census of India,* 1971, New Delhi.
2. *Census of India,* 1961, Paper No. 1 of 1962.
3. Kingsley Davis, *The Population of India and Pakistan,* p. 27.
Note: Before 1951 figures are adjusted for post-independence India.

persons per square kilometer), (B) low density (less than 50 persons per square kilometer), and (C) medium density (50-200 persons per square kilometer).

Areas of high density are peripheral to Peninsular India, and to the arid and semi-arid parts of the Thar Desert (west Rajasthan). These high density areas include: the Ganga Plains, North Punjab Plains in north India; Gujarat, Kerala (Malabar Coast) along the Western Coast; Tamil Nadu (especially the Kaveri Delta) in the extreme southeast; the eastern littorals of Orissa and Andhra Pradesh (especially the river deltas) and Brahmaputra Valley in Assam in the northeastern part of the country. All these areas are well-watered, arable lowlands of fertile soils and easy transportation, and contain old settlements (with the exception of the recently settled Brahmaputra Valley). The single most populous section within the belt of high density is the Ganga Plains and the adjoining areas of north Punjab — a vast territory of over 250 million persons. Average nutritional densities (number of persons per unit area of cultivated land) of over 6,000 persons per kilometer exist in several areas within the densely populated Ganga Plains, and part of West

TABLE 3.2

ESTIMATED CRUDE BIRTH RATE,
CRUDE DEATH RATE
AND NATURAL INCREASE IN INDIA 1901-1971

	Crude Birth Rate	Crude Death Rate	Natural Increase in Per Cent Per Year
1901-11	48.1	*	*
1911-21	49.2	*	*
1921-31	46.4	36.2	1.0
1931-41	45.2	31.2	1.4
1941-51	39.9	27.4	1.2
1951-61	41.7	22.8	1.8
1961-71	39.0	12.4	2.6
1971-76	38.0	13.0	2.5
1978 (Estimate)	34.0	15.0	1.9

*Data Lacking

Source:
    1. *Growth of Population in India,* Ministry of Health, Government of India, New Delhi, 1962.
    2. *Census of India 1941, 1951, 1961, 1971.*
    3. *1979 World Population Data Sheet,* Washington, 1979.

Bengal, north Bihar and eastern Uttar Pradesh, where some eighty per cent of the population is engaged in agricultural activities. Gujarat has high density in areas drained by the Sabarmati river. Increased urbanization consequent upon the industrial and commercial development of the last fifty years has raised the density of population. Along the western coast the plains of Kerala are well-watered and composed of fertile soils. The Kaveri Delta in Tamil Nadu along the eastern coast also has been a densely populated area of fertile alluvium for over two millennia and forms the core of Dravidian culture.

Areas of low population density are the Thar Desert (Western Rajasthan), the hill/mountainous areas of northeast India (Meghalaya, Nagaland, Mizoram, Arunachal

Pradesh) and the district of Bastar. These areas contain poor soils and rugged terrain, and are handicapped by a serious shortage of water supply for any large-scale agricultural activity. In parts of the Thar Desert population density is below 10 persons per square kilometer.

The remaining parts of the country contain only medium densities (50-200 persons per sq. km.). Most of the Deccan Plateau, South Bihar, Central India, eastern Rajasthan, and West Orissa belong to this category.

These patterns of population distribution and density have developed over long periods of time in response to physical and cultural forces. Some of the physical factors have been pointed out above. Cultural factors have also interacted to produce these patterns. Settlement during the ancient and medieval times was based on the original consideration of defense, water supply and caste affiliations, etc. The development of urban centers as foci of administrative and commercial functions, the development of roads, growth of railroads, development of canal irrigation facilities, growth of ports, and the opening up of new areas for settlement during the British occupation are some other factors that led to the differential rates of population growth in the various parts of the country.

Despite the differential growth of the various parts of the country, however, the overall population patterns, shown in Figure 3.1, have not changed noticeably except in Assam and in the Punjab during the last fifty years, although within this framework (areas of high and low densities) densities have been consistently rising. Growth rates between 1961-1971, however, suggest that population increases have occurred at lower rates in the high density areas (Uttar Pradesh, Bihar, Tamil Nadu), a situation suggestive of their probably having reached a saturation level in terms of supporting further increases. Punjab, Haryana and Rajasthan continued to show higher increase in densities resulting from intensification of irrigational facilities.

Figure 3.2 shows population change during the intercensus period 1961-1971. Areas showing a high rate of population increase include: (1) the Brahmaputra Valley in Assam, an area of intensive land reclamation programs for the last forty years, high human fertility and large in-migration, especially of Bengali refugees from Bangladesh since parti-

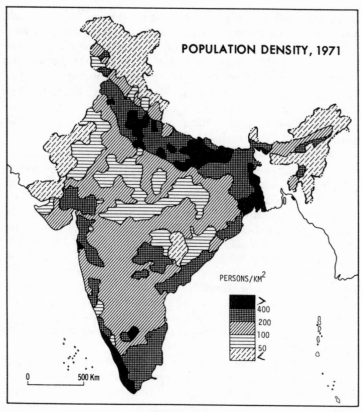

FIGURE 3.1

tion; (2) Tripura which also received large numbers of refugees from Bangladesh; (3) West Bengal, an area of industrialization and urbanization (and another area of substantial in-migration from Bangladesh); (4) East Punjab, Haryana, and north Rajasthan, an area of new settlement on reclaimed wastelands and the extension of canal irrigation in the 1950's and 1960's; (5) parts of Gujarat, Rajasthan and adjoining Madhya Pradesh, where rapid population growth has resulted from increased urbanization and industrialization; (6) the scattered areas of urbanized districts of Delhi, Hyderabad, Madras, Bombay, Ahmadabad (all grew over 30 percent). These urban districts received large numbers of rural immigrants. A noticeable feature of this

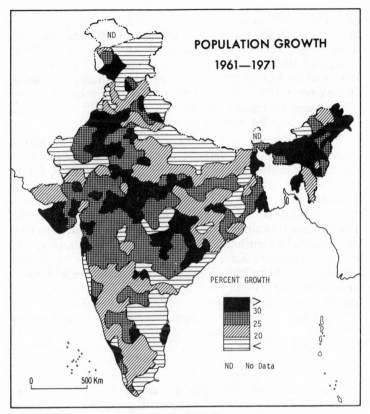

FIGURE 3.2

map is that very few parts of the country experienced a low rate of increase (below 20 percent).

PROBLEMS OF ILLITERACY

India has one of the largest illiterate populations in the world. Despite improvements in the literacy levels during the recent years, only 29.3 percent of its population could read and write in 1971. Although statistical increases in literacy are substantial—net gains of 56 million literates (from 104 to 160 million) between 1961-1971, as compared to that of 44 million (from 60 to 104 million) during

1951-1961 — 387 million were recorded as illiterate in the 1971 census. Allowing for the exclusion of children below six years of age, who would not normally know how to read and write, this figure would drop to 320 million. This fact of a vast illiterate humanity overshadows the significant gains in literacy since 1951. As a matter of fact, the actual number of illiterates increased by 92 million — 34 million between 1951-1961, and 58 million between 1961-1971.

Female literacy is even depressingly lower. By actual count, only 48 million females are literate, as compared to 112 million males (the male-female ratio thus being 2.6 to 1). In India, as in many other places, females form the backbone of tradition and conservatism. Traditionally, literacy has had little relevance for females in the rural areas. Their prime functions in the rural areas are to cook, to feed the household members, work as agricultural laborers, and to rear children. Since 1951, however, gains in female literacy have been higher than among males, especially in rural areas, largely due to increasing awareness among the masses as evidenced by increasing female enrollment in the rural schools. Government legislative measures encouraging compulsory and free education to the primary school level have helped to create public opinion favoring female education.

Literacy differences between rural and urban populations have been striking, but are slowly narrowing. Urban literacy is twice as high as for the rural population (52.4 percent vs. 23.6 percent in 1971). Although female literacy is universally lower, urban male-female differentials are smaller than those in the rural areas.

Figure 3.3, showing the distribution of literacy, brings out the broad regional disparities in the country. In general, areas of higher literacy (over 30 percent of the total population) are concentrated in the urbanized districts of Delhi, Calcutta, Ahmadabad, Baroda, Hyderabad and Madras; in Kerala and in a few districts in Assam, and Nagaland. In Kerala literacy rates are over 60 percent , the highest for any Indian state. About one-third of Kerala's population is Christian. Intensive Christian missionary activity, which was responsible for opening parochial schools and hospitals during British rule, accounts for its higher level of literacy. Christian missionary activity was also strong among the

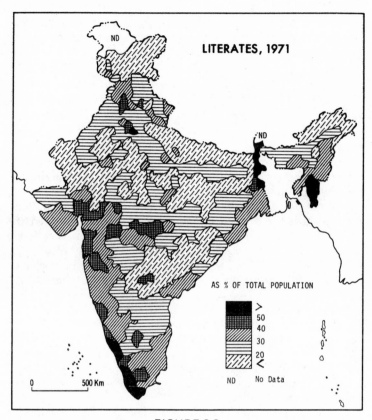

FIGURE 3.3

tribal groups in Assam and Nagaland. Here, low literacy (below 20 percent), is coincident with areas of low urbanization (less than 20 percent).

In 1966, the government set up a goal of imparting free and compulsory education to all children in government schools up to the primary grade. Furthermore, thousands of new schools, teacher training and technical institutions, libraries, vocational schools and degree colleges have been opened since 1951. Large outlays of funds (over a billion dollars for the five-year period of the Fourth Plan 1966-1971, and several billions during the previous plan periods) have been spent on such measures. The impact of these efforts is only slowly manifesting itself, but the goal of a completely literate society remains as yet a planner's dream. Large annual increases in population make the problem of rising literacy levels even more difficult.

POPULATION AND THE FOOD PROBLEM

In order to meet with the critical foodgrain deficiency during the last 25 years, the country spent large amounts of scarce foreign exchange on importing foodgrains. Foodgrain imports during this period averaged 3 to 5 million tons a year, rising to a peak of 10.8 million tons during 1966-1967, when the United States alone supplied 8 million tons. For the first time in 25 years, the government announced in 1971 that the country had achieved foodgrain sufficiency. Whether this status can be maintained in the future or whether demographic increases will outstrip foodgrain production is still problematic. Furthermore, the nutritional requirements of the people would have to be met. On the average, the caloric intake of an Indian is one-half of a North American. Possibly famines and large scale foodgrain shortages which plagued the country from time to time would be averted in the future. But it will be a long time before the nutritional requirements (quite apart from desirable improvements in the quality of the food) of the people can be achieved.

Eighty percent of the total cultivated area in the country is under foodgrain crops like rice, wheat, millets, and maize. Increasing their production is chiefly a question of increasing their output and yields, since a possible extension of the productive areas is limited. It is estimated that 20 percent of the area is in the form of culturable wastes (usually unused infertile patches full of weeds) and has been lying fallow since medieval times. Only insignificant parts of these so-called "culturable wastelands" can be reclaimed, and they generally show little promise for future development.

Between 1947 and 1966, foodgrain production increased over 50 percent, from 50 million tons to 80 million tons. The addition of another 10.5 million tons was recorded between 1966 and 1970. In a single year of 1970-1971 more than 5 million tons in foodgrain increase future gains in production enabled the country to show a production of 129 million tons by the mid-1970's making it sufficient in its foodgrain needs. It was officially claimed that whereas population could be expected to grow at a rate of 2.0 to 2.5 percent a year, foodgrain production could be expected to grow at 4 to 5 percent a year for several years. Officials claimed that India might never again have to depend on foodgrain imports. Official claims must, however, be interpreted with caution. By its own admission, the government report warned that the spectacular growth of 1970-1971 in food production cannot be indefinitely maintained. In fact, during 1971-1972 the country experienced a severe drought which forced the administration to import approximately 2 million tons of foodgrains from Canada, Australia and France. Since then foodgrain production has oscillated between 105 and 125 million tons. The country has now virtually attained foodgrain sufficiency. Future outlook would, however, depend on several factors: diffusion of new techniques, population increases and natural hazards, the last of which is of great importance.

Contrary to popular belief, sections of productive land in the Middle Ganga Plains (Uttar Pradesh, Bihar and West Bengal) are deficient in foodgrain supply. In these areas, population densities are very high, and despite large-scale foodgrain production, foodgrain requirements are not met. Among the factors creating this ambivalent situation are over-cropping, soil exhaustion, lack of fertilizers, backward farming methods, fragmented holdings, and the extreme poverty of the *ryot* (cultivator). These areas were also the hardest hit during the famine of 1966-1967. Other areas of high population densities and foodgrain deficiency are: Kerala, western Tamil Nadu, western Rajasthan, western Andhra Pradesh, parts of Karnataka, Assam and eastern Madhya pradesh. These areas suffer from poor rainfall, rugged terrain, infertile soils and/or limited irrigation facilities.

Reports of recent farming booms in many parts of the country, especially in the selected districts where the "Green Revolution" brought increases in wheat and rice production (e.g., Ludhiana district in Punjab, Tanjore district in Tamil Nadu) have given some hope for the future. The "Green Revolution" is largely attributed to the utilization of hybrid seeds of rice and wheat, better fertilizers, and pesticides.

however, the impact of the "Green Revolution" is yet to be felt in most areas of foodgrain deficiency. Regional deficiencies in foodgrain production continue to persist. Several studies have pointed out that the areas of foodgrain deficiency were hit hard during epidemics and famines. Movement of grain to these areas was hampered by poor transportation, inadequate storage conditions, faulty distribution facilities and administrative controls exercised by the states with surpluses. Administrative planning should be focused on narrowing the regional foodgrain production disparities. Geographically, the national problem of foodgrain self-sufficiency is in reality a regional problem. Planners should realize and deal with the problems faced by farmers in the various regions (Chakravarti, 1970). Efforts should be made to universalize the diffusion of "green revolution" techniques, to augment farm activities under the existing Community Development Programs, to enforce cultivator-assisting tenancy reforms and to promulgate tenancy laws in all the parts of the country. In addition, structural and institutional changes in the agricultural systems, such as the growing of alternative high yielding food crops like cassava, sweet pototoes or bananas in areas of lesser fertility have also been recommended.

The current near sufficiency, however, does not necessarily forestall an indefinite time-frame within which foodgrain production might outstrip population growth rate. It is, therefore, imperative that efforts to achieve and maintain foodgrain self-sufficiency should not be relaxed.

THE PROBLEM OF DISEASES
AND PUBLIC HEALTH

India has been the endemic home of several diseases, notably cholera, malaria, dysentery, pneumonia and typhoid. Occasionally recurrent epidemics of plague also brought death and destruction to millions especially in the urban areas and along routes of trade and pilgrimages throughout historical times. During the last fifty years plague has ceased to be a health problem primarily as a result of significant improvements in public sanitation. The last great plague arrived by sea to Bombay in 1896, and spread quickly inland along the trade routes (Learmonth, 1965). Until 1920, it ran in short six year cycles, and on the average one-quarter to one-half a million deaths a year were reported. Since then, mortality from plague has declined to about 150 in 1962. Until 1955, malaria was the major cause of mortality in recent times, claiming about 2 million deaths a year. Its chief foci lie in the Tarai areas and in the riverine plains and rainy plains and rainy slopes of the coastal *ghats* (hills). It has been prevalent in an epidemic form in the Ganga plains, and the coastal plains, in the interior parts of the country it has been endemic. There were between 60,000-65,000 yearly deaths from malaria in the 1960's, but since then there have been fewer cases. The virtual eradication of malaria has apparently been achieved by the large scale spraying of D.D.T. all over the country under the natural malaria control program aided by the World Health Organization during the 1950's. During the 1970's, however, D.D.T.-resistant strains of mosquitoes surfaced and the incidence of malaria increased.

Cholera incidence and mortality have also been significantly reduced during the last fifty years primarily as a result of a large-scale inoculation program during disease incidence and environmental sanitation program. However, it is still responsible for large numbers of deaths during religious pilgrimages. It spreads explosively along the pilgrim routes and in the pilgrim centers, especially during the mammoth gatherings of hundreds of thousands of pilgrims in Allahabad every twelfth year or every fourteen years in Hardwar, and at other places at the recurrent times of religious pilgrimages. Its normal and less violent occurrence zone lies in the Ganga-Brahmaputra delta, from where it generally fans upstream, often accompanied by violent outbreaks at places of poor drinking water facilities, and insanitary environment conditions.

Smallpox has been one of the major epidemic diseases in India, accounting for 30,000 to 40,000 deaths annually till 1978 when the W.H.O. claimed that it had been virtually eliminated. The chief areas of smallpox mortality were in Bihar, Punjab, Haryana, Rajasthan, Uttar Pradesh and Madhya Pradesh, where poor conditions of sanitation and overcrowding are associated with the disease. During epidemic years it branched out in all directions with the move-

ment of persons along the railroads and roads. A mass vaccination campaign extending over the last fifty years, particularly in the urban areas, has resulted in appreciable recent declines in the disease (from 85,000 reported cases in 1960 to about 10,000 cases annually since 1970). The major obstacle in the implementation of comprehensive vaccination program in the country is the lack of public cooperation of the illiterate, conservative masses.

Indian disease statistics are scarce, incomplete and based mostly on estimates. In addition to the above mentioned three main diseases, others accounting for a significant number of deaths are: tuberculosis, typhoid, diarrhea and pneumonia. A wide-ranging campaign of inoculation and pilot projects to reduce T.B. incidence are currently underway. Bronchitis and related pneumonia are among the important causes of death, particularly in north India during the winter, and among the poor in urban slums. Dysentery is another major health problem, and is the cause of several thousand deaths a year. Improved sanitation and personal hygiene, and better standards of living are slowly reducing mortality due to dysentery and diarrhea.

Morbidity control in India has rapidly reduced mortality in the last fifty years. Crude death rate has fallen from 36 to 1,000 a year in 1921 to 15.0 in 1978. Average life expectancy of an Indian has risen from 27 years in 1931 to 57 years in 1978. Maternal and infant mortality are still very serious problems, with their rates among the highest in the world. Excessive child-bearing, poor nutrition, low standard of living, inadequate maternity care in general, and unhealthy sanitation and public hygiene are largely responsible for high infant mortality.

Decline in mortality in India has been sex, status and residence selective. Men are comparatively healthier, and less prone to diseases than females. Men enjoying a higher socio-economic status are healthier, less prone to diseases, and have lower mortality rates. Mortality rate is lower for urban areas than in the countryside, where public health facilities and sanitation are poorer. Despite recent reductions in mortality levels, they are still very high (15 per 1,000 population in 1978 as compared to 11 per 1,000 for the world, as reported in *World Population Data Sheet, 1979*). Further reductions will depend on several factors, chief among which are: government health policies, a massive literacy drive, a rise in the standards of living and improvements in infant health care. India's difficulties in this regard are heightened by the vast size and poverty of its public and inadequate financial help afforded by the government. Public health was accorded low priority in the first three Five Year Plans. The doctor-population ratio remained at a low lever of 18/100,000 persons during the fifteen years of Indian planning from 1951-1966. In 1975 it was 40/100,000. An allocation of a little over $600 million for public health programs for the Fifth and Sixth Five Year Plans (1974-1978; 1978-1983) works out to 3 percent of the total outlay for each plan which was over 5 percent if the allocations for water supply and sanitation programs were added. Although this represents a substantial increase in total outlay of public expenditure from the previous plans, it is insignificant on a per capita basis (amounting to less than Rs 12 or $1.50 annually per capita for public health, medical service, and water-sanitation).

MANPOWER AND EMPLOYMENT

India's total labor force (15-65 age group) is estimated at 220 million. Babies born between 1965 and 1975 will add 90 million to the labor force during the 80's. On account of expected increases in life expectancy, only 26 million workers are expected to die or retire from employment during the same period. This would amount to an addition of 64 million to the present 220 million in the labor force. To provide employment for this vast labor force is one of the greatest challenges to the country. Current demographic trends indicate that there will be large surpluses of labor both in the urban centers and in the countryside.

Employment statistics in India are scarce, and are mostly in the form of estimates or intelligent guesses. The jobless are now numbered at nearly 22 million or over 10 percent of the labor force. In addition, under-employment is estimated to be 24 percent of the labor force. Furthermore, of the jobless over 5 million are educated persons who should be put to work in the development of the country, as engineers, doctors and nurses (Bhardwaj, 82).

While precise information on urban unemployment is

difficult to obtain, a recent U.N. study estimated that nearly 10 million urban residents registered with the government-sponsored Employment Bureaus were seeking jobs in 1976. A large proportion of unemployment among the literates and the educated resides in the urban areas. Nearly 58 percent of the urban illiterates are unemployed, as compared to the rural illiterate-employed figure of about 42 percent among the labor force. A small but steady stream of rural population composed mostly of illiterates pouring into urban centers in search of mythical jobs in the competitive commercial-industrial labor market will probably be intensified. This urbanward migration seriously aggravates the unemployment situation.

The employment situation in the rural areas appears equally grim. Although its exact size remains unascertained, a sizable portion of the population engaged in agriculture perpetually remains under-employed and seasonally idle. During the 1980's there will be an addition of 45 million people to the rural areas who would be faced with finding work on the farms. The creation of such a large under- and un-utilized reservoir of labor will undoubtedly intensify migration to the cities, which themselves will be feeling the crunch of inadequate additional job opportunities. By a conservative estimate, 120 million additional jobs will have to be created by the end of 1985. Obviously, drastic measures will be required to permit the absorption of the unemployed into the employment pool.

The problem is not merely one of idle manpower, under-employment or unemployment, but also that of raising workers' productivity. Tradition and sentiment emphasize the measurement of productivity per unit of land, or in industry by capital returns, and not according to the output per worker (Lewis, 57-60). Labor productivity in India is among the lowest in the world. Vast opportunities exist in the introduction of new, scientific and progressive processes of production in which the vast human resources of the country can be mobilized. Government's response to the employment problem has been to encourage cottage industries, subsidized by public funds, and protected by regulated markets within the framework of the Five Year Plans. Cottage industries, however, have failed to absorb a significant portion of the idle labor force. Private factory production has exceeded the government ventures in efficiency, consumer orientation and quality of production. The solution, therefore, lies not only in the development of cottage industries, but in the development of progressive minded new rural industrial estates and the funneling of rural surplus labor into these agro-industrial centers, spatially organized around the varying size-groups of villages and small cities. In order to establish functioning market centers, a vast amount of rural reconstruction is also required, such as building irrigation ditches, *bunding*, i.e., damming, well-digging, rural road construction, building of grain warehouses and building of public facilities (Lewis, 63). The idle labor force should be encouraged to adopt more productive, efficient and rewarding measures, like the introduction of labor intensive techniques of cultivation, increased utilization of forests and underground water. The newly developed agro-industrial market centers near the villages will absorb the rural migratory streams which are currently moving to the larger cities. The principle bottleneck in the implementation of these plans is the scarcity of required capital (Johnson, 1965).

DEMOGRAPHIC DIMENSIONS
AND POPULATION EXPLOSION

Perhaps the most disturbing aspect of India's population is its demographic structure. Birth rates, now estimated at 33 to 34 per 1,000 per year, have remained constantly high (from 40-45) during the twentieth century. Death rates, on the other hand, fell markedly during the same period, from 36.2 to 15 per 1,000 population (Table 3.2). Infant mortality experienced a particularly noticeable decline, as life expectancy at birth rose from 32 years in 1951 to 57 years in 1978. A combination of these forces pushed the rate of population increase from 1.3 percent a year in 1941 to nearly 2 percent in 1978 (it was 2.6 percent in 1971).

Universal and early marriages, low divorce rates, and lack of recognition and practice of birth control measures in a tradition-bound society have contributed to high fertility rates. About 43 percent of the population is under 15 years of age, causing the working population to carry a large dependency load. Such demographic representations as the

AGE—SEX PYRAMID, 1971

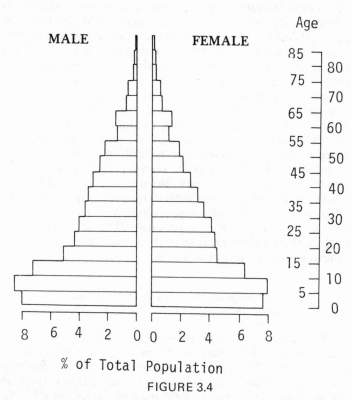

% of Total Population

FIGURE 3.4

age-sex pyramid only dramatizes India's population problems (Figure 3.4). In it, each five-year group (known as a
cohort) is larger than the one above it. Only in 1971, the 0-4
group, or the one at the base was slightly shorter than the
one above it. Such a trend, usually called progressive fertility, would, if continued, push the current population of 660
million to over 1 billion by the year 2,000. In sum, the total
population is already large, fertility is high and is progressive, death rates and infant mortality are declining, the
dependency load is large, and rates of population increase
are rising.

A careful analysis of the growth of India's population

suggests that even in the event of significant reductions of birth rates, India's population would still rise to the one billion mark at the turn of the century. One study's most optimistic estimate, which assumed that Indian women would beget only 2.4 children (as compared to the current figure of over 4) if birth rates are reduced by one half by the year 2000 A.D., appears to be a demographer's dream. This is one of the four possible courses that the country might take, according to the U.S. Census Bureau. Other projections estimate that India's population in the year 2000 A.D. might rise to the colossal figure of 1.5 billion (*India Ready or Not,* 6).

The population problem, or more specifically the problem of high birth rates, was one of the major pressing domestic issues confronting the Indian government after independence in 1947. When, in 1951, the government formulated its First Five Year Plan (1951-1956), family planning programs were included in it, and India became the first major nation among the developing countries to adopt a public policy aimed at achieving reductions in birth rates.

High fertility levels in India have resulted from many interacting demographic, cultural and economic forces. Youthful age-structure, near universal and early marriages, low divorce rates, cultural and religious attitudes favoring a large family, sharply declining mortality rates consequent on the virtual eradication of such diseases as smallpox, malaria, tuberculosis and typhoid during the last seventy years, and a lack of motivation encouraging a positive response to innovations regarding birth control and family planning efforts, are some of the deterrents to achieving reductions in fertility. In 1971 nearly one-half of the total population belonged to the most fecund age group (15-45 years of age). A predominant portion of this age group is in the married category. Available statistics point out that in the cities on the average 6-8 children are born to women who have completed fertility performance (15-44 years of age). This average may be even higher in rural areas, for which registration data are not available.

Specific targets to achieve reductions in birth rates from 45 to 32 per 1,000 persons annually for 1969 were fixed for the First Five Year Plan, and revised later to a figure of 25 per 1,000 for 1974. Initial government efforts were half-

hearted and slow. Policy was primarily designed to diffuse
information on birth control among the illiterate masses.
During the Second Five Year Plan (1956-1961) there was a
shifting of emphasis from mere publicity of voluntary
abstinence to more tangible and effective measures, such as
a large-scale male sterilization (vasectomy) program, and
free supply and servicing of the IUD (intra-uterine device) to
females. Several states even offered such inducements as
monetary awards and three days' paid vacation to go with
each vasectomy operation. During the Third Five Year Plan
(1961-1966) this drive was further intensified. However,
practical results were not forthcoming. The basic reason was
that the lifestyle and traditional beliefs of the people remained unchanged. By the end of the Third Five Year Plan,
it was clear that the achievement of the targets in birth rates
was merely a demographic pipe dream.

Allocations of men, materials and services were increased several-fold during the Fourth Five Year Plan (1966-
1971). The federal government's administrative set-up was
tightened up and coordinated with those of the various
states. Special recognition of the family planning activity
was provided by creating a new division in the Ministry of
Health to achieve greater efficiency. A federal "task force"
of doctors was newly constituted to train at least one doctor
specializing in family planning servicing for every 20,000
persons. Chief among the more recent innovations was an
effort to elicit the help of the private advertising media. It
was argued that the use of Indian manufactured condoms
known as Nirodh (literally meaning "prevention") might in-
might increase if a campaign were to be conducted by well-
known private companies. Condoms could be sold all over
the country, over the counters of tobacco, tea, soap and
flashlight shops for a price of one-half a cent.

Yet, tangible results were not forthcoming despite pious
wishes, enactment of budgetary allocations, and propagan-
dizing of new methods. By the mid-70's it was widely ack-
nowledged that government family planning programs had
failed. Government policy had indeed been, so far, unstruc-
tured, and its implementation was regionally selective.
Government efforts had been characterized by vacillation
and half heartedness.

Backed by the government, a dramatic drive during the

Emergency Rule helped push sterilization (vasectomies) programs to an unprecedented level of 8.2 million tons in 1976-77 (many performed on involuntary clients) as compared to the figure of 2.61 million tons for the previous year. Almost as an anticlimatic reaction to the excesses during the Emergency Rule, the new government reversed policies in 1977, and the vigor of 1976 gave place to complacency. During 1977-78 only 0.9 million vasectomies were recorded. The re-emergence of a previous political party with strong adherence to a vigorous family planning program in 1980 augurs the development of a new, rational, sustained and effective population policy.

The current birthrate figure of 34 per 1,000 persons per year is much higher than the projected target of 25 by 1981 despite the large expenditures in organization, personnel and expenditure during the twenty year history of the family planning programs. The Sixth Five Year Plan (1978-1983) aimed at reaching 100 million couples in the reproductive age group (15-45) for their voluntary adoption of birth control. Reliable estimates indicate that only 3 to 3.5 million couples are currently using contraceptives. If the birthrate is to be reduced to the targeted figure of 25 per 1,000 population for the year of 1981, about 50 million couples (or 48 percent of the reproductive age-group) must regularly use contraceptives. This can be accomplished only if the government increases its efforts by two to three thousand percent. A crash program involving large outlays of funds and personnel is required for the achievement of the targeted reductions in fertility. The expenditure out-lays for family planning during the Plans have remained at nearly 60 cents per head per reproductive age-group couple, a figure which is hopelessly inadequate to effectively deal with population problems.

In addition to inadequate resources, there is the question of managerial skills, and technical know-how to initiate improvements in the diffusion of family planning programs among the illiterate masses which the government teams lack. Public resistance to new gadgets and innovative techniques is also bound to be strong among the tradition-loving people, particularly when large families have been traditionally prized as labor help in agricultural production and as social security in old age.

CITATIONS AND SELECT BIBILIOGRAPHY

Agarwal, S. N., "Family Planning Program in India," *Asian Survey.* Vol. 7 (12), 1957, p. 859.

Bhardwaj, R. C., *Employment and Unemployment in India.* New York, 1969.

Bose, A., *India's Urbanization, 1901-2001.* New Delhi, 1978.

Bulsara, Jal R., *Problems of Rapid Urbanization in India.* Bombay, 1964.

Chakravarti, A. K., "Foodgrain Sufficiency Patterns in India," *Geographical Review.* Vol. 60, 1970, pp. 208-228.

Coale, A. J. and Hoover, E. M., *Population Growth and Economic Development in Low-Income Countries.* Princeton, 1958.

Davis, Kingsley, *The Population of India and Pakistan.* Princeton, 1951.

India: Ready or Not, Here They Come. Population Bulletin, Vol. 25 (5), 1970, specifically subsection by John P. Lewis on: "Population Control in India."

India, A Reference Annual. Publications Divsion, Government of India, 1970, 1971, 1973, 1977-78.

Johnson, E. A. J., *The Organization of Space in Developing Countries.* Cambridge, Mass., 1970.

Learmonth, A. T. A., *Health in the Indian Sub-Continent.* Canberra, 1965.

Learmonth, A. T. A., *Patterns of Disease and Hunger.* London, 1978.

Lewis, J. P., *Quiet Crisis in India.* Washington, D.C., 1962.

Maudlin, W. P., "Population Dynamics in Asia: A Research Focus," *Asian Survey,* Vol. 6, 1966, pp. 158-176.

Mishra, R. P., *Medical Geography of India.* New Delhi, 1970.

Nath, Pran, "A Study of the Economic Conditions of Ancient India," *Proceedings of the Royal Asiatic Society.* London, 1929, Chapter 5.

Schwartzberg, J. E. (ed.), *A Historical Atlas of South Asia.* Chicago, 1978.

Spate, O. H. K., and Learmonth, A. T. A., *India and Pakistan.* London, 3rd ed., 1967.

World Population Data Sheet. 1979, Population Reference Bureau, Washington, D.C., 1979.

CHAPTER 4

CULTURE AND SOCIETY

TRADITIONAL SOCIETY

This chapter tries to explore some distinguishing characteristics of Indian society, such as its rural agrarian base, the prevalence of diverse religions and languages, and the persistence of caste system.

Any study of traditional Indian society generally begins with the village as a functioning socio-economic unit. Approximately 80 percent of India's population resides in over a half million villages. A little less than three-quarters of the population depends directly on agriculture for a living. The innate conservatism of the society is reflected in its stubborn adherence to the caste system, backward agricultural practices, and an economic order virtually unaffected by modern technology and urban-based industrial output. Large metropolitan areas (of over 100,000 population) modified by modern technology and performing industrial-commercial functions account for only 10 percent of the population. Villages and metropolitan areas present two different worlds — two levels of living and experience. Linked poorly by transport and communications, and with a restricted exchange of goods and services, each world has crystallized into a distinct spatial reality.

Rural India remained largely untouched by outside influences. Within it, a complex system of socio-economic interdependence among the people has grown over the centuries. The various groups and castes are bound together in landlord-tenant (*zamindari*), patron-client (*jajmani*) and creditor-debtor relationships, in caste and ritual observances, and in a loose form of traditional self-government (*panchayat*). The British rule did not attempt or lead to the break-up of the traditional self-sufficiency economy of the village.

111

A typical village consists of a cluster of houses or huts, with agricultural fields around it, except where the settlement pattern is "dispersed" as in Bengal and Kerala. (For settlement patterns, refer to chapter 7.) Different groups in a village are bound together in social and economic relationships. The landlords, remnants of the feudal class structure (either by inheritance or as creations of British colonial policy), form the apex of a social hierarchy (Myrdal, 1051). This group enjoys a powerful political, social and economic position in the village since it owns most of the land and generally belongs to high castes. Landlords lease land to tenant-cultivators for agricultural work (usually as sharecropper). A section of this landowning group, the non-cultivating, absentee landlord section, is generally the one which can also acquire power from outside. The resident non-cultivating landowning section is generally poorer than the other landlords. Below these groups are ordinary peasants and sharecroppers, many of whom occasionally have to accept wage labor to augment their real incomes as cultivators. Finally, in such a socio-economic set-up the landless necessarily occupy the lowest ranks.

This division of the village population into the basic categories of peasant landlords, absentee landlords, other peasants and agricultural workers, is paralleled by social rankings as well. The highest order of social esteem is generally obtained by owning land, and those who perform manual labor are placed at the lower level. Supervisory work carries with it a traditional social status. A high social esteem is gained by abstaining from work. Sharecroppers and agricultural labor are held in low esteem. The lowest status, reserved for the landless agricultural laborer, arises from three factors: his landlessness, his performance of manual labor and the stigma attached to manual work under the regular supervision and control of another person (Myrdal, 1058). The hired landless laborer may be economically better off than the sharecropper, but he stands at a lower social status.

Most village land is owned by the high castes (e.g., Brahmans, Kshatriyas), regarded as "cultivating" castes. Brahmans are ritually and traditionally discouraged from tilling. They generally engage sharecroppers to do this work for them. Some middle ranking castes (e.g., Jats) are, however, traditionally farming castes, too. Lower castes (including the lowest of all, the farmer "untouchables" or "outcastes") are usually landless and are engaged as agricultural laborers. Each person is born into his caste and place in the village hierarchy and possibilities for upward movement are limited. The institution of caste is discussed in a separate section of the chapter. Land reforms since independence have resulted in land redistribution to the landless.

For centuries villages have remained self-contained, their economic links with outside world consisted of the transfer of agricultural surpluses to outside. Their basic needs of foodstuffs, fuel, cloth, sugar and a few manufactured items like agricultural implements and leather materials were fulfilled within the village. Castes traditionally looked after their time-honored occupations. Village castes, for example, included, *dhobi* (washer man), *teli* (oil presser, and *chamar* (worker in leathercraft). A complex system of exchange of goods between these castes and the upper castes in return for payments in kind and services grew up. (This system, known as *jajmani* system, is discussed in the section on Caste.)

Agricultural surpluses of the village which enter the monetized market are largely controlled by village landlords and moneylenders. The cultivators find it difficult to circumvent the powerful landlord to offer them their surplus produce on the open market, since in time of need, they have to turn to the landlord for credit. The landlords seek to monopolize the sale of surplus to their great economic advantage. This atmosphere of socio-economic parasitism of the privileged group has been perpetuated over the centuries. The cultivators are, therefore, usually disinclined to produce large surpluses.

Another crucial factor in raising land productivity and agricultural surpluses is the traditional tenurial system. The sharecropper is not enthused about attempting new improvements in agriculture, such as the adoption of modern techniques, and the use of fertilizers and pesticides, because of the insecurity of his tenure, his lack of capital and more importantly, his fear that the landlord would be the recipient of a major portion of the produce without working for it. Landowners are indifferent to investing more capital for improvement since their receipts from rents and crop-shares are adequate for their needs. The stigma attached to labor further impedes intensification of agriculture. Many would prefer semi-starvation on a tiny plot of rented land to the higher income possible from wage employment. One basic reason for the disinclination of the farmer to introduce improvements in agriculture is that traditionally agricultural production has been organized to maintain a conventional mode of living in caste-structured society rather as a means of acquiring profit for re-investment and expansion of production. In order to effectuate changes in such a traditional society, not only economic or structural changes in agriculture are needed but a thorough overhaul of the institutional structure is required.

The Traditional Agricultural Systems

Since agriculture forms a major component of India's economic activity and is basic to country's rural structure, its role in the socio-economic geography may be reviewed. Broadly speaking there are two main types of cropping systems: sedentary farming (irrigated or dry) and shifting cultivation. Each type is associated with a characteristic social and economic organization. In areas where shifting cultivation is predominant, as in the tribal territories of Assam and Arunachal Pradesh, the economic system remains largely self-contained and subsistence-oriented. In zones of sedentary cultivation, some surplus beyond the family's need has been occasionally produced and transferred to the local market or to the landlord in lieu of receipt of customary services and credit facilities from him.

Customarily, throughout ancient and medieval times, each family had a right to till the land for its own use and to dispose of the harvest. This family could be evicted only by a community decision. Authority to allocate the wasteland or reserve land surrounding the village in times of need rested with the village community. The village community was not only a geographic clustering of houses but also a social unit. Those who were born in it shared its religion and customs. The system of land tenure in which community held proprietory rights prevailed in most parts of the country, although in principle ultimate government ownership of land prevailed as far back as the Mauryan times. The Mughals introduced the system of granting extensive *jagirs* (land grants).

Under British rule several modifications in the tenurial system were introduced. Right of ownership was firmly transferred from the community to the government. Landlords who traditionally received tributes from the peasants became collectors of revenue for the government, and gained rights of evicting the peasant from the land or of increasing the rent if revenue was not readily forthcoming. The evicted land was then added to the landlord's private estate. A large class of private landowners, uninhibited by traditional tenurial rules, thus grew up. Landlords also received from tenants traditional "gifts" at specified occasions, in addition to the rents or land. Gradually, landlords grew in power through the annexation of vast amounts of land by peasant evictions. They hired agricultural laborers to work on their land and supervisory staff to oversee their land as well as for the collection of rents. Many lived in cities and left the working of land to the sharecroppers or hired tenants. Rent collection was delegated to local agents, who formed a growing cadre of intermediary rent collectors.

Often the peasants, fearing eviction for non-payment of rent or delay in rent payment, would borrow money at exorbitant rates from the village money lender, which in many cases would be the landlord himself. Landless peasants also needed loans for fulfilling customary obligations of children's weddings and other ceremonial functions. This indebtedness often remained unpaid and grew in proportion to the high rate of interest charged on it. Indebtedness even passed on from father to son. The landlords continued to profit from this situation and exploited the peasant proprietors over the years. The power of moneylenders in the traditional rural structure was further buttressed by their ancillary roles as merchants and landlords.

During the 19th and 20th centuries some other changes were occurring on the rural landscape. Population was rising, first slowly at 1 percent a year until 1931, since then at an increasing rate, without a compensating expansion in the cultivated area. In the absence of the laws of primogeniture among Hindus and Muslims, land was shared equally among all male heirs, resulting in subdivision and fragmentation of land under cultivation. Eviction of small delinquent peasants from their land combined with fragmentation of land holdership, contributed to the growth of a big landowner class, as well as that of the landless. The lot of a large peasantry of agricultural workers holding small inoperational units of land and landless peasants became increasingly miserable.

Over a period of time, many landholdings became inoperational. Due to excessive subdivision of land these interfered with the irrigational facilities, utilization of new techniques and mechanized farming. Small, scattered holdings have multiplied the labor involved in the application of fertilizers, and use of improved techniques. All these factors have contributed to the present agricultural inefficiency and low productivity.

Traditional social systems have also affected the utilization of agricultural labor. Absentee landlordism has removed a large section of agricultural population as a useful source of productive work. Hereditary caste groups like Brahmans and Rajputs have resisted manual labor. Female participation ratios have been lower due to religious and social taboos among Muslims and Hindus. High fertility rates among the population have increased their domestic responsibilities. The agricultural work year is very short and seasonal unemployment is estimated to be 4 to 6 months per year for most cultivators. Customs and religion usually claim a large part of the year for festivals, holidays and ceremonial occasions.

Selected Socio-Economic Aspects of a Village

This section deals with three selected aspects of a typical Indian village, namely the joint family system, village *panchyat* (council) and village handicrafts.

The *joint family* or *extended family* system is widely practiced in Indian villages. In a joint family, men (fathers, brothers, sons), their children, and wives (several nuclear families) are grouped together as a single consuming unit, and often as a single producing unit. These families reside together and share the same kitchen. The cultivating joint family works together in the fields. When members of a joint family migrate to cities, they find the urban environment not particularly conducive to continuance of the family structure. Brothers among urban immigrants may find different employment in different parts of the city, may experience transport and housing difficulties and the joint family thus often tends to disintegrate.

The *Panchayat* or village council is another characteristic feature of rural society. Since villages have, in general, remained isolated and relatively self-sufficient, the traditional council or self-government composed mainly of hereditary village elders (known as *panches*, literally "five") still persists. Such a local council looks after the fiscal needs of the village, is an arbiter of family and group disputes and has been traditionally headed by a member of a powerful local caste. The position of a village headman has largely been hereditary, passing from father to son. The village headman helps the local village officials, such as the *patwari* in the collection of taxes. The village *panchayat* has traditionally strengthened the political power of the local bosses, landlords, high caste persons and the moneylenders, who usually form the village council. Since Independence, the government has tried to democratize the election process for the formulation of village councils in several ways, especially by allowing membership to lower castes. Real power, however, is still wielded by the village social elites, the self-elected member class and the former hereditary title holder as a headman. The election process based on adult franchise itself is intended to reduce the power of the elite.

One other aspect of traditional rural life currently undergoing significant change is the gradual disappearance of the village crafts, as spatial links connecting the villages and the outside world are slowly developed. Urban influences are percolating to those villages which lie within the travel range of the cinemas, hotels, courts, military camps and schools of the nearby cities. Educated villagers, aspiring for clerical jobs in towns and cities, have now started to commute to newly-found urban occupations. Lower caste agricultural laborers are increasingly lured to work in the nearby towns to improve their economic status. Government instituted land tenancy reforms since 1950 regarding ceilings on landholdings, abolition of absentee landlordism, democratization of *panchayats* and the opening of co-operative credit banks for granting loans to the peasants, are factors contributing to a loosening of the traditional *jajmani* system, a shift in agricultural methods and the eventual replacement of village crafts by modern manufactured goods imported from urban areas. New development programs during the Five Year Plans and the construction of transport links are increasingly bringing villages closer to urban markets. Village self-sufficiency is being gradually eroded by a demand for outside goods such as cloth, tea, salt, sugar, oil, soap, *beedies* (native cigarettes), bicycles, fertilizers and agricultural implements. Occupational shifts among the castes in the villages are occurring, too. Lower caste groups like *chamar* (shoemaker), *teli* (oilman) and *dhobi* (washerman), find their traditional caste-based occupations no longer remunerative in the village, and are leaving for the cities in search of better prospects. This is leading to the decay of village crafts.

However, modernization of the rural socio-economic structure is still far off. Only drastic measures seem able to accomplish it. Increase in agricultural productivity appears to be a primary essential in this regard. Agriculturalists suffer from an acute lack of capital and their purchasing power for undertaking improvements is extremely limited. Accumulation of capital backed by private or government entreprenuership is highly desirable. Secondly, improvements in agriculture can be made if existing irrigation facilities are expanded, a more equitable distribution of land is carried out, and new fertilizers, better seeds and more agricultural implements are used. Thirdly, better labor utilization can be procured by dislodging the powerful landowning class from idleness. Under the traditional caste system some caste groups are discouraged from contributing labor and energy to effectuate improvements. In sum, modernization of the rural socio-economic system cannot be achieved unless the religious and social value systems are changed.

LINGUISTIC DIVISIONS

Like the Soviet Union, Canada, Switzerland and Belgium, India is linguistically a plural country, and like them, the distribution of many diverse languages has profoundly influenced its political, social and economic structures. In many ways, however, the linguistic configuration of India is unique and comparisons with other linguistically plural countries is misleading. In India, linguistic complexity has created a multi-dimensional problem as a result of several forces: a constant interplay between local, regional and all-India languages; an assertion of language-related territorial claims for the various states; interminable demands of the language elites seeking administrative privileges; and the overall problem of a national language for the country.

The *Linguistic Survey of India* of 1927 listed 179 languages and 544 dialects spoken within the country, while the Census of 1961 recorded 1018 different languages and dialects. The Constitution of the country recognizes 15 major languages, most of which (with the exception of Sanskrit) claims millions of speakers (Table 4.1). Twelve of these find territorial identification in large political units (states).

The seeming linguistic diversity, however, conceals certain basic traits. First, the various languages and dialects belong to four language families, Indo-Aryan, Dravidian, Sino-Tibetan and Austro-Asiatic. Second, 98 percent of the country's population belong to the first two large families. Third, with the exception of minor spatial scattering of the tribal languages, the major Indian languages are localized in compact territorial blocks. Fourth, only a handful of the languages have historically been used for administrative hegemony or cultural purposes. Until the 7th or 8th century, Sanskrit was the language for administration and of the cultural elite. Persian (later Urdu) was a court and administrative language of the Mughal and other rulers until the British assumed control in the late 18th-19th centuries. Under British rule, English replaced Persian as the language of courts, administration and higher learning. English, like its predecessors Sanskrit and Persian, did not, however, diffuse to the masses, but merely acted as a *lingua franca* and remained a possession of the social elites.

Perhaps no aspect of India's linguistic composition so vividly portrays the historic cultural-political cleavage between the north and the south as does the distribution of its two major linguistic families: the Indo-Aryan and the Dravidian (Figure 4.1). These two families are mutually exclusive in grammar, syntax, script and intelligibility. Throughout history, south India has possessed a general unity as an entity apart from the northern world of the Indo-Ganga plains; its cultural distinctiveness was intensified by the physical isolation created by the central Indian hills and tribes. Periods of imperial unification of the north and south were historically rare and brief.

TABLE 4.1

MAJOR LANGUAGES, 1971

A. Languages Specified in the Constitution

	Speakers in Millions	In % of Total Population
Hindi	163	30
Bengali	45	8
Telugu	45	8
Marathi	43	8
Tamil	38	7
Gujarati	26	5
Malayalam	22	4
Kannada	22	4
Oriya	20	4
Punjabi	15	3
Assamese	9	1.6
Kashmiri	2	0.4
Sanskrit	(2,212 persons)	(2,212 persons)
Sindhi	2	0.4
Urdu	29	5

B. Other Languages (Census of 1971)

Bhojpuri (Bihari)	14	2.5
Chhatisgarhi	7	1.3
Magdhi	7	1.3
Maithili	6	1.1
Marwari	5	0.9
Santhali	4	0.7
Rajasthani	2	0.4
Gondi	1.5	0.3
Konkani	1.5	0.3
English	2 to 3	0.4 to 0.6

Sources:
    1. *Census of India 1971.*
    2. *Pocketbook of Population Statistics,* New Delhi, 1972.
    3. *Census Centenary Monograph No. 10,* New Delhi, 1972.

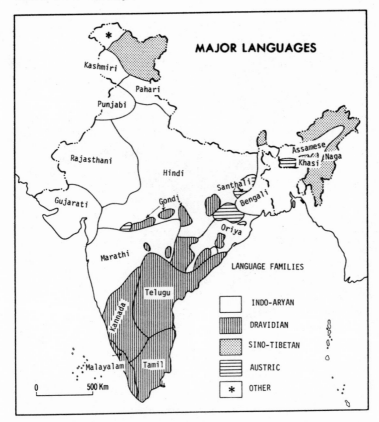

FIGURE 4.1

Within the Indo-Aryan family, Hindi claims the largest number of speakers (163 millions or 30.1 per cent of India's population according to the 1971 census), and is territorially spread over the states of Uttar Pradesh, Bihar, Madhya Pradesh, Haryana, Delhi and Rajasthan. Hindi-related languages of Bihari (14 million speakers), Rajasthani and Marwari (7 million speakers), Urdu (distinguished from Hindi in script and in vocabulary of Persian origin, with 29 million speakers), and Punjabi (16 million speakers), make the Hindi-related language group the largest language with nearly 231 million speakers or some 46 percent of the country's population (Figure 4.2). Other major Indo-Aryan

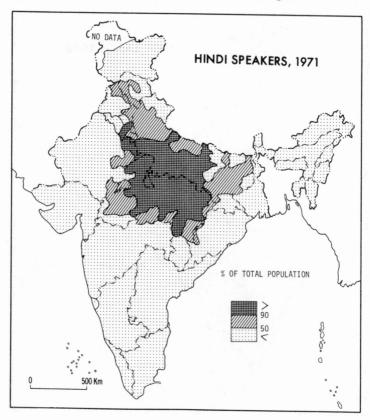

FIGURE 4.2

languages are: Bengali (45 million speakers), Marathi (42 million speakers), Gujarati (26 million speakers), Oriya (20 million speakers) and Assamese (9 million speakers), each contained within a separate state. Each of these languages possesses a mature literature and associated culture. Bengali boasts of a literary tradition surpassing that of Hindi. Marathi along with Bengali aroused national sentiment furthering India's struggle for Independence from the British. Kashmiri, localized mostly in the Jhelum Valley in the state of Jammu and Kashmir, is spoken by only 2 million persons.

The Dravidian language family includes four major languages with substantial number of speakers: Telugu (45 million speakers), Tamil (38 million speakers), Kannada (22 million speakers), and Malayalam (22 million speakers). They are inter-related and possess varying degrees of mutual intelligibility. Each is mostly contained within a separate state and only along the periphery of states is there some linguistic diversification. The fifteen languages recognized by India's constitution, including Sanskrit (Table 4.1), are spoken by 98 percent of its population; virtually all of the remaining population is divided among speakers of 226 Tibeto-Burmese tribal languages along the northeast borders of this country, and 65 languages distributed in central India. Sanskrit, with only 2,212 speakers, is retained in view of its cultural and religious significance; as is English because of its function as a "link" language between the various states.

Linguistic States

During the period of British rule, India was divided into provinces (roughly analogous to the present-day states) administered by governors appointed by the Viceroy in New Delhi, and a number of princely states. The provinces were created haphazardly in conformity with the exigencies of British annexations and often included territories of two or three linguistic communities. The province of Bombay, for example, included Gujarati and Marathi speakers' territory and several other language areas. The idea of linguistic states was, however, constantly espoused by the Indian National Congress, one of the major political parties in the struggle for Indian Independence. The proponents of linguistic patriotism pointed out that the creation of linguistic states would release energies which had previously been consumed by struggles between linguistic groups within multi-linguistic provinces.

Independence in 1947 thus became a signal for agitation favoring realignment of state boundaries. After resisting demands for linguistic states for six years, reasoning that centrifugal forces would gain at the expense of national unity, the federal government yielded in 1953 to the demand for a separate state of Andhra for the Telugu speakers of the northern part of Madras province. This opened the gates to other similar demands, and the federal government quickly appointed a states' Reorganization Commission to look into the question of formation of linguistic states. Following the

Commission's Report in 1956, the government carried out a
large scale reorganization of the internal political boundaries within the country. This resulted in the dismantling
of some of the former provinces, the emergence of new
states, and a sweeping modification of the boundaries of the
others. In effect, the government yielded to nearly all of the
major linguistic pressures. India was thus reorganized into
14 states, each of which, with the major exceptions of the
state of Bombay, and the Punjab, contained a clearly dominant language. Agitation for further changes, however,
persisted. Several revisions of state boundaries between 1956
and 1976 increased the number of states from 14 to 22. The
last of the major linguistic states to be thus created was Punjab, in 1966. As in this case, which was to placate Sikh
demands for a homeland for Punjabi speech, cultural moti-
vations generally accompanied linguistic demands seeking
political identification. A consequence of the boundary revisions is that most present day states are reasonably coincident with linguistic regions (Figure 4.1, compare it with
Figure 5.2).

NATIONAL LANGUAGE
AND NATIONAL UNITY

The assertion of a national language for a polyglot country like India, undoubtedly poses a real and serious problem. Since Independence, Hindi (in its Hindustani version),
spoken by the largest number of people and covering several
states, has been championed as the national language by the
Indian National Congress, the party which for a long time
was in control of the federal government in New Delhi. The
Indian constitution bestows upon 15 of the country's major
languages the status of official languages (Table 4.1), with a
pride of place for Hindi (in *Devanagari* script) which is
recognized as the official language for all-India communication at the federal level in New Delhi. The constitution also
provided that English would continue to be used for all purposes at the federal level for a period of 15 years (1950-
1965). At state level, the regional languages are recognized
as the official ones. English is accepted as a special language
for its role in Union government's transactions, in parliamentary debate, and as an instructional medium for special-

ized subjects for higher education, as well as for its value as a "link" language between various states. The 1963 Official Languages Act provides for its continuation beyond the 15-year period originally prescribed in 1950. Another enactment in 1967 reaffirmed its usage for communication between Union and states indefinitely.

The constitutional mandate that Hindi should become the federal language by 1965 always met with great resistance. Hindi is less developed than several regional languages, such as Bengali, Marathi and Tamil. Moreover, it has been steadily becoming a strange language in the past few years, as a result of its adoption of new Sanskrit vocabulary in order to enrich itself, and ostensibly to improve its quality. The main focus of resistance to Hindi has been the Dravidian language states in south India. Hindi's replacement of English as the administrative language at the level of the federal government and in the Public Service Commission Examinations was considered by many states to be a discriminatory imposition of "Hindi imperialism." To allay the fears of non-Hindi speaking states, Parliament passed in 1963 a language bill providing that English would continue to be used after 1965, in addition to Hindi. Nevertheless, as 1965 neared, apprehension might decide to keep Hindi as the sole official language at the federal level. Riots, based on linguistic nationalism, erupted in Madras, Calcutta and other places. The Central government swiftly and wisely responded in 1965 by allowing the continued use of English until all the non-Hindi states have consented to the use of Hindi, thus in effect retaining English virtually indefinitely. The feelings of the Dravidian states, who were at one time contemplating a secession of Dravidian areas from India to form an independent country of "Dravidistan," were particularly assuaged. English, therefore, remains an official associate language of the central government, along with Hindi, and is serving as a link between the different states.

In effect, Hindi has clearly failed to elicit universal popularity. In literary and intellectual appeal, it is seriously rivalled by such highly developed languages as Bengali, Marathi, Tamil and Telugu. Hindi enthusiasts, in their drive for modernization of the language, have injected into it a strong Sanskrit-based vocabulary and have thereby only increased the distance between the language and the masses. Furthermore, speakers of closely related languages like Urdu and Punjabi find themselves drifting away from the newly developing Sanskrit-based Hindi. These three closely related languages, Hindi, Punjabi and Urdu are mutually intelligible to a large extent, but are divided in scripts, which are favored by different religious communities. For Sikhs, Gurmukhi is the religious (therefore the favored) script for the Punjabi language. Urdu derives its script from Persian and is espoused by Muslims. Hindus favor the usage of Devanagari script for all these languages. In this context, the Sikh demand for a Punjabi-speaking state was interpreted as communal idea seeking a homeland for the Sikh community. In 1966 the demand was fulfilled when the state of Punjab was bifurcated into two states, the Hindi-speaking Haryana state and the mainly Punjabi-speaking state in which Sikhs possessed a narrow majority.

The important question of the future of English still remains. Undeniably, it has played a major role in India's national consolidation and development. During the British rule it was the official language at the provincial and national levels, universally used in civil and military services, in the judiciary, in politics and in the all-India struggle for Independence. It had created an intellectual elite on an all-India basis. It provided independent India with a modernizing leadership, and its place in the educational system became well established. Despite its wide ranging influence, however, the masses remained virtually insulated from it. This created a deep dichotomy between the elites trained in English and the uneducated masses.

Since Independence the role of English has been declining. The states have been advancing their regional languages as the primary media of instruction in the schools and public services at the expense of English. Circulation of regional language newspapers and films have tended further to weaken the usage of English as a *lingua franca*. Most educated Indians, however, consider the gradual disappearance of English as an intellectual tragedy. Already deterioration in the educational standards in the universities is observable in several states, a situation explained largely by the replacement of English as a medium of instruction in higher learning, as well as problems faced by graduates moving to other states where higher education is in a different regional language. These tendencies have once again underscored the need for the retention of English at the federal and state levels, in public services, and in higher education. Advocates of English further point out that such a retention would contribute to stronger international links, and internal administrative cohesion. Critics of English, however, are quick to point out that an alien language should never be accepted as an official language. One interesting suggestion favors the idea of several plural official languages, with the retention of English as an associate language in the government and higher education. The language problem is clearly putting India's overall structure of national unity to a severe test.

SPATIAL PATTERNS OF RELIGIONS

Religion has deeply affected the cultural and political life of India. The daily life of millions of persons is strongly colored by it. To a geographer the effects of religion may be observed at three spatially distinct levels. At the lowest territorial level of the village, religion is a pervasive force. Religious beliefs sanction caste restrictions on types of labor, the ritual value of cow dung and prejudice against certain cropping systems and veneration of cows have inhibited technological and agricultural progress. Religious groups and caste divisions have generated political disharmony in villages. Social stratification, based on religious and caste forms, has been manifested in residential segregation and has restricted cooperative and collective village efforts.

The second spatial level consists of urban centers which are well-linked between themselves but not well-linked with a vast rural society. At this level there is a greater diversity of religious adherence which has compounded the spatial interactions developing among the various communities. The urban world affords greater opportunities for the various groups to solidify their political forces into political parties. Sharp cleavages along social, linguistic and religious lines fuel inter-community riots which are often masterminded by religion-based political parties. Indian history during British rule and since Independence is replete with examples of

Hindu-Muslim riots, which were actively supported by political groups.

The third spatial level consists of groups of districts (administrative divisions) containing a religious community with a numerical majority. Such compact areas tend to exercise their political influence on state and federal administrations. During the closing days of British rule agitation for a separate homeland by Muslims was motivated by religious considerations. Their demand proved successful in 1947 when the independent country of Pakistan was formed by the union of territories in which Muslims claimed a majority status. In 1966 the political demand for a "linguistic homeland" (Punjabi-speaking state) within India by Sikhs was fulfilled when within the newly created state of Punjabi-speech they attained a majority status.

The Distribution of Religious Communities

Two major communities, Hindus and Muslims, together comprised over 94 percent of India's population in 1971. Hindus numbered 453 millions or 82.7 percent of the total population, and Muslims formed a little more than 11 percent of the population. Before partition, Muslim population was 92 millions, accounting for 24 percent of the country's population. In 1947 they numbered 36 millions, and the Muslim community has now grown to over 61 millions, making India as one of the major Muslim countries in the world. In addition, there are substantial numbers of Buddhists, Jains, Sikhs and Parsis (Table 4.2).

Hindus form majorities everywhere except in a few districts where Christians or Sikhs predominate. In fact, only in five areas do they form less than 84 percent of the population: (a) along the borders of Bangladesh and Pakistan; (b) the state of Jammu and Kashmir where Muslims account for 65 percent of the population; (c) areas of Christianity and tribal religions in Assam and Nagaland along the Tibet and Burmese borders; (d) Kerala state; and (e) scattered areas in Deccan and the Indo-Gangetic plains where large scale conversions of natives to Islam took place between the 16th and 18th centuries. Spatial ubiquity and predominance of Hindus has had a significant impact on the cultural and political geography of India. Other communities are, in general, dispersed among Hindu majorities,

TABLE 4.2

MAJOR RELIGIOUS COMMUNITIES, 1971

	Population (in millions)	As % of Total Population
Hindus	453	82.7
Muslims	61	11.2
Christians	14	2.6
Sikhs	10.4	1.9
Buddhists	4	0.7
Jains	2	0.5
Scheduled Castes & Tribes	80 + 38	19.8
Others	1.6	0.4

Sources:
> 1. *India, A Reference Annual, 1974,* New Delhi, p. 13.
> 2. *Census of India, 1971.*

and have been Hinduized in varying degrees. Many caste practices, characteristic of Hindu society, have been retained by non-Hindus, most of whom are the descendants of converts from Hinduism. Demographically, Hindus have shown a slight decline as a percent of the total population, from 75.1 percent in 1881 to 74.2 percent in 1901, to about 66 percent in 1941. After partition in 1947 (with most Muslim majority areas gone to Pakistan and the massive in-migration of Hindu refugees into India), the proportion of Hindus increased to about 84 percent of the population. By 1971 it had dropped again by 1.4 points. This declining trend is attributed to lower fertility among Hindus and loss through conversions to other religions. In the 1960's significant numbers of untouchables were converted to Buddhism.

Except in Jammu and Kashmir, Kerala and West Bengal, Muslims are nowhere in a majority status. Along the Bangladesh border in West Bengal, 20 to 50 percent of the population in several districts is Muslim. The share of Muslims in India's total population increased steadily, from 20 percent in 1881 to 24.2 percent in 1941. Since Independence they have formed 10 to 11 percent (11.2 in 1971) of the population. The higher fertility rate among Muslims results from their religious attitudes, especially from a greater tolerance

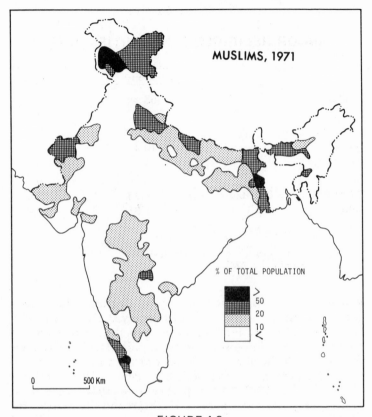

FIGURE 4.3

of widow remarriage. Muslims have been less literate and
less urbanized as a group than Hindus. They had fallen into
a position of inferiority to Hindus in government services
during British rule. Their demand for a separate homeland
derived partly from the prospect of advancing social and
economic power for the Muslim majority within a self-
governing territory. Figure 4.3 gives the geographical
distribution of Muslims in 1971.

The Christian population (14 millions) is dispersed mostly in the rural areas. Its main concentration lies along the
western coast around Goa, and in Kerala where Christians
represent 20-24 percent of the population. These areas have
had historical contacts with Christianity dating to the 1st

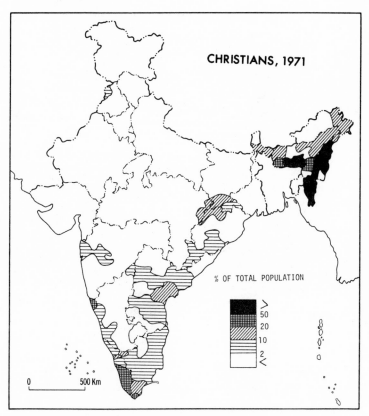

CHRISTIANS, 1971

% OF TOTAL POPULATION

> 50
20
10
2
<

0   500 Km

FIGURE 4.4

and 2nd centuries in Kerala and elsewhere since the Portuguese conquests in the 15th century. Christians are also relatively numerous among the tribal hill areas of Assam, Meghalaya, Mizoram and Nagaland, where Christian missionaries have been active and many were converted to Christianity during the British rule. A demand for a cultural and political homeland for the tribal population was fulfilled when the state of Nagaland was formed in 1970 in which Christian groups have a majority status. Christians have been gaining in their share of the country's population, from 0.71 percent in 1881 to 2.6 percent in 1971. Among the Christian population are the Anglo-Indian groups, offsprings of mixed European and Indian parents. Anglo-

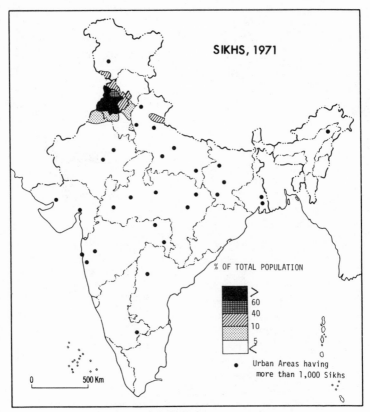

FIGURE 4.5

Indians adopted a European lifestyle and were preferred in the public services like the railways under British rule (Figure 4.4).

Sikhs, numbering nearly 10.4 million, are mostly concentrated in a small section of the country in the state of Punjab, their original homeland. Nearly 90 percent of all the Sikh population lives in a critical area bordering Pakistan (Punjab, Haryana), and in metropolitan Delhi (Figure 4.5). An offshoot of Hinduism, the Sikh religion retains many Hindu practices, and many Sikhs intermarry with the Hindus. In the 17th century, Sikhs were persecuted by Muslim rulers, and assumed a militant posture against Muslims. The partition of India in 1947 cut directly through their territory, and about 1.5 million Sikhs who found themselves in Pakistani territory moved to India in the state of Punjab. Since then Sikhs have been politically the most active religious group, and successfully agitated in favor of a Sikh-dominated state, which was created in 1966. Sikhs have experienced a remarkable growth in numbers since 1881 (from 1.8 millions to about 10.4 millions in 1971), and improved their share in the country's population from 0.75 percent in 1881 (in pre-partitioned India) to 1.9 percent in 1971. They registered a growth rate of 33 percent between 1961-71. Their fertility rates are among the highest in the country. They are also more literate than either Hindus or Muslims.

Jains and Buddhists are two older communities that originated in the early 6th century B.C. as a revolt against the caste system and ceremonial ritualism of Hinduism. However, their religious philosophies retain the basic Hindu beliefs of *Karma,* transmigration of soul and *ahimsa* (non-violence). Jains (population only 2 millions) are among the highly literate groups, and are mostly concentrated in the urban areas of Rajasthan, Gujarat, Maharashtra and Madhya Pradesh. Buddhists number about 4 millions, with 90 percent of the population concentrated in the state of Maharashtra (another major area is in Ladakh, Kashmir) where large scale conversion of mainly *Harijans* and low-caste Hindus took place following the example of Ambedkar, their famous leader. Parsi population is less than 100,000, concentrated mostly in the city of Bombay. The most literate and urbanized of all the communities, Parsis have played a significant entrepreneurial role in the business and commerce of Bombay.

The Indian census of 1971 enumerates a tribal population of over 38 million listed under the comprehensive category of "Backward classes." They are the descendants of the aboriginal population and are known as *Adivasis* (literally, "indigenes"). These tribes have long retained their distinctive languages and religious beliefs (a curious mixture of Christianity, Hinduism, and animism with a mixture of several rituals). These tribes are geographically scattered. The main areas of their concentration are generally hilly, forested and inaccessible: (a) Assam and Arunachal Pradesh along the Tibet border; (b) the central Indian hills and plateaus; and (c) hilly sections of Karnataka and Kerala. Relative geographic inaccessibility has no doubt imposed on them cultural, environmental and economic isolation from the mainstream of Indian society. Their isolation, comparative political autonomous status and primitive association with the physical habitat, have posed administrative and economic problems of integration of their territory into a unified national political system. These problems have become particularly critical in areas where they have developed marked cultural and political consciousness. Under British rule, missionary activity among them extended not only literacy but also a sense of tribal nationalism. The Nagas along the Burmese border belong to such a category. They actively agitated for the formation of a state in which they could further their cultural and religious interests. (Nagaland, a separate state, was created in 1967.)

Most other tribal groups, such as the Bhils and Gonds in Central India, the Santals in Bengal-Bihar and several minor tribal groups in south India remain largely poor, illiterate, and culturally remote. With increasing contact with the outside world, they are gradually being assimilated into Hindu society. Their lot is roughly analogous to the tribal Indian groups in the United States of America. On the one hand there is the problem of their integration into the mainstream of society, on the other there is a genuine concern regarding their prospective loss of identity and religion as they are acculturated into the main society. The federal government has established a semi-autonomous territory, Arunachal Pradesh, in which tribal religions and culture will be preserved and encouraged.

Religion and the Organization of Space*

Indian religious beliefs have found direct expression on the landscape in the form of religious structures, places of worship, cemeteries and burial places. Religious adherence has also indirectly affected the land. Hinduism, Islam, Christianity, Jainism and Buddhism have prescribed regulations regarding reproduction, life and death which in turn have affected the demographic-resource equation. Indian

---

*Sopher's *Geography of Religions.* (1967) has been particularly useful for this section.

landscapes are dotted with sacred places, holy rivers, and places of pilgrimage. Religious injunctions have stratified society into caste divisions, which have indeed influenced the whole range of man's activities and attitudes to space use.

Since Hinduism is numerically the largest and historically the most ancient of Indian religions, its imprint on the cultural landscape is the strongest. Hinduism has over the centuries grown into a highly complex, loosely organized group of diverse cults and sects incorporating beliefs ranging from polytheism to monotheism to monism. In its most intellectual form, it emphasizes the pervasiveness of the Supreme Being, the indestructibility and transmigration of soul, nonviolence, reincarnation of the physical body, and prescribed birth in a particular caste. Jainism, Buddhism and Sikhism which broke off from it as revolt against its ritual practices, have not escaped Hindu influences in their social stratification, and in the observance of rituals. These religious groups have, however, maintained their distinctive places of worship and their sacred shrines. Formal positive expression of Indian religions on the landscape is manifested in their sacred structures, use of cemeteries, and assemblages of plants and animals for religious purposes. Streets, parks, bridges, trees, and rivers are dotted with the statues or even symbolic figures of gods, which constantly receive the propitiations of the passersby. Sacred structures are widely and conspicuously distributed all over the country, ranging from minor inconspicuous village shrines (or even a small idol embedded in a roadside wall) to large Hindu temples, monumental mosques or ornately designed cathedrals in large metropolitan areas. Whether it is a Hindu temple, or a Sikh *gurdwara,* or a Muslim mosque, or a Buddhist monastery, such communal sacred buildings differ in size, form, space use and density depending on the ideological and organizational requirements of the religious order. All, however, perform a basic religious function.

A distinction between structures housing a god or those meant for congregation may be made. Hindu temples invariably enshrine a statue or a symbol of a deity, whereas mosques, *gurdwaras* or churches are basically designed for religious congregations. In addition to their basic religious functions, such structures tend to acquire secular attributes as well, and often maintain guest rooms for pilgrims and other visitors. Business and political conventions, folk festivals, and recreational activities are also arranged in areas specifically demarcated for such purposes within these religious structures. Most religious structures are located where adherents can regularly attend the services, their spacing and density parallel that of the hierarchy of settlements. Large Hindu temples are maintained by the various caste groups, wealthy people or charitable endowments. Over the years, a vast amount of wealth has been offered to the temple gods and priests. The total wealth of Hindu temples in the form of jewelry and property alone is estimated to be in billions of dollars. Hindu temples house many gods, since many Hindus are eclectic and propitiate not one, but several gods, believing that all gods are merely manifestations of one God.

A typical Hindu temple is distinctive in layout, architectural style and spatial features. Unlike a mosque or church, it does not necessarily require a large closed interior space for congregation where prayers are held. The statue of the chief deity is usually sheltered in an inner shrine. Surrounding it are the corridors (pavilions) for ritual circulation (*parikrama*) by the public. Elaborate temple gateways direct one's entry into the building. Jain and Buddhist temples also adhere to this basic plan. Sikhs do not enshrine a statue, and Sikh temples tend to adopt the congregational aspect of Islam and Christianity; space is allocated for the purpose. Islam and Christianity emphasize the congregational aspect of prayer. The focus of activity in their places of worship is congregational prayer space for which a hall or a compound is specifically allocated within a church or *masjid* or *jami*. In Islam, community worship is scripturally prescribed and universally practiced. Within the precincts of a mosque, an open space, usually rectangular in shape and enclosed by walls, is maintained.

The relative impress of religious structures on the land depends on the frequency of their distribution, the number of clients of the religious order, the wealth and enthusiasm of the religion's clientele and the ecclesiastic requirements of the various religions. In Goa, Kerala, parts of Assam and large urban centers, Christianity's impress of churches, mission houses and Bible libraries is pronounced. Areas controlled by Muslim rulers between the 13th and 18th centuries, especially urban centers like Delhi, Agra, Allahabad, Hyderabad and Lakhnau, clearly exemplify the strong Islamic impress on the cultural landscape. Mosques like *Jama Masjid* in Delhi and *Shahi Masjid* in Agra (both built by Shahjahan in the 17th century) are among the noble examples of monumental structures which dot most large Indian cities.

Religious functions can also be performed outside temples of worship, often in a home or even in an open space. Many Hindus keep household gods, symbolized by statues or paintings, located at a designated place in their homes where prayers are usually offered. Ritual prayers of Muslims (*namaz*) can be said anywhere at appropriate times, even in a moving train.

Cemeteries, burial places, and cremation grounds constitute other direct expressions of religious affiliation on the land. The Hindu, Buddhist, Jain and Sikh tradition of cremation of the dead is very different from the Muslim and Christian institution of burial in a community ground and thus leaves a different cultural imprint on the land. Burial grounds, for example, impose a squeeze on useful land within cities. Burial inscriptions, however, are instructive tools in deciphering the human geography and social history of the area.

Religions occasionally bestow on certain plants or animals a degree of sanctity or ritual function. Such plants and animals are kept in religious structures or dispersed along pilgrims' routes. *Tulsi, pipal* and *bo* trees, though of limited economic or decorative value, are sanctified by Hindus and Buddhists. The tumeric plant's sanctity is recognized because its pigment is used in Hindu rituals. Sandalwood's dye is considered sacred and is used in the ritual marks on the forehead by religious Hindus. Rice is a sacred plant because it is used in most Hindu and Buddhist ceremonies and ritual observances.

Associations between religions and places are developed in many other ways. The distribution of holy places and place names honoring thousands of Hindu gods and Muslim and Christian saints, indicate the direction and history of religious currents. Hundreds of places of pilgrimages express the direct formal expression of religion on the land. The geography of Indian holy places (Hindu, Jain, Buddhist and Muslim) is rendered complex by the large pantheon of Hindu gods, Muslim saints, Jain *tirthankars* (saints), and Sikh *gurus*. River sources such as Manasarowar Lake (in Tibet) and Badrinath in the Himalaya, river confluences (Allahabad), physiographic breaks in the course of rivers (Hardwar, Srirangam), mountain peaks (Mt. Abu), lakes (Pushkar) and caves (Amarnath) have all been sanctified by several religions. Large temples have been established in many of these locations, and these, in turn, have favored urbanization. Amritsar located at a spring lake (a holy place of the Sikhs) is another example. Many present day large urban centers originated with a predominant religious function as sacred places of pilgrimages like Varanasi, Madurai, Tirupatti, Allahabad and Mathura. In addition to their normal sanctified character as pilgrimage sites, these attract regular periodic pilgrim assemblages (*Kumbha Mela*) every 12 years.

Pilgrimage has been an important mechanism of religious circulation (*tirthayatra*) involving millions of Hindus (and Jains, and Buddhists to a lesser extent) each year, a number increased manifold during *Kumbha Mela*. These periodic pilgrimages afford a continuing forum for the exchange of religious ideas, often cutting across linguistic barriers. Pilgrims also generate cultural exchange, social mixing and trade and contribute to political integration. Pilgrim circulation, however, diffuses epidemic diseases, which accompanies each large 12 year *Kumbha* fair. An informal hierarchy of the distribution of pilgrim centers is recognizable at the national, regional and local levels, each level maintaining its religious hinterlands (Bhardwaj 225-228).

Religions have prescribed or encouraged taboos on work and food, which may be described as having a negative expression on landscape. General taboos against the killing of animals and meat eating among Hindus, Buddhist and Jains has resulted in a lack of development of the dairy and beef industry, and has upset the ecological balance in India. The taboo on beef eating by Hindus, an extension of the idea of *ahimsa* (non-violence), has resulted in the accumulation of an enormous cattle population, a large part of which is aged, diseased, unproductive and parasitic. It is a pity that very little attention has been paid to efficient stock breeding in India. However, future breeding should be controlled and the stock improved for the extension of a dairy industry within the framework of the ideals of *ahimsa* (Sopher, 40).

Religious mandates occasionally regulate human occupations. Hindu society is scripturally stratified into caste categories with associated occupations (expounded in the Laws of Manu). Basic notions of ritual purity among high-caste Hindus have affected their occupations. Occupations like fishing and leather tanning are downgraded as low-caste occupations. Cultivation is a lowly profession and high castes are reluctant to take up farming, which has traditionally suffered from neglect by castes who possess capital and managerial skills to undertake. Non-Hindus also display similar occupational traits. Jainism prohibits any form of agricultural occupation since plowing must destroy some insect life. Jains have, therefore, taken to trading and banking in large numbers, and are concentrated in cities.

Among Hindus, different castes display different food consumption traits as sanctioned by scriptures. Avoidance of meat eating is very strict among Brahmans, the highest caste. Lower castes, like the untouchables, who are considered ritually "unclean," do not avoid meat eating. Most upper caste Hindus abstain from fish and fishing as this occupation is accorded low social status. The fishing industry, in general, has not prospered in India. The development of a liquor manufacturing industry has also lagged, as most Indian religions forbid the consumption of alcohol. The other religions also mandate food habits. Sikh religion proscribes the use of tobacco and thus discourages Sikhs from entering into any related business.

The rhythm of farming activities is regulated by a ritual calendar affecting the quality of production. Religion festivals must be attended to even if growing crops need attention. Work in the fields is usually suspended at prayer time (devout Muslims observe prayers 5 times a day).

Religious mandates have indirectly affected the population-resource equation on the land. High and middle caste Hindus, Jains and Buddhists forbid widow remarriage, resulting in lower fertility rates among them as compared to the higher rates for Sikhs and Muslims. The Hindu desire for a child early in life encourages early marriage and higher maternity rates among young females. Another scripturally

Society and Development in India

sanctioned desire widely prevalent among Hindus is to have at least one male child (who is responsible for most ritual functions for the parents).

Religious beliefs also affect social and economic behavior. Based on the Hindu-Buddhist-Jain value systems, indifference to worldly gain has inhibited the formation of capital, investment and labor input. In this respect, Sikhs have proved to be more liberal and successful in farming and Parsis in business than have Hindus. The Islamic practice of segregating females deprives them of any economic functions (working in the field or in an office or factory).

Religious sentiments often dominate one's political behavior. Partition of the Indian subcontinent into two countries in 1947 was a successful goal of the Indian Muslim League, a strong political party inspired by religious motives. At several levels, local, district and state, religion-inspired political parties fight elections with the ostensible purpose of winning concessions and privileges for their religious groups.

THE CASTE SYSTEM:
ITS MECHANISM AND PERSISTENCE

Caste has been one of the oldest, most distinctive and persistent features of Indian society for the last three thousand years or more. It is a major force in the socio-economic and political systems of the country. Theoretically, Sikhs, Muslims and Christians are immune to the caste distinctions. But most non-Hindus in India are converts from Hinduism and their descendants. They socially and spatially interact with the traditional caste-based Hindu society every day, and have maintained the caste traditions of the Hindu society. Despite the weakening of caste structures in the cities, the lives of over 400 million villagers, an overwhelming majority of the population, are still profoundly shaped by the caste institution.

A precise definition of caste is difficult, but the concept includes at least two levels of comprehension. One is the philosophical and broad level comprehending caste as a hierarchical division of society on the basis of *varna* (literally "color") into Brahmans, Kshatriyas, Vaishyas and Shudras. From the original *varna* categories, the Hindu society evolved into hundreds of castes or *jatis*. Any visitor to India would soon discover that caste as a functional organic system is more complex than this classification of society into these four broad groups. The second level of caste comprehension is the segmentation of society into thousands of *jatis,* or castes, each internally bound by marriage, lineage, customs and was originally determined by occupational, religious, ritualistic, and social codes. With increasing urbanization, democratization and spatial mobility, the occupational affiliations of the castes have been undergoing social and structural transformation. The functional division of society into castes or *jatis* is a unique feature of India's human geography, and is of greater socio-economic relevance than the four broad *varna* categories.

Within the broad *varna* framework most *jatis* are traditionally stratified on the basis of their social status, ritual marriage ties and common descent by birth. The most simplistic explanation of the origin of castes may be traced to the Aryan settlement and expansion in India sometime in the second millennium. The Aryans, it is generally thought, were pastoral nomads in Central Asia, from where they migrated into northwest India and pressed into the Indo-Ganga plains. In the early days of their settlement, society was divided on the basis of color (*varna*) into fair-skinned Aryans and the dark colored natives, and perhaps additionally into nobility and commoners. Vedic literature (1500 B.C.-500 B.C.) suggests such a simple division of society. Gradually, as the Aryan movement spread to other parts of the country, increasing contact with and assimilation of the natives, and crystallizing the functional roles of the various groups, society was divided into a hierarchical strata of social classes. First, the four *varna* divisions emerged; later thousands of caste groups or *jatis,* distinctive in kinship, lineage, customs, and social taboos grew up within the *varna* framework. The precise procedures of this societal segmentation, and the formalization of ritual, lineage and social codes are not properly understood.

Caste mechanics, although grounded in antiquity and shrouded in mystery, are in general well known. Caste membership is hereditary and usually immutable for life. Birth, a basic attribute of one's caste affiliation, is a function of one's *karma* (reward or punishment for actions performed in a previous earthly existence). To play a desirable role in life, according to *karma*, is to lead a life prescribed by *dharma* (duty) rules of religious and social obligations and the observance of caste rules.

Caste territories are spatially demarcated on the basis of marriage links along endogamous lines. Physical contact with other castes is circumscribed by restrictions on contact, associations, dining or eating food cooked by other castes. Caste membership is emphasized by one's *jati* name, by the individual's identification with his caste in the eyes of the community, by one's conformity to the customs of one's caste and by one's subjection to the *jati* government. Ritual observances of the caste are strictly maintained. *Jati* solidarity is kept by its traditional occupations. *Jati* sanctions prescribe what forms of work one may or may not undertake, whom one should marry, what, how and with whom one may eat, and what rituals one may perform. Caste affiliations often affect local and state politics.

Polarization and Interdependence
of Castes in a Rural Society

In a traditional rural society, developed around a self-sufficient village community, various castes have performed their well-regulated functions. In ancient and medieval times spatial mobility and linkages were restricted to a few pilgrimages to sacred places, and to marriages. During the last fifty years, with the establishment of an increasing number of spatial links of the villages to the urban centers, caste structure is undergoing a few changes and its ritual role is declining.

In *varna* hierarchy, Brahmans stand at the top. Principle castes of this *varna* have been those of priests, teachers, custodians of sacred ritual practices and the arbiters of correct social and moral behavior. Geographically, they are the most ubiquitous since they must officiate in a variety of rituals. By virtue of their traditional prestige, they have been able to collect large amounts of land through grants by local rulers. Ritually barred from cultivation, they are now a prominent landowning and moneylending class. Their services are constantly in demand by other castes for all major ritual functions at births, marriages and deaths. Generally, Brahman households are few in a typical village, but Brahmans command a wide variety of services from other caste households as they own a large part of the agricultural land. Brahmans are generally better educated than the other groups. With increasing urbanization, they have shown a tendency to gravitate to the city for service in clerical and administrative positions. In many parts of South India, like Tamil Nadu and Kerala where they have historically played an unusually important role, anti-Brahman feelings have been building up over the last fifty years, and non-Brahmans have become active in the once Brahman-dominated administrative services. Many Brahmans who have adopted clerical and administrative occupations continue to perform ritual functions for other classes.

The Kshatriyas, next in *varna* ranking, are also very powerful. The traditional Kshatriya role of defense (warrior caste) is now largely submerged under the role of land ownership. When Kshatriyas form large majorities in a village, the village is usually identified by the *jati* name of the Kshatriyas, for example a Rajput village (in Punjab), Jat village (Uttar Pradesh), Thakur village (in Himalayan regions), and Nair village (Kerala). Vaishyas rank below Kshatriyas, but fall within the orbit of ritually high *varna*. Major castes within this *varna* were those who were engaged in occupations of farming and retail trade. Several prominent Vaishya groups have established successful monolithic businesses all over the country. Shudras, ranking below Vaishyas, belong to the lower category and are debarred from several ritual privileges. Shudras are mostly engaged in a wide variety of artisan services, such as carpentry, metal work, basket weaving, and cultivation. Shudras form the bulk of the country's population. In the middle and lower Ganga plains, they have been able to build a prestigious social status.

At the bottom of the social *varna* ladder are the "exterior" castes, the so-called "casteless," "untouchables" (now officially "scheduled castes"). During and since the British rule, they were listed in the special official schedules for administrative and representational purposes. Gandhi addressed them as *Harijans* (children of God). Their occupations are "unclean" (to the higher castes): disposal of the dead, flaying of the dead animals, janitorial and menial work, cleaning latrines, etc. To the upper castes they are the "untouchables." The practice of untouchability started with their original "unclean" occupations, and physical contact by the upper castes with them was prohibited. A complex code of physical contact, ritual purity and prejudice slowly grew up as society was formalizing codes of ritual conduct during the early crystallization of caste history. Untouchables were denied admission to temples, certain roads, schools and collective village social activities, and were also banned from the practice of occupations reserved for the high castes. Caste stratification can be seen in its worst form in south India. Until recently the Harijans were not permitted the use of sandals, residence in brick houses, or the wearing of an upper garment on their body in Tamil Nadu, Andhra Pradesh and Karnataka. By tradition, these were privileges enjoyed by the "clean" higher *varnas*.

The Hindu social system's organic functioning, though segmented into various castes (*jatis*), was based on the principle of caste interdependence. In theory, each caste has traditionally defined duties and obligations relative to its status and ritual purity in conformity with the needs of the village community. A unique system of hereditary service and patronage among the castes (and families) thus grew up. This system is known as *jajmani* system. The *jajman* or the hereditary patron receives the services of a hereditary tradesman or servant and pays in goods or cash on a regular basis for the performance of such services. For example, village landowning castes (usually upper castes) received ploughs, pots, and leather goods, as well as services connected with cleaning and repairing their households, from the lower castes (Harijans or Shudras); and pay for these in grains, vegetables and even landuse privileges. In certain ritual functions, the lower castes also act as *jajmans*, the patrons, as for example the Brahman performance of ritual (priestly) functions for the lower castes. Brahmans act as the keepers of village shrines. In lieu of these services, they obtain cash and other gifts on a regular basis. In essence, the *jajmani* practice sets up a social network of alliances among groups of people who exchange goods and services. Payment for goods and services is traditionally fixed and related to the amount of service rendered, the relative status of the caste involved in an exchange, and the needs of the receiving family. Payments by the *jajman* are also made in return for special services at ceremonial occasions such as births or marriage.

In a traditional, self-sufficient, caste-structured society, the need for such an arrangement is crucial for those castes whose ritual behavior keeps them from doing manual and menial jobs. Brahmans, for example, traditionally do not till the land, and Shudras or lower castes perform these functions for them in exchange for cash payments. Several castes perform the functions of craftsmen, such as carpentry, pottery, weaving, barbering, shoe making and the laundering of clothes for their *jajmans*, and receive regular fixed payments. Different castes carry specific social and religious obligations. In planning a marriage, or building a new house, or arranging entertainment, the householder must call upon the services of a wide range of castes in connection with sweeping the floors, performance of rites and procurement of goods needed for the occasion. Different castes thus perform traditionally defined economic, social and ceremonial roles within the village. The upper castes depend on the lower ones for labor, artisan goods and menial services; the lower castes look upon the upper ones for financial inducements and loans in times of need. This interdependence has preserved and strengthened the caste structure. Harmonious inter-caste relations are a guarantee of economic cooperation. It is advantageous for a landowning farmer to be on good terms with a carpenter, blacksmith, weaver or barber. The traditional cash payments to them were meant to be a hedge against the inflation of an urban commercial society, although inflation has clearly been eroding into its real value. Despite segmentation and polarization, the caste institution has, therefore, persisted as a remarkably cohesive force in a rural, self-contained society. The impact of the caste system is most clearly discernible in the rural areas.

Spatial Dimensions of Caste Distributions

No enumeration of the castes (except for "Scheduled Castes") has been made since the Indian Census of 1931 which listed 2,378 "main" castes, or *jatis*, for the country. Several of these claimed millions of followers. The present-day caste distribution in the country probably follows closely the lines of the 1931 Census. Although Brahmans and the "untouchables" (listed as "depressed" classes) perform wide-ranging services, and are more pervasively distributed, they still tend to show degrees of regional concentration. Other castes vary greatly in their regional distributions. At the micro level of a village, only a few of the castes are usually represented. Within a village the number and size of castes depends on the size of the village, its regional location, its economic structure and above all its historical experience. A tiny settlement of a few hundred farmers may contain only a few castes (farmers, shepherds). Neighboring larger villages provide it with ritual and other services. A typical average village contains a mixture of 5 to 15 main castes, a few land-owners (e.g., Brahmans, Jats, Rajputs), a few members of the lower castes performing menial jobs, and a large number of various farming castes.

Within the village, caste hierarchy is revealed by the residential segregation of the castes, the size of houses and the quality of materials with which they are constructed. Better houses belong to the higher castes and are usually located in the center, the other castes inhabit the peripheral parts. Residences of the untouchables generally occupy areas outside the main village. Muslims and other lower castes usually restrict their housing to one side of the village, but are not necessarily segregated in areas outside the village as are the untouchables.

The predominant caste may not necessarily be the *dominant* one. A *dominant* caste is the one which is economically and politically the most powerful. If a numerically weak caste holds most of the land, business, and public offices, it controls the politics and administration of the village as well and emerges as the dominant caste. Often a dominant caste possesses a high ranking on a social ladder.

Above the village level, two spatial levels of caste distributions can be identified: the exogamous caste region incorporating those villages which are functionally interconnected by marriage ties; and wide region grouping several hundred villages of a predominant caste.

Caste regions based on the marriage alliance are recognizable almost universally in north and west India. According to the rule of exogamy, one is not supposed to find a wife within one's own *gotra* (ancestral lineage traced to a patron saint). Marriage alliances are developed with the outside villages, usually in a 4 to 12 mile range. A few studies indicate that in Punjab the greatest clustering of marriage links lies within 8 miles, and in most parts of Uttar Pradesh between 8 and 12 miles. Usually no marriages are arranged within 2 miles of the residence. An average distance of marriage ties in Uttar Pradesh is 10 miles. A typical marriage circle covers about 300 villages, with about 80 villages accounting for half of all the marriage linkages. Spatially interconnective directions of the flow of girls in marriage ties are usually established and maintained. Spatially oriented marriage links also determine social ranks. "High" villages obtain the girls, and "low" ones supply them. Two sets of villages are therefore spatially organized; one set usually receives wives, and the other sends wives. Certain cases impose financial penalties on the families of their castes if territorial affinal boundaries are transgressed. The idea of hypergamy, i.e., men of higher caste taking wives from the castes below them, along with exogamy, helps to perpetuate the establishment of "high" and "low" villages. In Punjab-Haryana three marriage regions based on marriage ties have been identified: *Majha, Doaba* and *Malwa*. In south India, however, marriage alliances are encouraged within the same village because of the marriage preference for cousins and nieces.

Schwartzberg has identified caste regions by grouping several districts (civil divisions) of north India on the basis of predominant castes, caste dominance and rate of increase in the number of castes with increasing village size. He recognizes five distinctive regions for north India (Figure 4.6). Region *A* includes the Punjab plains and a contiguous area in Rajasthan. The predominant caste in this region is the farming caste of *Jats* (mainly Sikhs, but many Hindus as well). Whatever other types of castes they may contain, most are inhabited by one single caste, most often Jats. In some villages Rajputs (non-cultivating landowning caste of high ritual status), Sainis (gardeners), Kambohs (farmers) and Alhuwalias (cultivators) lead in villages. In a typical Jat village, there is often not a single household of Rajputs, emphasizing the mutual exclusivity of the two castes. Other castes well represented in the region are: Chamars (leather workers) and Mazabhis (Sikh sweepers). In some urban areas several Vaishya (merchant) castes are locally predominant. Region *B* lies to the east of region *A* in Delhi and Uttar Pradesh. Caste structure in this region is diversified with two

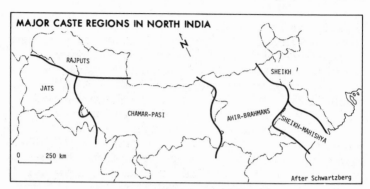

FIGURE 4.6

or three almost equally numerous castes coexisting, as well
as many less numerous castes. In some parts, the scheduled
castes are the most numerous ones. Several Muslim castes
are also represented. Chamars, Jats, Baniyas (merchant
caste), Rajputs, Ahirs (milkmen), and Kurmis (cultivators)
are numerically strong castes. Region *C* comprises the area
of lower Ganga plains in Bihar. Ahirs are predominant, with
Brahmans and Rajputs making up only 10 percent of the
population. Bhumihar, a cultivating Brahman caste, is also
locally significant in several areas. Region *D* stretches from
the eastern Nepal border to Bangladesh. Sheikhs (Muslim
caste) predominate numerically. Mahishya (cultivators) and
Kayastha (Kshatriya) castes are locally significant as landlords. Region *E* surrounds the Calcutta metropolitan area
but also extends to south Bihar. Brahmans, Mahishyas, and
Sheikhs are important castes. Tribal groups like Santals
predominate in several villages, and are being gradually
Hinduized (Schwartzberg, 1968).

The Changing Caste System

The caste system has persisted for well over three thousand years. Throughout these years, with the assimilation of
new elements, it has been continually expanding to form
new castes. Essentially it has worked reasonably well in a
rural, self-contained conservative society. Each social stra-
tum performed its assigned functional and occupational role
in the wider context of society. But it is a patently undemo-
cratic system based on absolute inequalities in social rela-

tionships, and it presupposes an unchanging environment and fixed needs of the society. However, traditional India is struggling to modernize itself, especially where the impact of increasing urbanization is being felt. The caste system, therefore, finds itself pitted against the forces of urbanization, constitutional democracy, and literacy.

In the cities, caste inequalities are being eroded perceptibly. City life prevents the observance of caste rituals in the matter of interdining, and polluting physical contact in public places like cinema houses, shopping areas, city transportation and restaurants, etc. Spatial diffusion of these social changes to the rural areas is still limited, but is on the increase. Since Independence, transport facilities have been extended to large number of villages and the traditional self-sufficiency of the villages has been reduced by the penetration of a money economy, and by a progressive disappearance of handicrafts and thus of the caste-related *jajmani* system. Chamars (a lower caste of shoemakers) are now lured to becoming milkmen to earn more money ever since factory-made shoes from the cities are being increasingly sold in the villages (Srinivas, 1960).

The three main forces responsible for bringing structural and institutional changes into the caste system are: *secularization, westernization* and *sanskritization*. *Secularization* may be defined as a process by which the scriptural and ritual behavior and symbols cease to possess the traditional mandate. Ritual purity becomes a matter of personal hygiene rather than a caste-prescribed social code. For example, "pollution" arising of interdining with lower castes is being replaced by interdining in washed teacups and dishes. The educated pilgrims are now more concerned with the polluting drains flowing into the river Ganga than the river's holiness. There is a gradual erosion of priestly authority. Ritual customs at weddings are becoming lax. All these are the outcome of secular processes (Srinivas, 1967).

Sanskritization refers to the adoption of the lifestyles, rituals, and beliefs traditionally associated with the upper. castes by the lower ones in order to achieve social elevation. The opening up of economic opportunities, the spread of education, and the concept of equality before law have all contributed to this process of vertical social mobility among the lower castes. In Karnataka, parts of Tamil Nadu, Punjab, and several other parts of the country, the Harijans are renouncing the consumption of liquor, meat eating and widow remarriage in order to claim higer social status by the adoption of these traditional castes mores of the upper castes.

Westernization is a process of adoption of the lifestyle of the western world, and gained initial popularity among the upper castes, who westernized their life pattern by adoption of the British social mores during and since British rule. The educated Indian elites (usually the upper castes) acquired such forms of British social behavior as drinking, adoption of western dress, and forms of greetings during their contact with the British in the clubs, officers' messes, civil departments and courts. Many rituals related to caste purity and physical pollutions were abandoned. The three processes mentioned above have made a greater impact in the cities where the vast, congested, mobile, secular, and somewhat westernized society would tend to diminish the original roles of the castes.

On the other hand, several forces have tended to perpetuate the caste institution, especially in the cities. Since Independence caste groups have been politicizing themselves by forming caste associations, a process started during British rule. The growth of caste hotels, caste-based religious schools, public dispensaries and restaurants has fostered caste kinship and interests of the individual castes. Caste lobbies have sprung up in the state legislatures. In the villages, the dominant castes have been tightening their hold on the village councils, despite the seeming democratization of the village councils (*panchayats*).

The most basic cleavage in the society, however, despite its apparent segmentation, remains in the form of its polarization into two basic groups: the "clean" and the "unclean" (polluting) castes. The "unclean" castes are the untouchables, or the *Harijans,* and number 81 millions or 14 percent of the population. Generally ubiquitous, they are concentrated in larger number in rural areas. Historically they have been oppressed, but they have functioned as an integral link in the socio-economic fabric of the society. Although they must reside in segregated quarters away from the main settlement nucleus, they work in the homes and fields of the upper castes, and receive *jajmani* payment from them, thus forming an inseparable part of the society. Geographically the north Indian plains contain about one-half of their population, although in no part of the country are they altogether absent.

Untouchability has been abolished by India's constitutional mandate, and its practice made a criminal offense since 1955. But these legal sanctions have proved fruitless. Social pressures against untouchability are still quite feeble. During 1951-1971, the untouchables increased from 50 millions to 81 millions, registering a higher increase rate than that of the general population. About 40 percent of the untouchables are tenant cultivators, 35 percent work as hired agricultural laborers, and most of the remainder work in household services and cottage industries. In rural areas, approximately two-thirds of them are in debt to the village landlords. Illiteracy is nearly universal (90 percent) among them (compared to 76 percent for the total population). The Indian government is keenly aware of their backward status and has, since 1955, adopted several measures to improve their condition. Special quotas of reserved seats in the state and federal legislatures, public services, and educational institutions have been established for them. Such legislative measures to compensate the Harijans for historic injustices have ironically encouraged their separateness from the rest of the community, and has even bred social hatred leading to occasional minor civil riots. Rather than accelerating their socio-economic advancement, social cleavages have often widened. Meanwhile exploitation against the *Harijans* continues by the more powerful, elite and unscrupulous high-caste groups. A report of the federal government in 1969 indicated that very little improvement in their status has been achieved. The institution of caste, the report points out, is still deeply entrenched in the society. The report recommended several institutional and structural changes to root out untouchability; such as abolition of the hereditary priesthood, biological assimilation of the social groups through intermarriages, and stricter enforcement of legal equality.

The future of untouchability is linked with society's modernization and urbanization processes. Undeniably untouchability is disappearing in urban schools, temples, hospitals, and public transport. In the villages where illiteracy and ignorance are more prevalent and where the traditional social taboos are deeply entrenched, untouchability remains a fact of life.

CITATIONS AND SELECT BIBLIOGRAPHY

Area Handbook for India. U.S. Government Printing Office, Washington, D.C., 1975.

Atal, Yogesh, *The Changing Frontier of Caste.* Delhi, 1968.

Bhardwaj, S. M., *Hindu Places of Pilgrimage in India.* Berkeley, 1978.

Brown, W. N., *The U.S. and India, Pakistan, Bangladesh.* Cambridge, 1972.

Brush, John E., "Distribution of Religious Communities in India," *Annals of the Association of American Geographers,* 1948, pp. 81-96.

Chatterji, S. K., *Language and the Linguistic Problem.* London, 1945.

Dasgupta, J., *Language Conflict and National Development.* Berkeley, 1970.

Dumont, L. *Homo Hierarchicus.* Chicago, 1970.

Dutt. A. K., "Religious Pattern of India," *Geo Journal.* Vol. 3 (2), 1979, pp. 201-204.

Fukutake, T., *Asian Rural Society.* Seattle, 1967.

Harrison, S. S., *India, The Most Dangerous Decades.* Princeton, 1960.

Kothari, R., *Politics in India.* Boston, 1970.

Lewis, John P., *Quiet Crisis in India.* Brookings Institution, Washington, D.C., 1962.

Maddison, A., *Class Structure and Economic Growth.* London, 1971.

Mahar, J. M., (ed.), *The Untouchables in Contemporary India.* University of Arizona Press, 1972.

Mason, P., (ed.), *India and Ceylon: Unity and Diversity.* London, 1967.

McLane, J. F., *India—A Culture Area in Perspective.* Boston. 1970.

Myrdal, Gunnar, *Asian Drama.* 3 Vols., New York, 1967.

Report of the Committee on Untouchability, Economic and Educational Development of the Scheduled Castes and

Connected Documents. Government of India, New Delhi, 1969.

Schermerhorn, R. A., *Ethnic Plurality in India*. Tuscon, 1978.

Schwartzberg, J. E., "Distribution of Selected Castes in the North Indian Plains," *Geographical Review*. Vol. 55, 1967, pp. 477-495.

Sengupta, B., *The Fulcrum of Asia*. New York, 1970.

Singer, M., (ed.), *Traditional India: Structure and Change*. Philadelphia, 1969.

Singer, M., *When a Great Tradition Modernizes*. New York, 1972.

Smith, D. E., *South Asian Politics and Religion*. Princeton, 1966.

Sopher, D. E., *Geography of Religions*. Englewood Cliffs, 1967.

Sopher, D. E., "India's Languages and Religions," *Focus*. Vol. 6, 1956.

Srinivas, M. S., *Social Change in Modern India*. Berkeley, 1967.

Srinivas, M. S., *India's Villages*. Bombay, 1960.

Tinker, Hugh, *India and Pakin—A Political Analysis*. New York, 1962.

Zinkin, T., *Caste Today*. Calcutta, 1962.

CHAPTER 5

INDIAN POLITICAL
AND ADMINISTRATIVE TERRITORY

The evolution of India's internal state structure, its administrative-territorial hierarchy, the external relationships of its political territory and the prospects of its external security are examined in this chapter.

INTERNAL ADMINISTRATIVE SYSTEM

Growth of the Indian States

On the eve of Independence, India was subdivided into a fragmented patchwork of large and small political units. Most of the large units, called provinces, were ruled directly by the British, while the remainder were the "native" states with their own rulers operating under British suzerainty. This complex system resulted from the historical consolidation of British interests in India, based in part on pre-British arrangements but greatly changed by subsequent military and political developments.

The British states' system of provinces which was in operation between 1857 and 1947 with only minor territorial modifications, largely evolved between 1747 (Battle of Plassey) and 1857 (Indian Revolt). Although some British conquests were gained by treaty, the bulk of India's territory was acquired by force of arms. By the end of the 18th century, the British had overcome French colonial competition in India and were firmly entrenched in the three key coastal locations of Bombay, Madras and Calcutta. From these three coastal strategic points British occupation began to penetrate inland. British conquest was achieved by the amalgamation of native states into provinces for political

154

and military convenience. Kingdoms or parts of kingdoms annexed by conquest or treaties were grouped arbitrarily into provinces under British governors without consideration for traditional boundaries, cultural affinities or regional bonds.

Those remaining parts of the country which escaped direct annexation largely occupied the interstices of the British provinces and were shared by more than 650 native rulers. About half these were in Kathiawad Peninsula in West India and most of the remainder in adjoining Rajputana and Central India. Each had its own ruling house and enjoyed a degree of sovereignty under the mantle of British power. At one extreme, some native states were as large and as populous as some of the world's large nations; for example, the states of Hyderabad and Jammu and Kashmir were each over 80,000 square miles in area, and the former had a population of 19 million people. At the other extreme, some states were very small, occupying areas of a few square miles, with a few hundred inhabitants, and receiving only a few dollars in annual revenues. Even the larger native states were unable to pose a united front to the British because they were flanked or isolated by the strategically located British provinces. By 1819 the British supremacy had become unchallengable. The British annexation of India had been completed by 1857. Only a few small insignificant coastal areas remained outside British control in the hands of the French and the Portuguese, relics of the colonial struggles of the 17th and 18th centuries. India's state structure in 1857 and the French and Portuguese possessions persisted essentially unchanged until 1947 (Figure 5.1).

In 1947 when India moved into Independence, the state system erected by the British underwent a major change through the creation of the Muslim state of Pakistan. Pakistan was formed in two separate blocks. West Pakistan, carved out of northwestern India, contained ten native states; East Pakistan consisted solely of the eastern part of the province of Bengal and a segment of the adjacent Assam province. Some Indian observers feel that one of the basic reasons responsible for the creation of Pakistan was British colonial policy in the 20th century which contributed to the Hindu-Muslim schism. This policy was apparently directed at granting the Muslims greater political recognition as a means of countering growing nationalist urges among the

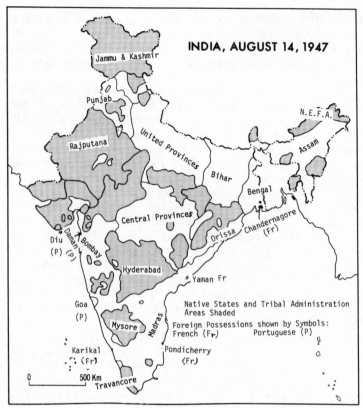

FIGURE 5.1

Hindus. During the 1930's and 40's, Muslims increasingly demanded a "homeland." After the Second World War, major parties were reconciled to the demand of a "homeland" for the Muslims, and cooperated with the British government to make plans for partitioning and Independence of the country. The basic procedure followed in partition was to create Pakistan from the portions of British provinces having Muslim majorities in the population according to the census of 1941.

Territorial Consolidation
of the States, 1947-1950

Immediately after Independence, the governments of both India and Pakistan started to tackle the difficult task of revising the complex and administratively illogical state structure inherited from the British. The main problem was not the key British provinces but the 562 native states falling to India's share, a heterogeneous mass of territories. In addition to their remarkable variations in size, population, and revenues, the native states had varying degrees of administrative cohesion and economic development. These territories, which were the accidents of history, did not coincide with the major economic, linguistic and cultural regions of the country. Futhermore, the British government had controlled the external affairs, defense and communications of the native states. Such arrangements, which bestowed upon the British virtual control over the native states, may have been suitable for colonial administration, but in independent India they were clearly anachronistic.

After the end of British rule in India, the native states were legally empowered to accede to either India or Pakistan. Most native states recognized their inadequacies as sovereign units and the wisdom of joining India or Pakistan. The new countries of India and Pakistan could ill-afford to allow the continued existence of independent kingdoms scattered throughout their territories, a situation which could seriously endanger the political stability and economic development of the new countries. Hence, the first job which the government of India undertook was to establish its control over the native states and to create through consolidation a more logical system of states. By a process of territorial consolidation and reorganization a union of all the native states into three categories within the overall administrative framework of the Union of India was achieved by 1950. The notable exceptions to this regrouping process were the large native states of Hyderabad and Jammu-Kashmir. The Muslim ruler of Hyderabad (population 87 percent Hindu in 1941) favored the idea of establishment of an independent state within the British Commonwealth with some political relationship with Pakistan. Under the Indian government's relentless pressure, followed by token military action, the ruler signed a treaty of accession in 1949.

The states of Jammu and Kashmir, another large area (over 84,000 square miles), posed a more formidable problem. The state was ruled by a Hindu, although 77 percent of the population were Muslims in 1947. The strategic importance of the state in proximity to the borders of China and the Soviet Union was heightened after partition because of its contiguity to both Pakistan and India. It was claimed by Pakistan on the basis of its Muslim majority status (the Indo-Pakistani dispute over this state is discussed later in the chapter). Immediately following partition and Independence, while the ruler was still contemplating a possible course of action, tribesmen from Pakistani territory (with the possible connivance of the Pakistan government) attacked the state, forcing the ruler to make a desperate appeal to the Government of India for military help. This was quickly granted, but only after he decided to accede the state to the Indian Union, an action which made the state a legal part of India. Soon after, Pakistan rushed its own troops to support the invading tribesman. India quickly moved its troops to halt the invaders. Thus the Indo-Pakistan war over the state started.

Rather than flushing the invaders out of the entire state, the Indian government took the case of aggression from the Pakistani side to the United Nations which immediately appointed a commission to investigate the states' boundary and territorial dispute. The United Nations Commission on India and Pakistan (UNCIP) proposed that a plebiscite be held to ascertain the wishes of the people of the state and also called on both Pakistan and India to establish a cease-fire line. The ceasefire line was demarcated, with areas of high altitude left undemarcated, and accepted by both parties on January 1, 1949. The ceasefire line left India in possession of two-thirds of the state including the fertile valley of Kashmir lying east of the line, and area west of the line remained under Pakistan's control administered through the so-called "Azad" (Free) Kashmir government. Since then, the line has crystallized into a *de-facto* boundary between the areas controlled by two countries. By 1950, all the native states had acceded to India or Pakistan, and the first phase of the territorial readjustments of the former native states and British provinces was over.

In this readjustment process there were three basic types of arrangements which led to the country's territorial consolidation. Most of the small princely states, not viable as separate units, and located within, or adjacent to, the Governor's provinces (during British occupation) were merged with them to create large Part A states (1st Schedule of the Constitution, 1950). Two hundred and seventy five of the medium-sized or small native states were integrated into five large adminstrative units (unions) with a separate legislature and a capital. Three of the largest states—Jammu and Kashmir, Hyderabad and Mysore—were allowed to retain their separate identities. These states and the unions of states were called Part B states. Finally, 61 medium-sized states were molded into new units as Part C states to be directly administered by the central government. Ajmer, Coorg, and the capital territory of Delhi were also accorded Part C status. Part C states were allowed limited powers.

In addition to the British provinces and the princely states there were a few French and Portuguese possessions in India, mostly located along the coasts. After Independence, India and France successfully negotiated, and in 1956 the French possessions of Chandernagore (near Calcutta) and Pondicherry (on the east coast) were made over to India by France. Pondicherry has been retained as a Union Territory. The Portuguese possessions of Goa, Daman, Diu, Dadra and Nagar Haveli, all along the western coast, proved a real problem. Portugal remained unyielding in retaining these, whereas public opinion both in India as well as in the Portuguese possessions, especially in Goa, strongly favored their merger with India. Unsuccessful in negotiations with Portugal, India forcibly annexed Goa in 1961, while the other Portuguese enclaves had earlier been taken over by India. Although India's occupation of Goa was practically bloodless, her annexation was widely condemned in the West. The former Portuguese territories have been retained as the Union Territories of i) Dadra and Nagar Haveli and ii) Goa, Daman and Diu.

Reorganization
of the Indian States Since 1950

We have seen how the integration of the princely states into the Indian Union produced a patchwork of different categories of state structures. The political units devised by 1950 in many cases, lacked economic viability or a suitable administrative machinery. Even while carrying out the sweeping modification in the state-system during 1947-1950, the Indian government had announced its intention of devising a more rational reorganization at a future date. Such a reorganization would necessarily involve the creation of new units based on such considerations as distinctive regional, linguistic, cultural and economic characteristics. Against this background, and under mounting public sentiment favoring linguistic states and growing government concern, the Indian government created the first linguistically based Telugu-speaking state of Andhra Pradesh in 1953. This quickly sparked renewed demands for political recognition by other linguistic and culture groups. This led to the establishment of a States' Reorganization Commission in 1953 which was entrusted with the task of making recommendations for a more rational subdivision of the country into states. The Commission's Report was submitted in 1955, and was put into law as the States' Reorganization Act of 1956. Although the Commission considered several factors, language apparently was the most important consideration in the creation of the new states.

However carefully designed, no system of Indian states could satisfy all the diverse pressure groups. After intense Gujarati pressure, a fifteenth state of Gujarat incorporating the Gujarati speaking areas of Bombay state was created in 1960 and the new Bombay state, incorporating the Marathi-speaking areas of the adjoining Hyderabad and Madhya Pradesh (Vidarbha), was designated as Maharashtra.

Numerous areas of political tension and many dissatisfied groups still remained. Two politically powerful groups were most vociferous in seeking territorial identification in the form of separate states: Sikhs in the Punjab and the Naga tribesmen in Assam along the India-Burma border. In addition, minor tribal groups were seething with discontent and agitating for their individual states. In the Punjab, the Sikhs sought for the creation of a Punjabi-speaking state. In reality, however, they used the linguistic issue to cloak their aspirations for a separate state in which their religion would be in a majority. Initially, such demands were resisted by the Indian government out of a fear that further subdivision of the country would lead to its undue fragmentation especially along the strategically located international borders (e.g., the Punjab and Naga areas). However, the government yielded to the pressures of these insistent groups and created a new state of Nagaland in

1963. In 1966 out of the existing Punjab State, Punjabi speaking areas were grouped into a new state of Punjab. The remaining parts of the former bi-lingual Punjab state was named Haryana. In a further revision in 1971, several hilly parts of Punjab were transferred to the already existing Union Territory of Himachal Pradesh, which was accorded the status of a state in 1971.

Sweeping territorial rearrangements in the Assam hills resulted in the new state of Meghalaya which was carved out of the territory of the state of Assam in 1973 in order to satisfy the wishes of the people of the Garo, Khasi and Jaintia Hills. These hill people did not wish to be dominated by the plainspeople of the Brahmaputra Valley in Assam. In a concurrent process of reorganization the centrally administered Union Territories of Arunachal Pradesh (formerly North East Frontier Agency or NEFA bordering Tibet) and Mizoram (along the Burmese border) were created. In 1973 when Manipur, Meghalaya, and Tripura were elevated to state status, there were 21 states and nine Union Territories. Following internal unrest, the Indian government accorded the status of an associate state to Sikkim in 1975, which had remained as a protectorate. The number of Indian states was raised to 22. Underlying the Indian government's motivation in the creation of all these states was the hope that the creation of these political units would relieve tension in these border areas.

The Vidarbha part of Maharashtra, and Telangana area of Andhra Pradesh may be cited as two examples of regional aspirations. In 1969 there were serious riots, work stoppages and demonstrations in favor of the creation of a separate Telangana state.

In contrast to these desires of smaller cultural groups to gain identification as separate states, the desirability of creating larger states has long been voiced. Even during discussions regarding the States' Reorganization Bill in 1956 in the Parliament, a proposal for the creation of a United State of Bengal and Bihar was advanced but fell through for want of public support. Another proposal for the creation of a large southern state consisting of Dravidian India, to be known as *Dakshinapath* or Dravidistan also failed to bear fruit. The proponents of larger states felt that factors of national security and economic progress were more important than cultural considerations. According to them, smaller cultural states would lead to the ultimate balkanization of the country, and be a potential hazard to the development of a viable spatial political organization. However, in several instances the clamor for cultural "homelands" as separate states are localized in less developed areas and stems from alleged discrimination against or lack of recognition for the underdeveloped regions by political leaders from more developed parts of the state. The creation of new smaller states, therefore, can fulfill local politicians' aspirations toward personal administrative roles, and a greater participation in state politics.

Administrative Territorial Hierarchy

An experimental step toward the formation of larger political units was made in 1956 in the form of Zonal Councils. The State's Reorganization Act of 1956 divided India into five large zones, each containing a number of states and union territories functionally tied to an advisory body known as a Zonal Council. These were invested with purely advisory roles of liaison between the states and the federal government in matters of such interstate disputes as border quarrels, water distribution and economic planning. Shorn of administrative, legal or legislative powers, their effectiveness was seriously limited. In view of the sensitive nature of the northeast India-Tibet border, a special advisory body similar to the Councils but invested with special functions was set up in 1972 for the states of Assam, Manipur, Meghalaya, Nagaland, Tripura, Mizoram, and Arunachal Pradesh.

At the time of the states' reorganization discussion in 1956, the Prime Minister pleaded unsuccessfully for the creation of larger states of the size of the Zonal Councils. Such a move envisaged five or six big administrative states for the country, each with a secretariat, legislature, one cadre of public services, one governor and a capital. It was argued that within such a large multi-lingual and multicultural state, various groups would not be apportioned among two states, reducing the chances of clamor for cultural subdivision of a country. More importantly, the creation of a few states would be more conducive to the launching of coordinated economic development plans, and would result in substantial savings of public funds.

Unlike the 22 states, the nine Union Territories are directly administered by the federal government in New Delhi through an administrator appointed by the President. Their legislative bodies possess reduced powers. The Territory of Delhi is in fact a Federal District. The Anadaman and Nicobar Islands, as well as the Lakshadweep Isles (formerly Laccadive Isles) are the outlying island territories. Three are former French or Portuguese holdings; Goa, Daman (Damao) and Diu; Nagar Haveli; and Pondicherry (ex-French) plus three other smaller territories. Other Union Territories lie on the northeast strategic borders with Tibet and Burma (Arunachal Pradesh, Mizoram). Figure 5.2 shows the major political units of India.

The states and the union territories are subdivided into over 350 local administrative units, known as districts, below which are the sub-units of *tahsils, taluks* or subdivisions, each comprising several (typically 100) villages.

*Administrative Integration
and National Security*

The territorial integrity and internal stability of India depends upon how well its administrative authority at the national level is balanced against the regional pulls of castes, languages, religions, and other pressure groups. In a federal system in which the states are accorded a large measure of internal administrative power, the overall administrative and social cohesion of the country has to be effectively protected by investing the federal government with special power to cope with the centrifugal tendencies which might be set in motion in the different states. In view of this, and despite the avowed federal structure of its administration, India's Constitution provides for the government at the national level a large measure of centralized power. In fact, the rights of the states can be taken away from them by the federal administration by two-thirds majority of those voting in each of the two houses of the Union Parliament. States themselves can be created, abolished or divided by a majority vote. Since the complete revamping of the old state boundaries in 1956, several revisions of state boundaries have taken place, including the dismantling of old states and the creation of new ones.

The division of powers between the Union and the states

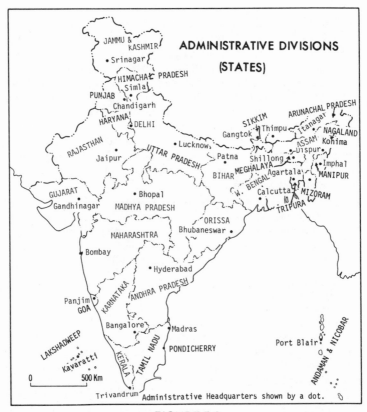

FIGURE 5.2

is clearly defined in the Constitution. Powers not specified in the Constitution (i.e., the residual powers) rest with the Union. The federal government (the Union) has jurisdiction over national defense, foreign affairs, interstate trade, regulation of mines, communications, railways, incorporation of banks, and national insurance. The states have control over police, local government, public health, education, agriculture, and irrigation. In addition to the "Union" and "State" lists, there is a concurrent list on which both the federal government and the states can legislate. This list includes price controls and treatment of refugees, among other things. Although the states can exercise the power to tax, a large part of state revenues are derived from the revenue-sharing formula with the federal government. The federal government pays for many of the states' major economic development projects, hydro-electric dams, heavy electric machinery, locomotives or aircraft factories. Despite these overriding federal powers over the states, in actual practice states have been exercising a good deal of political power since most states have been so far under the administration of the Congress Party which has also controlled the federal government.

In practice, inter-state conflicts occasionally arise, e.g., disputes over boundaries, over the location of federal government development programs, and even over the location of steel mills or the sharing of river waters by several states. Such issues have often generated conflicts, even including acts of violence and riots carefully timed to draw the central government's attention to the depth of regional feelings.

An important limitation on the powers of the states is the exercise of emergency powers by the federal government at times when the security of India or any part of the territory thereof is threatened whether by war, internal disturbance, or external aggression, including domestic violence, failure of parliamentary government to function, or a breakdown of financial stability. In such cases the President's Rule is imposed on the state, an act which must be approved by the Union Parliament within two months, and revoted every six months. The federal government has exercised these emergency powers over two dozen times. Major examples of President's Rule are Kerala (1959), Bihar (1959), Haryana (1968), Rajasthan, the Uttar Pradesh (1973, 1977), West Bengal (1972, 1979). Indian administration has been, therefore, called federal in theory and unitary in practice.

The federal government tries to maintain the overall unity of the country by such measures as the institution of all-India services, notably the Indian Administrative Service, Indian Foreign Service, Indian Police Service, and the various Economic Services. It has established integrated Indian defense services. The personnel of these services are obliged to serve anywhere in the country and help bring an inter-regional point of view wherever they serve. Furthermore, English has been retained as an associate language to promote national integration.

Governing the Administrative Territory

Reference has been made earlier in this chapter to the hierarchical structure of India's administrative divisions from the state to the *tahsil* level. This pyramidal hierarchical structure is presided over at the top by the President of the Union, from whom the chain of command flows unbroken almost down to the local, *tahsil, taluk* or subdivision level. States are divided into districts. Perhaps the district is the most important of the units in the administrative hierarchy. Administrative machinery at the state level is in many respects a replica of the federal government. Each district is administered by a district officer who exercises power over a million or more people in his district. From the district level up, the administrative positions are held by Indian Administrative Service personnel (IAS), the professional, permanent, and generally well-trained government servants, the successors of the famous British Indian Service (ICS) personnel. The *tahsils* or *taluks* are administered by the assistants of the district officers, which manage their own affairs through the village *panchayat,* composed of elected headman and village leaders.

This tightly centralized administrative set-up was liberalized in 1952 when the Community Development Program was instituted. New administrative divisions known as Development Blocks, comprising approximately 100 villages with a population base of 60,000 to 70,000 were set up, each served by a block officer, and assisted by a technical staff for advice on agriculture, public health, animal husbandry and rural industries. Block officers' staff looked after the "village level" workers. This well-conceived but poorly organized Community Development Program did not produce expected changes in the rural landscape, a failure explained by a lack of motivation among the ill-paid staff, who in turn failed to motivate the villages and dislodge them from their ingrained traditional habits. It was realized by 1957 that the Community Development Program was not working well. Another three-tier system of self-government (*Panchayati Raj*) within the district was adopted by most states by 1959. At the base was the *Village Panchayat,* at the block level was a *Panchayat Samiti* elected by the village *panchayats* within the Development Block. At a still higher level *Zila* (District) *Parishad* (Council) elected by the *Samitis* which proscribed policy at the district level. This system was called "decentralized planning."

It is probably too early to determine the degree of success of this "decentralized planning" program in terms of the economic development of the country. At the lowest level, however, it has been observed that the *panchayati raj* has been responsible for aggravating factional tendencies and caste frictions in village elections as each caste seeks to gain control over the *panchayats*.

The legislature of the Union government is bicameral. The upper house of 250 members is called the *Rajya Sabha* (Council of States), and the lower chamber, *Lok Sabha* (House of the People) contains 500 members. Members of the both houses (with the exception of a few Presidential appointees and reserved seats for specific tribes/castes) are elected; for the *Lok Sabha* directly and for the *Rajya Sabha* by the elected members of the state legislatures. Most states also have bicameral chambers.

A striking feature of the Indian administrative system is the multiplicity of parties and independent candidates of wide-ranging political persuasions, representing the diversity of economic, social, political, religious, caste and regional interests. During the mid-term general elections of 1969, as many as 75 parties were registered with the Election Commissioner. Five parties, the Indian National Congress, Communist Party, Socialist Party, Swatantra (Freedom) Party, and Jan Sangh (Hindu party) have nationwide following. Only a few parties are regionally important, for example, the DMK (Dravidian Party), the Akali (Sikh) Party, and the Muslim League. The Indian National Congress (known as the Congress Party) has been the main political force in the country until 1977. It has controlled the Union government and most of the states in five of the seven elections since Independence (1952, 1957, 1962, 1967, 1971, 1977, 1980). Although it has never commanded an absolute majority of the popular vote, it has always polled consistently close to 40 percent until 1971. Since then it experienced a set-back when it not only lost its controlling position in several states where it failed to form cabinets, but its position progressively declined. In 1977 it was fragmented into 2 major groups, one led by Indira Gandhi (Congress I) and the other known as Congress O (Original). The reverses of the Congress Party

Society and Development in India

TABLE 5.1

PARTY POSITIONS IN LOK SABHA
IN INDIAN ELECTIONS

	1952	1957	1962	1967	1971	1977	1980
Congress	364	371	361	283	352	153	13
Congress (I)	—	—	—	—	—	—	351
Congress (O)	—	—	—	—	—	50	—
Janata Party	—	—	—	—	—	270*	32*
Praja Socialist	—	19	12	13	—	—	—
Communist Party of India	23	27	29	23	24	7	10
Communist Party of India (Marxists)	—	—	—	19	26	22	35
Dravida Munnetra Kazhgam (DMK)	—	—	—	—	18	1	16
All India DMK (ADMK)	—	—	—	—	—	19	2
Jana Sangh	3	4	14	35	19	—	—
Swatantra Party	12	—	—	23	—	—	—
Lok Dal	—	—	—	—	—	—	41
Other Parties	28	12	79	40	56	41	41
Independents	38	42	—	42	12	2	3
TOTALS	489	494	494	520	518	542	524

*Includes Jana Sangh, Congress (O) and Praja Socialist Party.

Sources:
  1. *India, A Reference Annual, 1977 and 1978.*
  2. *The Hindustan Times,* New Delhi, Jan. 10, 1980, p. 11.

have been attributed to internal infighting, the Sino-Indian border War in 1962, and the country-wide droughts of 1965-66. The opposition parties gained control of the administration in Bihar, Uttar Pradesh, West Bengal, Tamil Nadu, Kerala, and Punjab, dislodging the Congress Party from its dominant position for the first time. Table 5.1 gives the status of the major parties in the *Lok Sabha* since 1952.

Two interesting developments on the political scene were the elections of 1977 and 1980. Precipitated by a wide popular resentment against the Emergency Rule of 1976, the government had hastily arranged a special election in 1977 in which the leading party (Congress) in power was overthrown by a newly-formed right-wing party known as Janata Party (literally "People's Party") which was created by a coalition of the disgruntled elements of the Congress, Jana Sangh and the Praja Socialists. The Janata Party, however, was again overwhelmingly routed by Congress (I) ("I" for Indira, the Prime minister of India from 1966 to 1977), thus creating a most spectacular political comeback in modern history.

Of the other parties, the Communist Party has enjoyed a broad nation-wide following. It has been specially strong in West Bengal, Kerala, Tamil Nadu, and Bihar since 1967. In 1960 it formed a government in Kerala which did not survive. Since the Sino-Indian War of 1962, its appeal has declined, and it has split into two groups, pro-Russian and pro-Chinese. The various Socialist parties are hopelessly disunited. The Swantantra Party has been regionally important in Bihar, Rajasthan and Gujarat, and among the landlords and former princes between 1967-72. Its economic and social platform was mainly similar to the Congress Party. The Jan Sangh is a right-wing communal party espousing the cause of the revival of Hindu culture, and calling for a Hindu orientation in administration. It has called for complete control over Kashmir, and a stricter attitude toward Pakistan.

The DMK, Akali Dal, and the J & K Congress have been dominant political forces in Tamil Nadu (since 1967), Punjab, and Jammu and Kashmir respectively. Furthermore, a large number of independent candidates have been entered in elections. They have been able to capture only a few seats in the *Lok Sabha* but have been somewhat more successful in the state assemblies.

At the state and local levels, political parties which seek to occupy the seats have often strong local caste-affiliations. Often two rival parties will choose members of such castes as their candidates. Occasionally several independent candidates court the traditional caste strongholds. Caste rivalries thus play a major role in state politics.

India contains the world's largest electorate (of over 330 millions), although only 30 percent of it is literate. In each

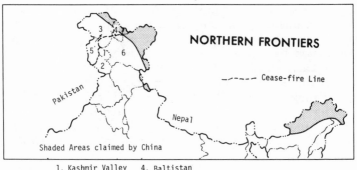

1. Kashmir Valley   4. Baltistan
2. Jammu   5. Pakistan-occupied Kashmir
3. Gilgit-Hunza   6. Ladakh

FIGURE 5.3

general election over 50 percent of the eligible voters have cast their ballot (69 percent in 1971, 55.5 percent in 1980) which compares favorably with elections in western countries.

EXTERNAL POLITICAL RELATIONS

Sino-Indian Border Dispute

India has a common, extensive and difficult border of over 2,400 miles with China, separating China from the Indian states of Kashmir, Himachal Pradesh and Arunachal Pradesh. Virtually impossible to demarcate on the ground because of rugged terrain and harsh environment, the boundary was ratified, though imprecisely, on the maps between India and Tibet (over which China has long claimed suzerainty). The boundary has been disputed by China since 1914, although even earlier the National Chinese Government never properly accepted it. The Chinese government has laid claims to nearly 50,000 square miles of territory controlled by India during the British rule. In addition, China laid claims to areas in Bhutan which is tied to India by special treaties.

The Sino-India border easily divides itself into three sectors: the western sector extends for about 1,400 miles from the easternmost tip of Afghanistan to the southern tip of Ladakh in the state of Kashmir; the middle sector lies for a few hundred miles between the Indian state of Himachal Pradesh and Uttar Pradesh and Tibet; and the eastern sector of about 800 miles separates southeastern Tibet from the state of Arunachal Pradesh in India (Figure 5.3).

The western sector was never delimited on maps. The Chinese claims rest partly on ethnic grounds, and on the assertion that the wastelands of the Aksai Chin in the disputed territory were always linked more with Tibet and Sinkiang. Ethnically this area is an extension of Tibet in language, religion, and culture. But the Chinese documentation regarding the actual occupation of the area by Tibet is unconvincing. The Indian case rests on the claims that the area has been historically administered by the state of Jammu and Kashmir since 1849, and that the Indo-Tibet Treaties of 1684 and 1842 confirmed the traditional boundary between Tibet and Ladakh (a part of Kashmir), although the precise boundary alignment was never undertaken (Van Eckelen, 165). China also claimed a part of the Hunza-Gilgit area in north Kashmir (ceded to her in 1963 by Pakistan), although the whole territory has been effectively under British sovereignty since 1895.

The disputed territory in the middle sector is very small, touching the international boundary at few places. The disputed area in the eastern sector lies to the south of the line, usually referred to as the McMahon Line, which in general follows the crest of the Himalaya between Bhutan and Burma for about 800 miles. India has stressed that the McMahon Line as the international boundary between Tibet and India was agreed to between the two governments in 1914 and marked as such "on the map attached to the draft convention initialled by the plenipotentiaries of India, China and Tibet" (The Sino-Indian Dispute, 12-13). However, China has considered the McMahon Line illegal and unacceptable (The Sino-Indian Boundary Question, 57), claiming that Tibet had no right to sign the 1914 Convention held in Simla which delineated the McMahon Line on the map. India challenges such a position, maintaining that Tibet was independent and in fact concluded several independent treaties which were considered valid by all parties, and were in operation for decades (The Sino-Indian Dispute, 12-13).

China denied the validity of the McMahon Line as an international boundary and laid claims to areas south of the line up to the foot of the Himalayan Range in the Brahmaputra Valley in the state of Assam in India. The disputed territory in Arunachal Pradesh of about 32,000 square miles has been administered by India since 1947. It has been inhabited by several tribal groups, such as the Miri, Abors, Daflas, Apa Tanis, Mishmis, Akas, and Monpas; each speaking its own distinctive tribal language of the Tibeto-Burmese family, and functioning more or less as an independent political unit under Indian jurisdiction. Racially the tribes are closer to the Mongolian Tibetans. The Monpas have generally adopted Lamaistic Buddhism, although several are animists. Their contacts with the outside world have been few and varied from tribe to tribe, but more with the Brahmaputra Valley than with Tibet. Until the 19th century the British showed no interest in the tribes or their territory. It was only at the Simla Conference in 1914 that the status of the area was formalized.

Chinese governments never formally questioned the validity of the agreement between India and Tibet until 1959. From the Indian point of view there are two crucial elements in controversy; first, the fact that from 1914 onward Britain and since 1947 India exercised jurisdiction, however weak it might be, over the area, and second that China did not dispute or formally protest against Indian control until 1959. Even in 1956 when the Chinese government's attention was drawn to certain Chinese maps showing the areas to be a part of China, Chou En-lai, the Chinese Prime Minister, promised to look into the alleged "cartographic errors" in the Chinese maps (The Sino-Indian Dispute, 16-17).

India's relations with China were marked by friendliness until 1959. Strangely, China's annexation of Tibet in 1950 which traditionally formed a part of the "outer ring" sphere of British influence was designed to keep other major powers out. In fact the leaders of independent India had disapproved of the British defense policy of keeping British influence in Tibet, which was based on the security system consisting of concentric "inner" and "outer" rings. During the British rule in India the Himalayan countries of Nepal, Sikkim and Bhutan formed the "inner" ring in which complete border security was developed by a skillful alliance with the border states. Afghanistan and Tibet formed the "outer" ring in which diplomatic pressure kept other major powers out. After Independence, this defense policy for India's borders was abandoned. India's recognition of Chinese sovereignty over Tibet was accompanied by only a mild protest. In 1954 it relinquished its special privileges in Tibet which had been acquired from Britain, such as the right to keep military contingents in the town of Gyanste, and the control of Tibet's postal and electric services. These traditional rights were given up without trying to obtain Chinese endorsement of the McMahon Line (Van Eckelen, 193-197).

Chinese attempts to establish normal relations with India during the early 50's when they were tightening administrative control over Tibet proved illusory. The Chinese moved slowly at first, consolidating their gains in Tibet, which they later extended to Ladakh and the NEFA. By 1956 border incursions were growing in intensity. India, meanwhile hoped that the insurmountable barrier of the Himalaya would leave China no choice but to follow a policy of peaceful coexistence. Indian apprehensions grew when in 1956 it was discovered that China had been building a road through Ladakh linking West Tibet with Sinkiang, and had quietly moved into Aksai Chin, an area formerly under Indian control. Advances into the NEFA were also viewed with alarm and dismay. India formally protested in 1958, diplomatic notes were exchanged and both sides adopted increasingly hostile postures. Prospects for settlement through negotiations became clearly remote. Repeated small-scale armed clashes along the border between 1959-1962 escalated into a fullscale war in the summer of 1962 when China launched a major offensive in both NEFA and Ladakh. It was not quite clear how much territory China actually wanted to annex. Its demands kept shifting. As rapidly as the offensive was launched, China announced at the end of November that it would make a unilateral withdrawal from its advanced positions. The sudden withdrawal of the Chinese forces closer to the McMahon Line in the eastern sector puzzled most observers. Chinese forces had penetrated deep into the Himalaya, crossing the crest or the "watershed." Despite shipments of arms and ammunition from western countries, India could hardly withstand a swift bold push to the Brahmaputra lowlands in Assam. The Indian armed forces were out-numbered and outgunned. They were not well trained to fight a modern war in mountainous terrain. Surprisingly, the Chinese forces pulled back without annexing the disputed territory in the eastern sector, a large portion of which had already fallen to them. In the western sector, however, they did not pull out of Aksai Chin.

The China war taught India many lessons. The myth that the Himalaya was an effective defense barrier was exploded. India's naive confidence in China's friendliness had dulled her perception regarding effective security measures in the India-China borderlands. The prompt and positive response of the western countries in rushing military supplies to the war zone helped to improve the image of the West in Indian eyes. India realized that the posture of "non-alignment" was no substitute for defense preparedness.

The reason of expediency has been advanced for the sudden unilateral decision by China to withdraw its forces. Her advance troops would have been cut off from supply bases in Tibet in the winter of 1962 when the high passes in the Himalaya would have been closed by snow. The Chinese explanation was that they had no further territorial ambitions.

Since November 1962 an uneasy truce has been in force along the border. Unfortunately neither side has called for a negotiated settlement of the dispute since the winter of 1962. India has tightened her security measures all along the border and only a few minor clashes have been reported. The Colombo powers, spearheaded by Ceylon (now Sri Lanka) tried to mediate a settlement, but failed to persuade China to vacate the annexed areas in Ladakh and NEFA. The Soviet Union afforded some moral support to India without helping her with arms. Several countries condemned China as an aggressor. Cuba, Albania, and Portugal supported the Chinese viewpoint.

One significant indirect effect of the war was the emergence of China as a superior military and political force in Asia, a position which was later bolstered when China became a nuclear power in 1973.

Clearly it is in the interest of these two major neighboring powers to reach agreement in the interest of peace in the area. In 1970 India's Foreign Minister spoke of his country's basic policy toward China in this manner, "Neither China nor India can change the geographical fact that our countries have a long common border. It is in the interest of both countries to settle the border question peacefully and normalize relations . . . when China is willing to take a concrete step in this direction, she will not find us lacking in response" (*India, A Reference Annual,* 1971-1972, 524-525). More recently Chinese leaders have expressed similar views.

Border with the Himalayan Kingdoms

Landlocked between India and Tibet, the Himalayan Kingdoms of Nepal, Sikkim and Bhutan cover an area of a little over 75,000 square miles and share common boundaries totaling about 750 miles with India. Historically they were maintained within the "inner" ring of the British defense interest as "buffer" states. The current aggressive policy of China in the Himalaya has brought sharply into focus the strategic aspect of their location.

Nepal managed to survive as an independent country during the British rule over India, but established close attachments to India by treaties of friendship and protection from external aggression. Bhutan is protected from external invasion while retaining autonomy in internal administration. In Sikkim, which became an associate state within India in 1976, India exercised control over its external policy as well as its borders and internal administration. China has allegedly laid claims to Bhutan. Since the Sino-Indian hostilities of 1962, India has adopted defensive postions along the Sikkim-Tibet border designed to guard several strategic passes, and has reportedly stationed 25,000 men in areas which were the scenes of Chinese intrusions in the 1960's.

India formally protested in 1959 against China's claim over Bhutanese territory. China responded by denouncing Indian rights of protection of Bhutan, and asserted that any border dispute with Bhutan could be settled directly with Bhutan without Indian interference. The Indian government maintained its right to defend Bhutanese borders. It has been closely helping Bhutan in its defense efforts, although no Indian soldier has been stationed along the Bhutan-Tibet border.

Like Bhutan, the independent kingdom of Nepal is sandwiched between Tibet and India. Neither China nor India has laid any territorial claims over it. China disputed

Nepal's Tibetan border, but its claims were relinquished in 1961 following a treaty, and the entire northern border has now been demarcated.

Nepal has carefully pursued a policy of non-alignment, and has allowed both India and China to construct roads linking its capital city of Kathmandu with its two big neighbors. India considers Nepal to lie within its perimeter of defense interests and she is acutely aware of the dangerous potential of any possible future southward expansion by China made easier by the Tibet-Kathmandu road constructed in 1968-1970.

The Burma Border

The 960-mile Burma border, extending from the eastern offshoots of the Himalayan ranges southward roughly along the watershed between the Brahmaputra and Irrawady river systems, has only been demarcated recently. The border passes through the mountainous territory inhabited by several tribal groups, such as Nagas and Mizos. Distinct in culture, language and race from the plainspeople of the Brahmaputra Valley, these tribesmen have shown considerable independence from the Indian and Burmese authorities and have occasionally used Burmese territory as a staging point for anti-Indian activities, often abetted by Communist guerrillas in Burma. In the pacification program of this border the Indian government, as has been noted, yielded to political pressure and created the state of Nagaland in 1963 as a cultural-political "homeland" for the Nagas, and the centrally administered territory of Mizoram in 1972.

India and Burma have maintained good neighborly relations, despite Burmese deportation of much of its Indian population between 1948 and 1952. Mutually, they have tried to tighten border security against the insurgent guerrillas. Both countries reached an agreement in March 1967 regarding the demarcation of a portion of their common border.

India Bangladesh Border

The partitioning of the Indian subcontinent in 1947 into the two countries of India and Pakistan, created a common border of 1,150 miles in East Pakistan (which since December 1971 has been separated from West Pakistan as Bangladesh). Never fully demarcated on ground, this border criss-crossed numerous streams and contained a number of (foreign) enclaves lying in Indian and Pakistani territories. Only a few railroads crossed the international boundary of East Pakistan linking the Indian states of West Bengal and Assam. Rivers generally served as the main arteries of communications. East Pakistan, separated from West Pakistan by over 1,000 miles of Indian territory was linked with its larger and politically more powerful western counterpart via the Bay of Bengal and Indian Ocean.

East Pakistan constituted a wedge of land in eastern India, separating Tripura and Manipur from the rest of India until a new railroad constructed after Independence restored an effective communication link. Of crucial concern for India along this border was the possibility of the Bay of Bengal becoming hostile waters which could shelter nuclear vessels of Pakistan's allies in the event of a major Indo-Pakistan confrontation.

No major dispute arose along the border, although minor tension always prevailed. The question of "enclaves" was never solved. The continuously shifting streams also created territorial claims and counter-claims. Following the Indus Water Agreement between India and Pakistan in 1960, dispute arose over the use of the Ganga River Waters in East Pakistan. India had been planning to construct a barrage across the Ganga River at Farakka about 140 miles north of Calcutta, to rejuvenate West Bengal's river system. The Farakka plan was aimed at controlling floods, for producing more efficient water distribution between the northern and southern parts of the state of West Bengal, and helping to desilt Calcutta harbor. Pakistan feared that India's diversion of waters within the Indian state of West Bengal would seriously reduce water flow into East Pakistan, thus threatening its new irrigation projects and food-sufficiency drive. India argued that the Farakka plan would not affect East Pakistan's water needs.

Negotiations failed to produce a settlement on the question of Farakka plan. India meanwhile started work on the barrage in the mid-1960's fearing that delay in construction would further jeopardize the shrinking water supply for Calcutta's metropolitan area as well as the rapidly deteriorating condition of Calcutta's harbor. Since December 1971 the emergence of an independent and generally friendly country of Bangladesh in place of East Pakistan raised the prospects for an amicable settlement of this dispute. In 1980 an agreement appears imminent.

Indo-Pakistan Relations
along International Borders.
Dispute Over Jammu and Kashmir

Unquestionably the most critical problem between India and Pakistan has been the dispute over the territory of the former princely state of Kashmir (more accurately the state of Jammu and Kashmir), which has led to war between the two countries in 1948, 1951, 1962, 1965, and 1971. Both countries have large political, economic and strategic stakes in Kashmir and for both the dispute has become a symbol of national prestige and international justice.

The state is not a single geographic, economic, cultural or linguistic unit, but a conglomeration of six distinctive regions which were brought (under the administrative power) as a united political unit by Maharaja Gulab Singh, who entered into a subsidiary alliance with the British within the Indian Empire in 1849. In the current dispute both India and Pakistan have claimed the entire territory as if it were a homogeneous unit. Among the various regions the most significant is the historic Kashmir Valley, a well-developed center of tourist attraction and politically the seat of central authority. Until quite recently it was accessible from India by a single road, which was seasonally snowbound until the introduction of snowplows in 1948 (Figure 5.3). It is reached from the Pakistani side by a few roads. Overwhelmingly Muslim in population, this region is the most critical in the dispute. The minority of Kashmiri Brahmans have traditionally held positions of economic, social and political power, whereas the Muslim peasantry have remained abysmally poor. The second region, Jammu, lies in the southern part and contains only one-seventh of the total territory. More than half the population of the Jammu region is Hindu (about 50 percent in 1971). Its capital city of Jammu has been the state's winter capital, as well as the home of the state's ruling dynasty, the Dogra Rajputs. The third region, Gilgit, in the northern part of the state, is mountainous and predominantly Muslim. It is reached from Srinagar, the state capital in the Kashmir Valley, by crossing high mountain plateaus and glaciers, and is only tenuously linked with the other regions. The fourth region is that of Baltistan in the extreme northern part of the state, to the west of the Gilgit-Hunza region. And like it, is not easily accessible and contains high mountains. It is reached by a road along the Indus river in Pakistan. It is predominantly Muslim. The fifth region, Punch, lies to the north of the Jammu region and west of the Kashmir Valley. It is mostly Muslim, adjoins the Pakistani border, and is easily accessible from Pakistan. Two important rivers, Chenab and Jhelum flow into the region from the Kashmir Valley and through it into Pakistan where the waters are utilized for Pakistan's agriculture. The sixth region is that of Ladakh (literally "Little Tibet") occupying over one-third of the state in its eastern portions. It is a vast, barren, high plateau resembling Tibet in culture, Lamaistic Buddhism, and Mongolian language and race.

We have noted earlier that Kashmir state acceded to India in 1947. India's acceptance was subject to the determination of the wishes of the people by a plebiscite. Immediately Pakistan claimed that state had violated the Maharaja's previous agreements with India and Pakistan, and that the accession was based on "fraud and violence."

Pakistan's claim to Kashmir is largely based on religious and economic considerations. Kashmir state as a whole is a Muslim state, contiguous to and connected with Pakistan by several communication links. Furthermore, the four rivers, Chenab, Jhelum, Ravi, and Indus, vital to Pakistan's agricultural production, flow through Kashmir (more particularly the portion occupied by India). Pakistan has consistently maintained that a plebiscite of the entire state as recommended by the United Nations would result in a clear decision in her favor, and that India has been acting irresponsibly in her backing out of its original acceptance. India has held the position that Kashmir's accession had given India sovereignty over Kashmir. It had at first agreed to a plebiscite on condition that the Pakistani invading forces were withdrawn, a condition which was stipulated by the United Nations' resolution, but had never been realized. India, therefore, stresses the illegality of Pakistani support of the raiders and the Azad Kashmir government. Pakistan blames India for failing to withdraw its own forces from the

Indian-controlled territory, and for supporting a regime prejudicial to the holding of a plebiscite.

Agreement on the demilitarization, considered essential to a fair plebiscite, was never achieved by either side. To India, Pakistan was an agressor and should first withdraw its troops and its hold over the "Azad Kashmir" territory. Pakistan feared that if it withdrew its own forces, Kashmir would be left unprotected. The position of the two parties has been perceptively analyzed by Brown: "India has resolved not to permit a plebiscite, and Pakistan has not been able to force it. Whether or not India's stand on this issue is morally or legally justifiable, Pakistan's condonment of the invasion by the tribesmen, if not connivance, and later assumption of hostilities itself are seriously questionable . . . Each nation has pursued a policy in its own interest, and has had a less than a perfect case. The most potent consideration might possibly be that of need; Pakistan's was greater in 1947, but having reached an agreement with India on the Indus Basin's Waters in 1960, the extent of Pakistan's need seems to be diminished" (Brown, 200). (The Indus Basin Waters' Dispute is discussed later in this chapter.)

Ever since accession, the Kashmir government in Srinagar has maintained a close relationship with India, and in 1952 negotiated a pact which has given it a special status within India. Since 1956 India has outright rejected the possibility of a plebiscite, blaming the United States for its military aid to Pakistan and thus its "tilting" in favor of Pakistani claims. India has feared and openly declared that American military aid to Pakistan would be used against India in the event of any resumption of Indo-Pakistani hostilities.

India has vigorously promoted several economic and development plans in Kashmir's Indian-controlled territory. In 1956 it arranged for the establishment of an elected Kashmir constituent assembly which voted to make Kashmir a regular state within India. Since then, India has treated Kashmir as a constituent unit of the country, no longer open to a plebiscite.

Meanwhile the United Nations has over the years tried several times to mediate in the dispute and has arranged Indo-Pakistan bilateral negotiations, but the two countries have not been able to resolve their differences.

Apart from the purely legalistic view of Kashmir's accession to India, two other major considerations have guided Indian policy toward the dispute. First, India has declared and considered itself to be a secular state. Surrender of Kashmir on religious grounds would be a denial of the nation's essential principles. Secondly, the strategic location of Kashmir close to the Soviet Union and China is of critical importance to India. China's aggressive policy in the late-1950's in its annexation of Tibet, and later its occupation of Ladakh and building of a road through Aksai Chin in Ladakh, as well as its threatening posture toward India have all lent urgency to the strategic aspect of Kashmir's location.

During and after the Sino-Indian border conflict in 1962, India and Pakistan negotiated under pressure from the U.S. and Britain to resolve their differences, and agreed, in principle, to partition Kashmir. Talks fell through, however, for want of an agreement in the precise delimitation of the division. India appeared agreeable to accepting with minor adjustments in the ceasefire line as a basis for such a division, but Pakistan insisted on acquiring the Kashmir Valley.

The Chinese occupation of Ladakh in 1956-1957 has already compounded the issue of Kashmir's partition. In 1963 a new dispute arose when China and Pakistan entered an agreement regarding the borders of Pakistani-held Kashmir, a move which represented a reversal of Pakistan's foreign policy. Before that time, Pakistan had always posed as a staunch western ally, a good member of CENTO and SEATO and had received large amounts of military aid from the United States, all ostensibly to meet communist aggression. In fact, prior to the Sino-Pakistan border pact on Kashmir, Pakistan had been loudly proclaiming the need for joint Indo-Pakistani resistance to the Chinese threat to the Indian subcontinent. China not only agreed upon the demarcation of the border, but also helped Pakistan to build a new road across its occupied area to Sinkiang. Pakistan in return ceded a large territory (2,000-2,700 square miles), a move denounced as illegal by India, as it claimed that the entire state (including the area controlled by Pakistan and ceded to China) belonged to India.

Meanwhile Indo-Chinese clashes all along their common border erupted into a war in 1962. With occupation by

China of a part of Ladakh, India was forced to open a Kashmir front against China in addition to the deployment of forces against the Pakistani-held parts of Kashmir. In 1965 Indo-Pakistani fighting broke out in the Rann of Kutch (at the southernmost end of India's border with Pakistan), and later developed into a large scale war along the entire India-Pakistan border and the ceasefire line in Kashmir. With the efforts of the Soviet Union and the U.N. Security Council, Indo-Pakistani agreement on cessation of hostilities was reached.

Twenty-two years after Kashmir's accession to India, the dispute remains unresolved. A more recent Indo-Pakistan conflict in 1971 (in East Pakistan) and the emergence of Bangladesh in 1972 has added another element of bitterness to relations between the two countries. Since the prospect of holding of a plebiscite as a means of resolving its problem appears to become remote, other means to solve the problem should be explored.

The main bottleneck in the solution to the Kashmir problem has been treatment of the state as one homogeneous unit. Legal, moral, and economic grounds have been advanced by both parties claiming the entire state. In reality, the ceasefire line, adjusted in 1972, has already crystallized into an international boundary and part of Ladakh has been occupied by China. Students of the Kashmir dispute, including some in the United Nations, have favored the settlement on the basis of partitioning of the state. We have already seen that the state is only a conglomeration of regions. Under these circumstances the best solution would probably be a partition formula. The Valley of Kashmir could possibly be made an internally autonomous state whose territory could be jointly guaranteed by India and Pakistan under international trusteeship with both sides having access to it for trade. Jammu and Ladakh could go to India while the Muslim areas of Gilgit, Baltistan and Punch could go to Pakistan (Harrison, 56). In 1950 Owen Dixon, head of the United Nation's Commission for India and Pakistan had also suggested that the only hope for a settlement of the Kashmir question lay in some scheme for partition. Currently, however, both parties are inflexible in their negative attitude toward a settlement negotiated on the basis of a partition formula.

The Indus Basin Waters Dispute

Among the major problems that faced India during the early years of its Independence was the distribution of the waters of the River Indus Basin between India and Pakistan. One unfortunate result of the partition of the Indian subcontinent in 1947 was Pakistan's critical dependence for its irrigated agriculture on river waters obtained from the River Indus and its four major tributaries (Sutlej, Ravi, Chenab, and Jhelum) which flowed through India or Indian-controlled Kashmir territory before entering Pakistan. Pakistan's irrigated area in the Indus River Basin was nearly 20 million acres as compared to about 10 million acres that fell into India's territory. However, several of the headworks for the irrigating canals lay at sites in India. Thus India could, if it wished, exercise control over the water of Pakistan's canals. Pakistan feared that India would divert this water to its own territory, thus seriously injuring Pakistan's basic economy (i.e. agriculture). Luckily for Pakistan, such fears were never realized. However, during times of hostilities, India did possess an edge over Pakistan through this threat.

Related to the problem of the Indus Basin water allocation was the dispute over the construction of a large dam by India on the Sutlej river at Bhakra to provide irrigation facilities for India. Pakistan pointed out that India was trying to divert water to its advantage, thus depriving Pakistan of her share of water. India explained that the Bhakra scheme was an old scheme planned almost 30 years prior to partition.

Immediately following partition the water allocation problem of the Indus waters surfaced, and the negotiations between the two countries began in 1952. After eight years of hard bargaining and mediation by the International Bank for Reconstruction and Development (I.B.R.D.), an agreement was reached in 1960. According to the Indus Waters Treaty, waters of the three eastern rivers (Ravi, Beas and Sutlej) were allocated to India to use to the maximum of her needs, while the western three rivers (Indus, Jhelum and Chenab) were awarded to Pakistan. Since it was along the three eastern rivers (which were alloted to India) that most of Pakistan's irrigated territory lay, the Treaty called for the construction of costly link canals from the Jhelum and Indus rivers (awarded to Pakistan) to the Ravi and Sutlej rivers in order to keep the eastern rivers supplied with water. These extensive engineering projects were to be financed by loans from the International Bank (IBRD) and by contributions from India and Pakistan.

The two countries have displayed remarkable prudence in adhering to the terms of the treaty, even during the hostilities in 1965 and 1971. Irrigation development schemes have recently been expanded, and now encompass over 35 million acres. It might be observed, however, that instead of water-allocation, an integrated water-utilization scheme for both countries would be more beneficial in terms of economy and efficiency. Such a scheme, however, depends on the normalization of political relations between the two countries (Michel, 521-5).

THE INDIAN OCEAN

India's long coastline of about 3,775 miles projects into the Indian Ocean. Over 85 percent of India's trade is maritime, carried through the coastal ports. Imports of raw materials used for the country's industrialization and economic development arrive entirely by sea.

The Indian Ocean is strategically located with reference to India. The Indian subcontinent forms a roof over it. It is also girdled by land on the other two sides as well with the continent of Africa forming its western, and Southeast Asia and Australia its eastern walls, leaving its southern side open. This "landlocked" nature of the Indian Ocean has thrust upon India a commanding position. From the eastern coast of Africa and the shores of the Persian Gulf to the Strait of Malacca no other country rivals India's dominant location in the Indian Ocean.

For over 1,800 years Indians have used the Indian Ocean for trade, defense, colonization and diffusion of their culture particularly in Southeast Asia. As early as the 4th century B.C. the Mauryan kings had established ports on the coast of the Bay of Bengal. The large naval kingdoms of the Cholas and Chalukyas were set up in south India. After the downfall of the Sri Vijaya empire and the Chola dynasty in the 13th century, control of the Indian Ocean passed to the Arabs. The European thrust into the area started in the 16th century, after Vasco da Gama's landing on the west coast of India in 1498. Major European powers were eventually drawn into a long and bloody struggle for power in the Indian Ocean. Eventually, the British gained supremacy over the Indian Ocean and the Indian subcontinent.

The history of British control in India illustrates the basic geopolitical principle that the power which rules the sea eventually rules the adjoining land. Panikkar observes that the pre-British invasions and land-directed conquests of India led to the founding of political dynasties, which in a short period were Indianized. Only the British rulers could remain unassimilated as they could draw their strength from England through the naval pipelines (Panikkar 7).

India's current defense posture necessarily includes adjustment in the political and strategic role of filling up the vacated role of the British in the Indian Ocean. The United States and the Soviet Union have also shown interest in the area. The indivisibility of the seas makes it possible for them to exercise their power even though they may be far removed from the Indian Ocean. India should see that outside interests remain limited to trade. This is only possible if she maintains an adequate defense capability, and can play the role of a dominant power.

Since 1970 the Soviet Union has been steadily building trade and economic connections with India and the countries bordering the Indian Ocean. It is constructing naval radio stations and ammunition depots at the mouth of the Red Sea. It has obtained access to port facilities in Somalia, Maurituis, and Singapore. The Soviet Union is also trying to gain a foothold in the oil-producing states of the Middle East. The Russian push in the Indian Ocean is reportedly aimed at containing Chinese influence in the African and Arab countries, and in Southeast Asia. Since Indian and Australian naval capabilities are poor, the Western countries are deeply concerned over expanding Soviet presence in the Indian Ocean. The United States has gained a foothold in the Indian Ocean by the establishment of bases in Diego Garcia, a move opposed by the Indian government. India's current preoccupations with her domestic economic development programs, and her modest financial resources make it beyond her means to develop a strong naval capability to

deter encroachment by other major powers on India's legiti-
mate role in the Indian Ocean.

INDIA AND THE WORLD

Earlier in this chapter, problems related to India's international borders were discussed. India's international trade
and associated aspects of her foreign relations are examined
in Chapter 10. Only a brief review of some other aspects of
India's foreign relationships is presented in this subsection.

Immediately following Independence, India was too en-
grossed with her numerous domestic problems to be particularly concerned about the outside world. Basically, her
foreign policy was that of non-involvement in the cold war
between the West and the Communist countries. Soon, however, her size, large population, resource base, location in
the Indian Ocean, and newly attained free status thrust her
into prominence among the developing countries. She possessed a great cultural heritage, a long history of struggle for
independence and a responsive leadership; and the newly
independent countries thus looked to her for guidance. Her
policy of non-involvement commanded respect. It was in
1962, during the Sino-Indian War, that her policy of
nonalignment suffered a setback when India had to reassess
the basic premise of her foreign relations, and fixed new
priorities regarding her defensive posture. The Indo-Pakistani War of 1965 pushed her further into a defensive build-
up. Since 1963, India has sought successfully to strengthen
relations with her immediate neighbors: Nepal, the Himalayan kingdoms, Burma, and Sri Lanka. It is only with
Pakistan and China that border issues remain unresolved.

In addition to the Indo-Pakistan conflict over Kashmir,
problems rooted in the partitioning of the subcontinent
itself existed in some other areas. The first problem was that
of the rehabilitation of millions of displaced persons who
had crossed the borders, and the related issue of the
disbursement of the evacuee properties abandoned on both
sides. Relations between the two neighbors were strained on
the matters of the evacuee property compensation by both
governments. The question of the settlement of the cash
balances and assets the new administration of Pakistan left

in India posed another threat to Indo-Pakistan relations. In 1960, after years of negotiations, these issues were resolved. In addition to the war over Kashmir, Indian and Pakistani forces clashed on the mudflats of the Rann of Kutch over minor boundary disputes in 1965. The two sides agreed to demarcate the boundary lines suggested by an international tribunal, a work completed in 1969. Indo-Pakistani relations deteriorated again as a result of the conflict in Bangladesh in December 1971. Efforts to normalize relations are being attempted. The recent Indo-Pakistan-Bangladesh agreement of 1974 regarding the issues of the recognition of Bangladesh and evacuation of all the Pakistani prisoners of war contributed toward normalization of relations between these countries and toward stability in the subcontinent.

The international boundary partitioned the Indian subcontinent with inadequate regard to lines of communication, canal waters, and the complementary nature of the economies of the countries. India and Pakistan have so far lived under a shadow of mistrust and hostility and, therefore, have not been able to establish the most desirable goal of coordinated regional, economic and defense planning. With the recent prospect of normal relations such a scheme of coordinated planning in the subcontinent can be achieved.

India has been concerned about her friends along the Himalayan border and has stepped up economic aid to Nepal, Bhutan and Sikkim. Nepal has consistently pursued a policy of non-commitment to either India or China, and has accepted economic aid from both. India built a highway linking Nepal's capital at Kathmandu with north India, and China has similarly linked it with the Lhasa-Sinkiang road across difficult terrain and high altitudes. India does not particularly appreciate Nepal's policy of non-commitment, and would favor a more pro-Indian policy. Nepal's entry to the outside world is essentially through Indian ports, and thus would make her more dependent on India. Bhutan is an Indian protectorate and India is responsible for their defense. Sikkim's merger into India stemmed mainly from tightening India's defense along the Tibet border. Bhutan has exhibited some signs of achieving a degree of independence in its foreign affairs.

Indo-Burmese relations have generally been friendly. The principle irritant in the relations has been the status of about 0.5 million Indians (in 1960) in Burma. During the 1950's and 1960's Burma passed for them strict land-appropriation laws, nationalized their trading companies, and subjected them to discriminatory treatment, and large numbers moved to India. As of 1969 less than 100,000 Indians were left in the Burma. Relations between India and Sri Lanka (formerly Ceylon) have been somewhat strained over the issue of about a million persons of Indian origin who were working on tea plantations. They had not applied for Sri Lanka citizenship and after India's Independence had lost their rights to Indian citizenship. Sri Lanka refused to grant citizenship to these "stateless" persons. In 1964 an agreement over this issue was reached which called for repatriation to India of a portion of the involved persons. Furthermore, Sri Lanka's population includes a sizable Tamil-Hindu minority (22 percent of the total population) whose relations with native Sri Lanka Buddhists (68 percent of the population) have not been harmonious. Since the 1964 agreement, however, relations between India and Sri Lanka considerably improved.

India's relations with the West, especially with the United States, stem from her basic posture of non-alignment. She has looked upon the western military alliances, like NATO, CENTO, and SEATO as creators of tensions in an already troubled world because these alliances bring more arms and armaments and lead to a chain reaction of communistic defensive postures. To India, containment of communism, an implicit objective of the western military alli-military alliances, is of secondary importance. India has argued that peace can best be achieved by non-entanglement in such military postures. India has suggested that world peace will not be promoted by generating ideological confrontation between Communism and democracy, but by peaceful coexistence.

The West, on the other hand, has not been able to reconcile India's posture of non-alignment with her attitudes toward Pakistan and her annexation of Goa. Indo-American relations deteriorated markedly after 1954 when the United States started providing military assistance to Pakistan. The U.S. assurance that her arms could not be used against India did not convince Indians, who feared that U.S. arms would eventually be used against them in the event of Indo-Pakistan hostility. India's fears were realized during the Indo-Pakistani wars of 1965 and 1971. To counteract military assistance to Pakistan, India purchased arms and technical help from the Soviet Union to build armaments in Indian factories. Many persons in the United States accused India of having gone over to the Communist side. Indo-American relations, which had appreciably improved in 1962 when the West rushed military supplies to check the Chinese advance into Indian territory along her Chinese borders, deteriorated again in 1972 on account of the pro-Pakistani stance of the U.S. government during the Bangladesh crisis. Despite these fluctuations in Indo-American relations, there has always flowed a strong undercurrent of mutual goodwill. The U.S. has remained one of the leading trading partners of India. India's continuing dependence on the United States for economic aid makes it imperative for her to gain American goodwill. Her geographic location, size, population, resource-base and democratic form of government have given her an importance which the United States cannot easily ignore. As Lamb points out, "India is not only worth aiding, but even vital to American strategic interests" (Lamb, 343).

Since Independence India has maintained cordial relations with Britain and has remained an influential member of the Commonwealth of Nations. Britain has consistently adopted a friendly attitude toward Indian foreign policies, and has cooperated in resolving a few Indo-Pakistani disputes (e.g. the Rann of Kutch dispute). Britain has pulled her land, sea and air forces out of the Indian Ocean. The British stand on the Kashmir issue has been one of the few irritants in Anglo-Indian relations.

Indian relations with the Soviet Union have been friendly especially since the downfall of the Stalin regime. Close economic and diplomatic ties, and a degree of military cooperation have been maintained. The Soviet Union's open support of India over the Goa and Kashmir issues has been widely appreciated in India. The Soviet Union has aided India with her economic development programs. After 1966, however, a more evenhanded policy aimed at Indo-Pakistani power parity in the subcontinent has been pursued by the Soviet government. Soviet decision in 1968 to aid Pakistan militarily had generally been interpreted in India as the formation of a Soviet lever against Pakistan's growing dependence on China for arms and friendship.

India's relations with other communist countries, with the exceptions of China and Albania, have been marked by economic and diplomatic cooperation. Trade between the East European countries and India has been growing.

India has tried to play the role of a spokesman for several African and Asian nations and has often inspired the cause of their national freedom movements. It enjoys good relations with those countries with the exception of South Africa, Portuguese colonies and Israel. Her cool relations with Israel basically result from her conciliatory attitude toward the Arabs. India has adopted a pro-Arab stance in the Arab-Israeli conflict. She imports large amounts of oil from the Middle East. Her relations with Turkey and Iran are diplomatically correct although a bit cool in view of their membership in the CENTO alliance. During the 1965 Indo-Pakistani War, Turkey and Iran provided military and moral support to Pakistan. Indo-Afghanistan relations have been particularly friendly, especially in view of India's firm moral support to Afghanistan on the Pakhtunistan issue.

Many countries in Africa and islands in the Indian Ocean, Guyana and the West Indies, contain large population components of Indian origin. In Uganda, Kenya, Tanzania, Mauritius, and Fiji (in the Pacific Ocean), Indians have achieved success in banking, commercial and trade enterprises. In 1971 many Indians were dispossessed of their residence status and properties and were expelled from Uganda.

India's relations with Japan have been more economic than political. India considers Japan to be the most developed country in Asia and its industrial strength to be a major factor in Asian power-politics. Both countries are major trading partners in Asia.

CITATIONS AND SELECT BIBLIOGRAPHY

Bondurant, Joan V., *Regionalism versus Provincialism: A Study in Problems of Indian Unity.* Berkeley, 1958.

Brown, W. Norman, *The United States and India, Pakistan and Bangladesh.* Cambridge, Mass., 1972.

Frankel, F. G., *India's Political Economy, 1947-1977*. Princeton, 1979.

Hardgrave, R. L., Jr., *Government and Politics in a Developing Nation*. New York, 1970.

Harrison, S. S., *India, the Most Dangerous Decades*. Princeton, 1966.

Harrison, S. S., (ed.), *India and the United States*. New York, 1961.

India, A Reference Annual, 1971-1972. New Delhi, 1972.

India, A Reference Annual, 1976. New Delhi, 1977.

Kothari, Rajni, *Politics in India*. Boston, 1970.

Lamb, Alstair, *The China-India Border*. London, 1964.

Lamb, A., *The Kashmir Problem*. London, 1966.

Lamb, B. P., *India—A World in Transition*. New York, 1975.

Maxwell, N., *India's China War*. New York, 1970.

Menon, V. P., *The Story of the Integration of Indian States*. New York, 1956.

Michel, A. A., *The Indus Rivers: A Study of the Effects of Partition*. New Haven, 1967.

Morris-Jones, W. H., *The Government and Politics of India*. New York, 1967.

Panikkar, K. M., *Geographical Factors in Indian History*. Bombay, 1955.

Panikkar, K. M., *India and the Indian Ocean*. London, 1945.

Schwartzberg, J. E., (ed.), *A Historical Atlas of South Asia*. Chicago, 1978.

Sen Gupta, B., *The Fulcrum of Asia: Relations Among China, India, Pakistan and the U.S.S.R*. New York, 1970

The Sino-Indian Boundary Question. Peking, 1962.

The Sino-Indian Dispute. Government of India, Delhi, 1963.

Spate, O. H. K., "The Partition of India and the Prospects of Pakistan," *The Geographical Review*. Vol. 38, 1948.

Tinker, Hugh, *India and Pakistan: A Political Analysis*. New York, 1962.

Van Eckelen, W. F., *Indian Foreign Policy*. The Hague, 1967.

SECTION THREE
Developmental Processes

CHAPTER 6

AGRICULTURAL ECONOMIES

AGRARIAN ECONOMY:
STATUS AND PROBLEMS

Agriculture has played a central role in Indian economy for centuries and will undoubtedly continue to do so in the near future. Close to three-quarters of the population (72 to 73 percent) derives its livelihood from occupations related to agriculture. Nearly one-half (49.7 percent) of the country's national income is derived from the agricultural sector. Such major problems of the country as food sufficiency, rural unemployment and economic, political, and social discontent are directly related to its agricultural systems.

In statistical terms, India ranks high among the producers of agricultural goods. She stands third in the world in wheat production, after the Soviet Union and the United States; second in rice after China; and second in millet production after China. Producing between one-quarter to one-third of the world's tea, jute, peanuts and hemp-fiber, she leads all nations in their productions. She produces exportable amounts of several other cash crops in which her world status is high: third in the production of sugar-cane, tobacco, and oilseeds and fourth in cotton. She has the largest bovine cattle (290 million or one-quarter) herd of the world. These impressive agricultural productions must be matched against a large population rising at about 1.6 to 2 percent a year, low agricultural yields and poor per capita production. Although subsistence levels in foodgrains have been recently reached and prospects for future foodgrain increases have brightened up as a result of technological diffusions of agricultural modernization in selected parts of the country, the race between food and population remains a close one.

Despite spotty breakthroughs, the basic structures of the

194

agrarian economy remain traditional. Established centuries ago, these structures of a self-contained rural economy, founded in caste-derived occupational land tenures made complex by absentee and parasitic landlords, have been slow to respond to modernization. Linked as these are to other segments of society such as food self-sufficiency, industrial development, unemployment, foreign trade, social organization and administrative stability, agriculture became a major problem in the post-colonial India.

Agriculture is a multi-dimensional problem, its various components are so inextricably interconnected as to render analysis and classification of problems difficult. One example of the interconnectedness of the problems is the land tenure system. Landholdings are tiny, fragmented, and not particularly amenable to modernization efforts. The problem is at once social, economic and political. Inheritance laws, the colonial *zamindari* system, caste-based agricultural practices, all are bound up with the problem. Legislative efforts to ameliorate the situation are tied up with the social and political systems. Compounding the situation has been the mounting demographic pressure, which has wiped away gains in agricultural productions during the last three decades. The process of agricultural rehabilitation, therefore, would consist of effecting improvements on several fronts, in techniques as well as social institutions, as well as in reducing demographic pressures. Some major agricultural problems are analyzed below as units, although each is interconnected with the other.

Land Tenure Problems

Statistics regarding land-distribution among rural families have been few, and based on estimates. Table 6.1, prepared by the National Sample Survey, Seventeenth Round, in 1966 indicates the general pattern of the problem. At the bottom of the ladder are the 39 percent of households which own less than one hectare of land. It is estimated that within this category 10 percent of the families are totally landless. By comparison, one-half million families, or the richest one percent of the households, own 11.6 percent of the land used for agricultural production. While this highly unequal distribution of agricultural land suggests a serious land problem, even more serious is the unequal

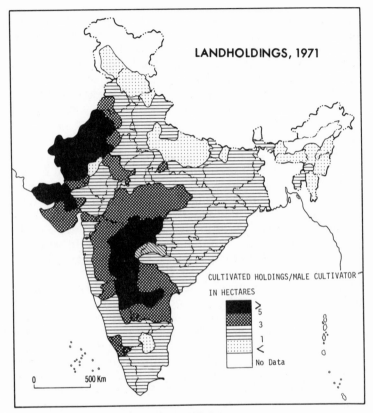

FIGURE 6.1

farm wealth or income. In reality, the smaller farms are not
only uneconomic but also suggest a serious problem of agricultural inefficiency. Figure 6.1 shows the distribution of
spatial variations in landholdings in India.

A major problem of landholdings has been their fragmentation. One household may own tiny bits of scattered
plots. The origin of fragmentation relates to Hindu and
Muslim inheritance laws, under which all sons would receive
equal share in good and bad sections of the land based on
soil conditions, type of crops, topography, drainage and fertility at the time of inheritance. Further fragmentation
resulted from partial confiscation of a lot by the revenue intermediary (*zamindar*) in case of delinquency of payments.

TABLE 6.1

DISTRIBUTION OF AGRICULTURAL LANDHOLDINGS, 1961-62

Size of Landholding	Households		Area	
	(Number in Millions)	Per Cent	Million Hectares	Per Cent
0- 1 hectare	19.8	39.1	9.2	6.9
1- 3 hectares	18.0	35.5	32.1	24.1
3- 5 hectares	6.1	12.0	23.0	17.2
5-10 hectares	4.5	8.9	30.6	22.9
10-20 hectares	1.8	3.5	23.1	17.3
20 hectares and above	0.5	1.0	15.5	11.6
TOTAL	50.7	100.0	133.5	100.0

Source: *India, Pocketbook of Economic Information, 1972.* Government of India, New Delhi, 1972, p. 52.

For the poor cultivators, a part of the land must go to the landlord as a payment of the debt incurred. Often villages of the size of 5,000 to 6,000 ha would be divided into 50,000 to 60,000 fields. Since the enactment of recent legislation on Consolidation of Holdings, millions of tenancy suits lie pending in the overburdened civil courts.

Fragmentation clearly creates uneconomic holdings. Apart from the duplication of effort in irrigation and cultivation of scattered fields, a farmer must lose much land in the earth-ridges (he has to erect to separate his fields from others' crops). For the same reasons fragmented fields do not lend themselves to mechanized farming or the application of chemical fertilizers.

Another problem is that of landless or tenant cultivators. The rise of landless cultivators, though common in most countries, assumed tragic proportions in India during British rule. The dominant prevailing system of land tenure during Mughal rule was the *ryotwari* or peasant-proprietor (small holding) system. The peasant was the owner of land and possessed the decision-making and inheritance rights. The government collected revenues from the peasants directly through the village governments. During the late Mughal period revenue collection was increasingly assigned to the intermediaries or *zamindars,* who during British rule

virtually became the landowners. Often repressive in collection practices, the *zamindars* were given rights to confiscate
lands of delinquent revenue payers. At the time of Independence there were two main systems of land-tenures,
the *ryotwari* and the *zamindari*.

A characteristic feature of the *zamindari* system was that
the actual cultivators had no contact with the government,
and were at the mercy of the intermediaries. The *zamindari*
system became a fundamental issue in the land reforms after
Independence. In the wake of such slogans as "land to the
tiller," several laws of land redistribution, land consolidation, land ceilings and the abolition of the *zamindars* and
absentee landlords were enacted during the 1950's and
1960's. Progress undoubtedly has been achieved in a number of States in requisite legislation, but implementation remains difficult. Before Independence 40 percent of the
cropped area was under the *zamindari* system which by 1972
had been largely eliminated. After 1947, nearly 20 million
farmers were given landowning rights and nearly 6 million
hectares of land was alloted to the landless farmers. By 1972
scattered land holdings of 32.6 million ha of land had been
consolidated. Land ceilings ranging between 4 and 30 ha
have been fixed by the different States. Despite these
legislative measures, nearly one-half of the households still
possess landholdings of 20 hectares or more.

A related problem was that of the absentee *zamindars*
(landlords). A large cadre of absentee landlords has arisen
under British rule. Although owning most of the cultivable
land, the *zamindars* resided in the urban areas, leaving the
chores of cultivation to the tenant farmers (share croppers)
who in turn would occasionally hire laborers to do the work.
A system of sharecropping was soon established. Periods
of economic depression, unforeseen weather and constant
borrowing of money from the *zamindars* often ruined the
sharecroppers, but enriched the *zamindars*. Improvements
in agricultural practices by the sharecropper under such
conditions were impossible. The absentee landlord was content with whatever returns he could get, and was disinclined
to make investments for agricultural improvements, whereas
the tenant-farmer did not possess the capital necessary to do
so. He was content with whatever share of the crop he could
get without any additional investment, in the true fatalist
tradition.

Agricultural Productivity

As the Table 6.2 of major crops of the selected countries indicates, Indian agricultural yields are among the lowest in the world, although a steady rise in the yields during the two decades between 1950 and 1971 was recorded.

The absence of scientific fertilization of the fields is commonplace. An average farmer, deep in debt, does not have the resources to apply nitrogen, potash, or potassium to the crops. Investment in chemical fertilization can lead to his complete economic ruination. Burnt stubble, branches, leaf mold, an occasional oil-cake or animal manure application are his chief means of fertilization. Even these are inadequately applied. Social customs frown upon the utilization of human excreta for the fields. Occasionally cow dung is used, but 60 percent of it is burnt as a fuel or lost as a plaster coating to floors or walls in the rural areas. Recent experience has demonstrated the need for fertilization. Recent breakthroughs in yields by the introduction of high-yielding varieties, or HYV of crops have demonstrated the need for chemical fertilization. The Five Year Plans, therefore, rightly emphasized expansion in the output of chemical fertilizers.

The use of chemical fertilization has steadily gained ground since the early 1960's. The most rapid growth in the use was in the Haryana-Punjab area, which was responsible for 16 percent of national nitrogenous fertilizer consumption during the Third and Fourth Plans, as against an annual rate of 4 percent. Another area where fertilizer consumption markedly improved was in Tamil Nadu and parts of Andhra Pradesh. Other areas have been slow to accept fertilizers, partly because these parts were poor in infrastructural, economic and other capabilities such as irrigation, water management and rural electrification to sustain the consumption of fertilizers.

Potentials for diffusion of scientific fertilizer utilization appear bright if other capabilities are improved. By 1970 about three-fourths of the area given to wheat and rice cultivation and 80 percent devoted to other foodgrains were still not utilizing chemical fertilizers. The success of fertilization would vary with different regions. A universal diffusion is neither possible nor required, but considerable potential for diffusion exists for the watered areas of the Ganga Plain and Maharashtra.

TABLE 6.2

AVERAGE YIELD OF PRINCIPAL CROPS, Kg/Ha

| | India | | | 1971 | | | |
	1950-51	1960-61	1970-71	U.S.A.	U.K.	Japan	U.S.S.R.
Rice	668	1,013	1,134	5,200	*	5,220	4,000
Wheat	663	855	1,299	2,280	4,400	2,650	1,410
Jowar	353	533	470	*	*	*	*
Sugar Cane (gur)	3,342	3,289	4,966	9,210	*	6,270	*
Cotton	88	88	108	490	*	*	840
Jute	1,043	1,183	1,177	*	*	*	*
Groundnuts	775	745	832	DNA	*	*	*

*   Crop Unimportant

DNA   Data Not Available

Source: 1. *India, Pocketbook of Economic Information, 1972, op. cit.*
           2. F.A.O. *Production Yearbook, 1971,* Rome, 1972.

Peasant Indebtedness
and Capital Formation

To an extent peasant indebtedness is universal among subsistence farmers, but its impact is nowhere as crushing as in Indian farming. Estimates of the extent of Indian peasant indebtedness vary, but all point to an incredibly high level. Following a period of depression in the 1930's, rural debt in British India (excepting the Native States) was estimated to be over Rs 12,000 or $1500 million approximately which probably equalled the averaged annual rural income. This, in all likelihood, has been on the increase since then. An estimate of the All-India Rural Credit Survey of 1954-56 indicated that nearly 70 percent of all the cultivating families were in debt. Recent statistics only confirm the continuance of large-scale and deep-rooted rural poverty in the country. The average annual income of an Indian farmer (cultivators, landlords, and moneylenders included) is about $50, whereas the average indebtedness of the rural families in debt (70 percent of the total) amounts to $68 (in the early 1970's).

The lot of the landless cultivator is even more pitiful than indicated by the average figures. To an average farmer indebtedness is a way of life. Factors responsible for indebtedness are many: uneconomic, fragmented landholdings, vagaries of monsoons, capital deficiency to tide over sickness, drought, floods, cattle diseases, lack of storage facilities forcing sale of the harvest even at unprofitable times, and above all, the incurring of customary extravagant expenses on certain social occasions, such as the birth of a son or the marriage of a daughter.

Rural credit is notoriously inept in organization and poor in service. Although government-run cooperative societies offering credit facilities to farmers in 1971 numbered 320,000, these served only 31 million agricultural families or catered to no more than one-third of the agricultural credit requirements of the country. Between 1951 and 1972 the number of credit societies increased by 50 percent and loan advances rose from $131 million to $242 millions. Specialized cooperatives for sugarcane, fishing, marketing, agricultural management, and the processing of agricultural output were also established during the period. Undoubtedly, the facilities have been improving, but only

for the upper class farmers who are more credit-worthy. The
bulk of farmers lack vision, initiative and resourcefulness
to make use of the facilities. They still approach the local
moneylender, usually the big landlord, who charges exhor-
bitant rates for commercial loans. Interest on loans of 20 to
36 percent a year is not uncommon.

Problems of Mechanization

In large measure, the Indian peasants' agricultural inefficiency had resulted from the work of nature and society,
e.g., lack of irrigation facilities, poor soils, a caste-based
system of exploitation and deficiency of capital, efficient
tools and implements. His conservatism was not merely an
expression of his utter imperviousness to new ideas or techniques. It stemmed from traditional practices, which were
intimately adjusted to the environment. His tools and practices were simple and the land yielded enough. He remained
a small part of the closed society in which his role and duties
were prescribed by caste, tradition and government statutes.
As the society opened to the world, and as new demographic, tenurial and economic pressures began to build up
on the land, the peasant sank into poverty.

The need for diffusion of innovations to pull the peasant
out of tradition and poverty has been widely recognized, but
the farmers' resistance to innovations still persist. A correc-
tive to traditional perceptions must be vigorously
demonstrated to the average farmer. Evaluation of innovations before initiation have also to be clearly undertaken.
The use of an ordinary light plough may serve as an example. The criticism that the light plough merely scratches the
surface of the soil is not entirely tenable for conditions under
which an average Indian farmer has been working. The
traditional "surface scratcher" light plough is all that his
bullocks can draw and that he can carry on his shoulders to
and from his scattered fields. Furthermore, it has been
demonstrated that deep plough is useful only for certain
crops and in specific soil conditions. The key to good
ploughing is the efficient use of soil-moisture and irrigation.
Only in areas of precarious rainfall is deep ploughing with
tractors especially useful.

The introduction of innovations in techniques (machines,
irrigation, better crop varieties and seeds) must therefore be

based on and coincide with the given circumstances of farmers' capital resources (credit facilities), tenancy laws regarding viable and consolidated landholdings and infrastructural bases. Simple, improved tools such as the seed-drills, threshing and winnowing appliances, water lifts or electric wells are cost-effective devices that can be more useful than the huge machines to an average Indian farmer. Mechanization, in conformity with Indian conditions, however, has to be introduced. Undoubtedly simple farm implements are useful and in the long-run cost-effective. For example, small tractors can perform a multiplicity of farm jobs from clearing, cultivating, and harvesting, to the transport of produce and implements, although its initial expense for an average farm could be large. A large harvester-combine on the other hand may not be suited for small Indian farms. In 1976 there were 251 million tractors in operation.

Associated with mechanization is the problem of unemployment among agricultural labor which would undoubtedly be further aggravated if mechanization programs are carried out to their logical limits. The problem of agricultural unemployment has indeed taxed the minds of agricultural analysts. An answer to it is the proposal that this massive agricultural laborforce, released from the farms consequent upon mechanization, could be usefully channeled into newly developed agro-based rural industries. A recent study by Billings and Singh regarding the impact of farm mechanization in Punjab and Maharashtra where new HYV of wheat were introduced, concluded that under those conditions substantial growth in human labor requirements could result from the development of agro-based industries and farm services. Mechanization, if accompanied with technological innovations (fertilization, electrification and irrigation), requires the development of infrastructure which is capable of absorbing labor.

The use of mechanical implements has been on the rise in the country since 1961. An efficient iron plough has replaced the traditional wooden one in several parts of the country. Its use has become significant in the Western Uttar Pradesh and Tamil Nadu, where 100 iron ploughs were used for each 1000 ha of cultivated land, as compared to 26 ploughs/1000 ha for the nation in 1966, a dramatic rise since 1961. By 1966 tractors had become widely used in

Punjab Haryana (4 to 5/1000 ha of cultivated area); elsewhere the use was negligible. In 1966 about 50,000 tractors were in use in the country. The use of specialized implements, namely seed-drills, threshers and sprayers was more common in Gujarat, Karnataka and Andhra Pradesh. Powerdriven water-lifts had become widespread in Punjab, Haryana, Gujarat and parts of Tamil Nadu (15 electric or diesel wells per 1000 ha of cultivated land) during the same period. Great regional variations clearly exist in the diffusion of these innovations. The most noticeable shift from the traditional farm operations to mechanization in Punjab and Haryana has paralleled the initial diffusion of HYV of wheat and millets in those States.

Infrastructural Problems

Rural communication in India is generally inadequate, although its road network is one of the largest in the world. Poor unsurfaced roads serve most rural interiors, straining the transport of goods by bullocks. This has been one factor which has hampered development of industries based on agricultural produce, such as canning and dairy farming.

The Community Development Projects during the early phase of planning (1951-1966) laid considerable emphasis on the development of communications in rural areas. Nearly $1,400 millions were spent on improvements and expansion of rural-linked road tracks. Road track connected with the rural interiors expanded from 243,000 kms to 721,000 km between 1951 and 1966 (in 1971 it was 880,000 km).

Another major task of rural development is the provision of marketing facilities for the middle class and small farmers. Only in a few States such as Punjab, Maharashtra, Andhra Pradesh and Gujarat does a fairly well-developed network of officially-inspected markets exist. Elsewhere, conditions for the storage, credit and transportation of commodities are poor. Even in areas of regulated markets, the small farmer rarely utilizes the existing facilities. Moreover, he is still at the mercy of unscrupulous traders in obtaining a fair price for his commodities since a national, effective pricing policy has not been strictly enforced even in the regulated markets. A small farmer is easily exploited by secret brokerage, false weights and inflated commissions.

The crux of agricultural progress, therefore, lies in the creation of an adequate infrastructural base.

THE USE OF LAND

Records of India's land classification have been faithfully maintained since the beginning of the 20th century, although their quality has suffered for lack of statistical verification, or improvement in terminology and classification systems. The reporting agencies, mostly at the village level, have not been above reproach. Terminology is often ambiguous. For example, the category of "culturable wasteland" has never been clearly defined. Although it suggests potentially usable land for cultivation, in reality it contains only a fraction of land presently fit for cultivation. "Area not available for cultivation" includes permanent pastures, grazing land, and land under miscellaneous tree crops. "Current Fallow" represents area lying fallow for less than one year. "Other fallows" are lands which have not been ploughed for between one and five years. Areas not cultivated for over five years relapse into the "culturable waste" category. Problems are compounded by the use of such terms as "adjusted," "unadjusted," "provisional," "final estimates," and "not reported." Table 6.3 gives a detailed idea of the land uses in India between 1950-51 and 1973-74.

Topographically, two thirds of India's surface area is usable. The rest is either in high and rugged terrain (mostly over 7,500 feet altitude), is climatically unsuitable for cultivation, or is barren.

About 161 million hectares of land is given to cultivation, representing nearly one-half the surface area of the country, a figure placing India among the leading countries on the basis of percent of its land devoted to cultivation. On a per capita basis, however, it amounts to only 0.26 hectares. About 18 percent of the cultivated area is double-cropped (cultivated more than once), while one-fifth of the cultivated area and most of the double-cropped area is under irrigation. Surprisingly, a mere 3.9 percent of the land is in permanent pasture and grazing, in a country which contains the largest bovine population (290 million

TABLE 6.3

LAND UTILIZATION
(In Million Hectares)

	1950-51	1955-56	1960-61	1965-66	1970-71	1972-73	1972-73 (in % of total area)
Total Geographical Area	328.0	328.0	328.0	328.0	328.0	328.0	100
Forests	40.5	51.3	54.1	61.6	66.2	67.4	20.5
Area Not Available For Cultivation	47.5	48.4	50.8	49.5	45.4	43.7	13.3
Other Uncultivated Area	49.4	38.9	37.6	35.8	33.8	33.2	10.1
Fallow Land	28.1	24.1	22.8	22.4	19.7	24.4	7.4
Net Area Sown	118.7	129.2	133.2	136.2	140.4	137.1	41.8
Area Sown More Than Once	13.1	18.2	19.6	19.1	24.7	24.8	7.5
Total Cropped Area	131.9	147.3	152.8	155.4	165.1	161.9	49.3
Area Under Irrigation	22.6	25.6	28.0	30.9	37.0*	39.2	12

*Estimate

Sources: 1. *India, Pocketbook of Economic Information, 1972*, New Delhi, pp. 50-51
2. *India, A Reference Annual, 1976, and 1977-78*, New Delhi.
3. *Times of India, Directory, 1978*, Bombay, pp. 32-33.

cattle) in the world. Could it be that part of the "culturable waste" belongs to the "grazing" category also?

A steady but modest extension of cropland amounting to 30 million hectares has taken place during the two decades between 1950-51 and 1972-73. Area given to forest also increased, while fallow lands decreased in area. A more notable increase was in the area under irrigation and in double-cropped land. Wastelands, however, did not shrink appreciably.

In 1972-73 net sown area was 137 million hectares, only 25 million ha of which yielded two or more harvests. Cropping intensity, therefore, remained low. In geographical distribution, both the amount of cropland and cropping intensity showed great regional variations. In most parts of the Indo-Ganga Plains, eastern Gujarat and the lava regions of Maharashtra nearly 80 percent of the land was under crops. Rajasthan and eastern Madhya Pardesh had the smallest proportion of land (less than 20 percent) given to cultivation. The double-cropped area, however, did not positively correlate with regions containing high proportion of cultivated land. In fact, double cropping was more significant in a few hilly areas, such as Himachal Pradesh (where in places the double-cropped included up to 60 percent of sown land). In these areas of poor economy farmers generally depend on a second cash crop. In addition to growing cereal crops (wheat, maize and rice) in these areas of adequate rainfall, a second crop of potatoes, ginger and vegetables are grown as cash crops on small hillside (or valley) holdings. Elsewhere, the double-cropped area in general amounted to less than 20 percent of the cropland.

These two measures, the amount of cropland and the double-cropped area, reflect the intensity of cropping and the relationship between the two, e.g., percent of net area sown (Figure 6.2) is particularly significant. A refinement which incorporates the duration of crops in the field as a measure to indicate cropping intensity has been proposed by Dayal (Dayal, 1978, 289-95) who assumes that the length of crop duration accounts for the inputs of labor, land and irrigation water. His index gives crop months per hectare of net area sown. A map based on such an index helps identify areas capable of enhanced crop intensity. For example, areas of already high intensity (with values of 9 months or over) hardly offer any further prospects for raising intensity.

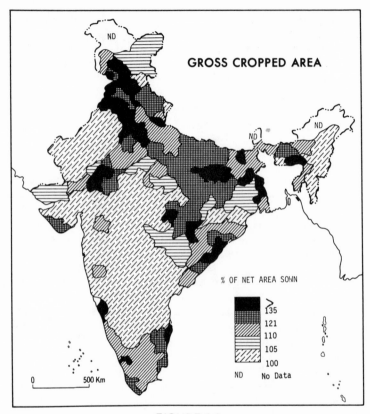

FIGURE 6.2

Figure 6.3 utilizes the result of the application of this formula.

Areas of high-intensity cropping are: North India
Plains, Brahmaputra Valley, Kerala and scattered delta
plains along the eastern coast. These correspond with the
densely-populated river basins, deltas and coastal plains
where either rainfall or irrigation is adequate, and soils are
fertile. Subsistence crops are generally cultivated. The hilly
areas bordering the North India Plains in Himachal Pradesh
and the Kashmir Valley also have high cropping intensity.
These hill districts also specialize in such cash crops as tea,
fruits and vegetables. In Kerala high intensity results from
double cropping of rice and the cultivation of long-duration

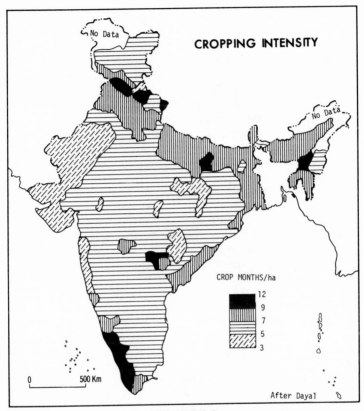

FIGURE 6.3

cash crops such as rubber, coffee, coconuts, black pepper and tapioca. Medium-intensity areas cover two-thirds of the country in Central India stretching from Gujarat to Tamil Nadu. Multiple cropping of short-duration foodgrain crops (jowar, millets, pulses, ragi) is common. A conclusion that can be drawn from the map is that most parts of India have already been over-cropped. Only with large inputs of fertilizers, irrigation and mechanization can further intensification of cropping be realized.

IRRIGATION SYSTEMS

At least two considerations highlight the importance of irrigation in India: inadequate moisture for crops in large sections of the country and the generally low crop yields even in the moist alluvial plains. Recent experiments in the introduction of HYV crops in Punjab and Tamil Nadu have further demonstrated that best results can be obtained only if irrigational facilities accompany the diffusion of High Yielding Variety crops. Indeed the future of the "Green Revolution" rests in a large measure upon the expansion and intensification of irrigation.

In 1972-73 roughly one-fourth (24.1 percent) of the total cultivated area was irrigated. Canal systems accounted for 35 percent, wells, 30 percent, and tanks, 12 percent of the irrigated area. The Fifth Plan estimated that by the end of 1973-74 43 million hectares of cropland were irrigated and that the potential exists for future extension to twice the current level of irrigation by 1979. It further estimated that if the potentials can be realized, India could attain foodgrain self-sufficiency by the end of 1979.

Within the country there are wide spatial variations in the amount of irrigation provided to farmlands. They range from 8 percent in Tripura (high rainfall area) to 16.5 percent in dry Rajasthan to as much as 76 percent of the cultivated land in Punjab where irrigation facilities are the most extensive. Generally speaking, irrigation facilities are most widespread in the North Indian Plains, serving one-quarter to one-half of the farmland. It was here that the most extensive network of irrigation was initially laid out during British rule. In hilly sections of the country (States of Himachal, Pradesh, Kashmir) where cultivated area is restricted, a comparatively large part of it (9 to 15 percent) is under irrigation. Inter-state variations result from differences in physical features but also from the developmental processes during the 19th and 20th centuries. An extensive irrigation network was developed under British rule, and has been extended since Independence. Irrigation became a key element in Indian planning. By the end of the Fourth Five Year Plan (1969-1974) 45 million hectares or 25 percent of the cropped area was under cultivation.

As a natural consequence of rapid population growth and economic development programs during the 1960's and

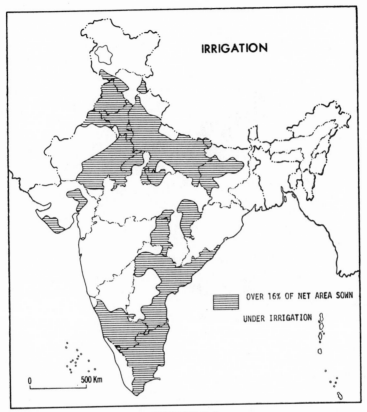

FIGURE 6.4

70's, demand for water — both for extension of irrigation as well as for power generation — increased sharply. Population pressures made foodgrain imports necessary, and increasing food production through extension of irrigation facilities became a matter of urgency. Many new canals and other facilities were constructed. By the end of the Fourth Five Year Plan (1969-74) the irrigated area had increased to 45 million ha from 22.5 million ha in 1947, covering roughly one-quarter of India's farmland. Irrigation expansion under the Fifth Plan focused mainly on the areas where the HYV crops were introduced. This plan also proposed the creation of a comprehensive system of irrigation facilities to be prepared by a team of engineers, agronomists, soil scientists and agricultural economists.

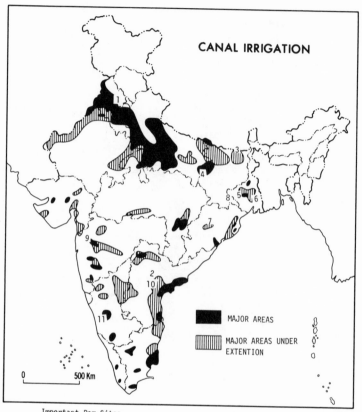

Important Dam Sites

1.	Nangal						
2.	Nanaksagar	4.	Son	7.	Hirakud	10.	Nagarjunsagar
3.	Kosi	5.	Durgapur	8.	Panchet	11.	Bhadra
		6.	Mayurakshi	9.	Gangapur		

FIGURE 6.5

Figures 6.4 and 6.5 show major areas of irrigation in the country. The distribution reflects the federal nature of Indian planning which mandates the states to seek financial support from the central government. Although India's Planning Commission, within the federal framework, articulated a policy of achieving so-called "balanced regional development" for the purpose of location of new schemes of irrigation, most schemes became objects of political pressures, each state advocating location of such schemes within their boundaries. Revision of political boundaries in 1956 and adjustment since then often complicated the picture in some instances. For example, the Tungabhadra project, originally planned before 1947, was held up for several years on different occasions. Placed in Karnataka, its service area fell inside Andhra Pradesh after the 1956 revision of state boundaries.

Occasionally, two states sponsor a scheme. Bihar and Uttar Pradesh thus utilize the Gandak project and even share it with Nepal under the 1956 Indo-Nepal agreement. A major part of it is now complete. Noteworthy among the inter-state projects is the DVC (Damodar Valley Corporation) which was conceived for the integrated development of a river basin. It envisaged comprehensive planning of the Damodar Basin in irrigation, flood control and power generation on the TVA pattern. Commissioned in 1948, by 1973-74 it provided irrigation to 350,000 ha and had reached roughly 90 percent of its target. Another scheme, Bhakra-Nangal, is a unique multi-purpose project aimed at providing irrigation to 1.5 million ha in the States of Haryana, Punjab and Rajasthan. A special beneficiary will be the semi-arid lands of Haryana and Rajasthan. An integrated system of link canals designed to raise agricultural productivity has already been responsible for the diffusion of HYV crops in these areas.

Most *irrigation canals* are aligned along the river-interfluves so as to provide irrigation to a large territory. The North Indian canals are fed by the perennial rivers and are never completely dry as their flow is regulated at masonry headworks (Figure 6.5). Those of the Deccan rivers rise in the deltas of the eastern coast during monsoons and are only seasonal.

Among the disadvantages of the perennial system is the collection of fertile silt at headworks, leaving little for the canal to carry to the irrigated land. Another problem experienced has been over irrigation in areas of poor drainage and excessive flow causing the accumulation of alkali pans and salts (known as *thur*) in the cultivated lands, a result of rapid evaporation and the rise of salts on the ground in dry areas. Problems of waterlogging and salt formation have become serious in parts of Haryana, Punjab and Rajasthan. Waterlogging has also been reported in the Gandak and Kosi project areas in Bihar.

In the Deccan Plateau problems are different—those of water storage and flow since rivers are non-perennial and canals become dry for a considerable time. Water has to be pumped from the natural storage points in the river. Conversion of innundation to perennial canals has been recently attempted. It entails a costly procedure of enlarging river storage areas to a certain level for adequate water distribution.

Unique among the recent projects is the proposed construction of a National Grid System linking the Ganga and Kaveri river basins and carrying the surplus water of the Ganga 2,200 miles southwards into Kaveri by hydraulic techniques. This ambitious plan is likely to take 25 years. The project has been designed to irrigate 2 million ha of land when completed.

Irrigation by *wells* (traditional and more recently power driven) amounted in 1972-73 to about 30 percent of the irrigated area and occupies an important role in agriculture. The use of power driven wells has been on the increase during the 1970's particularly in the states of Punjab, Haryana and western Uttar Pradesh, but the traditional well-irrigation operated by human or animal muscle has remained the backbone irrigation in north India. Suited admirably to the construction of wells with high watertables, absence of hard subsurface, and consequent ease of digging, these plains became important for well irrigation. The traditional well, whether masonry (brick or *pukka*) or non-masonry, despite its ease of construction, is cost-effective only for a small farmer, who has to irrigate only a small patch for growing vegetables, sugarcane, or pulses as cash crops. Larger holdings demand a more efficient system. Big farmers utilize canal irrigation or power-driven wells. In the states of Punjab and Haryana, rural electrification has reached the 100 percent mark, and power driven wells have come of age. Elsewhere, in Tamil Nadu and Uttar Pardesh, their use is on the increase. Figure 6.6 shows the chief areas of tank and well irrigation.

Tank irrigation is most extensive in Deccan Plateau. Low earth embankments in natural depressions, sometimes rock-lined, trap rain water to form tanks. These are usually aligned with the contour of topography and a small mound at the lower elevation side helps to trap water. Hard, geologic formations help water retention. A common

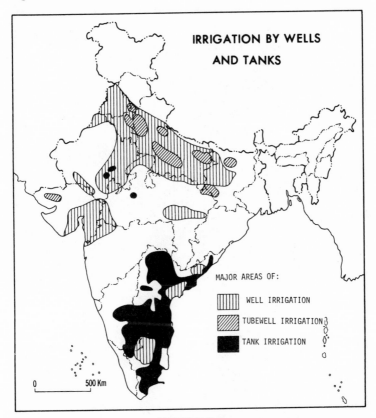

FIGURE 6.6

feature of the landscape in Karnataka, Andhra Pradesh and Tamil Nadu, tanks form the major means of farm irrigation. Canals or wells are difficult to dig in hard rocks and where the water table is deep. Rivers are non-perennial and canal flow is only seasonal. Tanks have a large surface area in relation to the volume of water, are prone to evaporation, and generally make unsatisfactory sources of irrigation water. Over time these are silted up and often have to be abandoned; their raised floor is then used for cultivation.

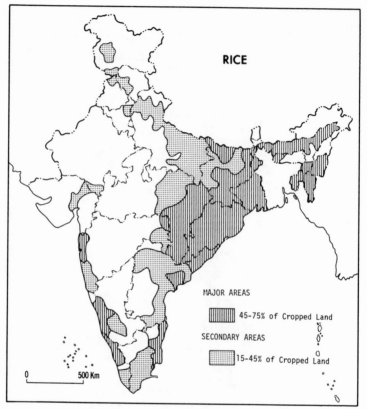

RICE

MAJOR AREAS

45-75% of Cropped Land

SECONDARY AREAS

15-45% of Cropped Land

0   500 Km

FIGURE 6.7

REGIONAL CROP PATTERNS

Subsistence Food Crops

Rice is the leading crop, grown over a quarter of the cultivated land; it accounts for one-third of the production of foodgrains in the country (Figure 6.7). The most favored areas of production are in the Ganga Delta and the coastal lowlands (especially the Kaveri plains) where high temperatures (mean of 75° F/24° C), ample rainfall (60 to 80 inches/150 to 220 cms annually) during the growing season, and conditions of clayey loam soils in the low lying floodplain of river valleys offer an ideal environment for growth. In these areas and in Tripura, Manipur and Mizoram more than 60 percent of the cropland is devoted to rice cultivation.

In a few districts rice is virtually monocultural. It ranks as the premier crop in the Middle Ganga Basin (Bihar, eastern Uttar Pradesh), Assam Valley, Maghalaya, Maharashtra coastal plains, and Kashmir Valley where 15 to 25 percent of the cropland is under rice cultivation. Essentially a "wet-crop," only in western Uttar Pradesh, Punjab, Haryana and central India, is it grown under irrigation. Tolerant of heavier alkaline soils, its cultivation has recently expanded in the waterlogged, alkaline areas of Haryana, Punjab and Uttar Pradesh.

The area given to rice cultivation has steadily increased between 1950-51 and 1974-75, growing from 30 million ha to 38 million ha. Production nearly doubled (from 20 to 40 million tons per year) during the same period, suggesting modest gains in the extent of cultivated area but substantial gains in yields. Increased irrigation facilities in drier areas, reclamation of waterlogged soils, and introduction of HYV crops (particularly in Haryana and Tamil Nadu) made this possible. Yields have benefitted particularly from the introduction of high-yielding, short-duration, fertilizer-responsive varieties. Crop yields are now over 1500 kg/ha. The national figure still remains low at 1000 kg/ha, which is one-fourth that of Japan and about one-half that of China. Improvement in rice yields has been slower than that obtained by other foodgrain crops (wheat, millets, maize, bajra) for a number of reasons. Rice cultivation is less adaptable to mechanized farming and chemical fertilization. Rice has had to compete with wheat cultivation in Punjab and Haryana where farmers could switch easily from the traditional to the innovative practices for wheat rather than for rice cultivation. The "Green Revolution" had less impact on rice yields than other foodgrain crops in such areas. Tables 6.4 and 6.5 give statistics regarding areas and productions of major crops for selected years between 1950 and 1975.

Paddy (wet rice) is a *kharif* crop sown after the rains have set in from June to August, and harvested between November and January. In West Bengal two to three crops are the general rule: *aus* (June to September) and *aman* (November to January), normally account for most of the cultivation, with an occasional third crop or *boro* (February

TABLE 6.4

AREA UNDER MAJOR CROPS
(In Million Hectares)

	1950-51	1960-61	1970-71	1973-74	1974-75
Rice	30.8	34.1	37.4	38.0	38.0
Wheat	9.7	12.9	17.9	19.0	18.1
Other Cereals (jowar, bajra, maize, ragi, millets, barley)	37.7	45.5	46.2	46.2	46.1
Pulses (gram, *tur*, & others)	19.1	23.6	22.4	22.9	22.6
Foodgrain totals	97.3	115.6	123.9	126.1	126.2
Sugar Cane	1.7	2.4	2.7	2.7	2.7
Oilseeds (linseed, rapeseed, sesamum, mustard, castorseed, peanuts)	10.7	13.8	15.3	15.3	15.6
Cotton	5.9	7.6	7.6	7.6	7.6
Jute (mesta)	0.6	0.6	0.8	0.7	0.9

Sources: 1. *India, An Annual Reference 1977-1978.*
        2. *Times of India Directory, 1978.*
        3. *India Pocketbook of Economic Information,* 1972.

to March). In such areas rice tends to be monocultural. In-finitely painstaking, it is intensely raised in tiny, flooded, heavily-manured beds, transplanted by hand, and is harvested manually. Climatically, topographically, and in the provision of plentiful farm labor, the densely populated Lower Ganga Basin and the coastal plains are ideally suited for rice cultivation.

In terms of caloric value per hectare rice crop yields are more productive than other foodgrain crops. Not surprisingly rice is the major crop in densely populated areas, provided that the environmental conditions are also favorable. In Punjab, western Uttar Pradesh, and central India, wheat and other grain crops are the staple food of the common man; rice is used for festive occasions.

TABLE 6.5

PRODUCTION OF MAJOR CROPS
(In Million Tonnes)

	1950-51	1960-61	1970-71	1973-74	1974-75
Rice	20.6	27.6	42.5	43.7	40.2
Wheat	6.5	11.0	23.2	22.0	24.2
Other Cereals	15.4	23.7	30.5	28.1*	26.2
Pulses	8.4	12.7	11.6	9.7*	10.3
Foodgrains, Total	50.8	82.0	107.8	103.6	101.0
Sugar Cane	5.7	11.4	13.9	13.8	14.3
Oil Seeds	5.2	7.0	9.2	8.5*	8.6
Cotton	2.9	5.2	4.6	5.8*	7.1
Jute (mesta) (in 1,000 bales)	3.3	4.9	4.9	7.5*	5.8

*Estimates

Sources: As for Table 6.4

Wheat is characteristically different than rice in its climatic preference. It grows best in dry, irrigated areas during the cool season (*rabi* crop). Particularly adapted to the dry, irrigated lands of Punjab, Haryana, and western Uttar Pradesh and the Malwa Plateau, it is grown there as a premier crop and is the main staple food. Its "core area" is Sultej basin, the Ganga Plains and the Malwa Plateau where nearly one-third of the cultivated area is devoted to its cultivation. Its proportion of cropland declines eastwards in the Middle and Lower Ganga Plains where rice gains primacy, and southward from the Malwa Plateau where millets, groundnuts and oilseeds predominate. In the Peninsula, wheat cultivation extends from Gujarat to as far south as Karnataka on black-lava soils but on merely 4 to 5 percent of the cropland. Generally, the crop grows best on the alluvial, well-drained clayey loams of Punjab-Haryana and western Uttar Pradesh, but adapts well to varying types of soils excepting the sandy or the waterlogged. Nearly one-half of the country's wheat lands are found in these areas, which account for 60 percent of the total production.

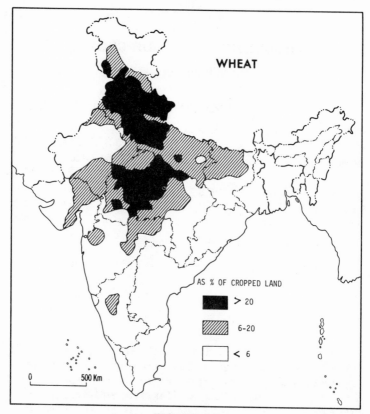

FIGURE 6.8

The area under wheat nearly doubled between 1950 and 1975 (10 to 18 million ha), but production increased fourfold (6.5 to over 24 million tons a year) during this period. Significant increases were in Punjab, Haryana and western Uttar Pradesh where increases between 10 to 15 percent a year were normal. Extension of wheat cultivation to Bihar, West Bengal and Orissa as a dry, winter crop has also been attempted. Yields are still among the lowest in the world, averaging between 800 to 825 kg/ha. Recent improvements in yields have resulted in the "core area" following the introduction of HYV (Figure 6.8).

Millets as cereal crops are intermediate between rice and wheat lands in terms of location and environmental controls (climate and soil conditions). Several types, principally *jowar, bajra,* and *ragi,* are extensively grown, collectively accounting for more area than is given to rice cultivation. Both production and area have increased modestly during the last twenty years. A long-standing prejudice against these crops as inferior cereals fit for consumption only by the poor has traditionally relegated their cultivation to the poorer soils. This prejudice stems from the fact that millets are a coarser grain, although in nutritional content they rank higher than either wheat or rice.

Bajra, a staple of the poor, tolerates drier conditions and sandier soils than *jowar,* and is grown best in Rajasthan, south Haryana, western Uttar Pradesh and Gujarat where it is grown on 20 percent of the cropland. Its cultivation also extends to most of the northwestern sections of the Peninsula. It is primarily a *kharif* (summer) crop and thrives best under warm temperatures.

Jowar is grown in an extensive area stretching from Punjab to Tamil Nadu, with the greatest concentration of cropland in the northwestern and central sections of the Deccan Plateau where it is a leading crop and claims over 30 percent of the cropland. In Tamil Nadu, it is grown as a *rabi* (winter) crop, its growing period coinciding with the winter monsoons. Elsewhere it is a summer crop.

Ragi is a *kharif* millet grown in a wide-ranging area from the Himalaya in the Uttar Pradesh to the uplands of Tamil Nadu. It is a secondary foodgrain crop to rice in Tamil Nadu, and occupies generally heavier, poorer upland soils. Its main value lies in providing unfailing dependability during the lean famine years, particularly in the poorer sections of the Deccan Plateau. The "core area" of production lies in the uplands of southern Karnataka where it occupies one-third of the cropland, and is consumed locally as a staple food. It is nutritionally superior to rice and has a high calcium content, but the grain is coarse like other millets.

Maize (corn) and *barley* are two cereals grown typically under temperate conditions in north and central India. Maize has a larger cultivation distribution and extends well into south Rajasthan, Madhya Pradesh and Andhra Pradesh. It has the status of a coarse, secondary cereal crop, but its cultivation covers a large area (nearly 5 million ha) because it is also used as a fodder crop. A deep-rooted, leafy crop, it grows best on well-drained, deep, heavy loams in areas of assured rainfall or irrigation. The nucleus areas are in the hills, principally in the Kashmir Valley were it occupies 15 to 30 percent of the cropland, and in the uplands of southeast Rajasthan. Yields are very low by world standards, and hybridization has been recommended for the improvement of strains. Barley is grown as a minor cash crop in the Uttar Pradesh Himalaya, and in southeast Rajasthan.

Among other cereals, *pulses* of various kinds are grown extensively, covering over 22 million ha of cropped land. Grown ubiquitously over the country, their cultivation exhibits a few areas of concentration in central Rajasthan, Bihar, Orissa, Kutch and Madhya Pradesh. For the diet of millions of Indians these provide a rich source of protein, although ecologically most responsive to areas of low moisture and light soils, pulses can be grown in wider environmental conditions. Both *rabi* and *kharif* varieties exist; best known among these are: *gram* (chick-pea), *moth* (brown grain), *tur* or *arhar*, *moong* (green beans), and *masur* (lentils). Regional distributions vary with different types, which are adapted to local soil and moisture conditions. In most parts of the country the cultivation of pulses forms a necessary activity in agricultural calendar for these also provide a useful leguminous rotation for retention of soil fertility. *Gram* and *tur* account for over 10 percent of the total cropland. Most pulses are used as *dal (dahl)* or a puree to be eaten along with Indian curries or are roasted/fried for snacking.

Cash Non-Food Crops

Both refined sugar and *sugarcane* have long been used in India. Raw cane, probably native to the country, grows ideally in the tropical climates. The largest producing areas lie outside the tropics in the North Indian Plains from Punjab to the Middle Ganga Basin. In the moist, tropical, coastal parts of Kerala which are ecologically best suited to its growth, the crop cannot successfully compete with grain crops and other cash crops. Its total cultivated area amounts to a mere 3 million ha which yields, however, nearly 15 million tons of raw sugar (*gur*) annually. Despite encouragement to augment sugar production, areas given to the cultivation of cane did not increase. Extension of cultivated land in the country was instead occupied by cereal crops.

Some extension in its cropland occurred during the First and Second Plans (1951-56/1956-61). After reaching self-sufficiency and providing a modest exportable surplus in the 1960's, sugarcane cultivation expanded only slightly.

Indian yields are low because its areas of greatest production do not coincide with the climatically most-suited region in south India. The crop is highly demanding, requiring rich soils and abundant moisture during the growing season. In the western Uttar Pradesh Plains and the *tarai* areas, cane occupies over 10 percent of the cropland. Nearly one-half of India's cane-cultivation area lies in Uttar Pradesh, the remainder is shared among the states of Punjab, Maharashtra and Bihar, leaving only a minor portion of its surface scattered in the deltas of the Godavari, Krishna and Kaveri, despite the existence of ecologically optimal conditions of rich alluvial soils, cheap irrigation and year-round high temperatures in the southern states. In the North Indian Plains where rich alluvial soils have been traditionally utilized, a long growing period, widely-practiced irrigation, and cheap, abundant labor partially offset the disadvantages of a less than ideal environment.

Ranking after Cuba and Brazil in output, India is one of the most important sugar-cane producers in the world. Its cultivation area is the largest among growers but the native variety is of thin cane containing little juice and yield per ha is low particularly in the subtropical north Indian growing region. In the Peninsula (Maharashtra, Andhra Pradesh and the Kaveri delta) where most favorable ecological conditions prevail, yields are 2 to 3 times higher (6,000 kg/ha) than in the north.

Oilseeds, used both as cooking media and as animal feed, are widely grown in the country. Five major varieties: linseed, rapeseed/mustard, sesamum seed, castor seed and groundnuts collectively occupy 11 million ha of the cropped area. Rapeseed/mustard and sesamum are the principle winter-weather (*rabi*) crops, utilizing about one-fifth of the area of oilseed cultivation. Sesamum is mostly a *rabi* crop in southern India, but *kharif* in the north. Major cultivation areas are central India, the Malwa Plateau, east Rajasthan, Madhya Pradesh and Kerala, which account for about 15 percent of the area given to oilseeds. Groundnut ("peanut" of the U.S.A.) is a leading crop in Gujarat and parts of

Maharashtra, but is also grown extensively in Tamil Nadu, Andhra Pradesh, Karnataka, Punjab and western Uttar Pradesh. It is an important cash crop grown widely in warm, tropical lands and is well-adapted to poor, light soils. India is the leading producer in the world, accounting for nearly one-third of the world's total output. Newer high-yielding strains have recently been tried, but with little success.

Spices, coconuts, areca nut, palms, and chillies are grown chiefly along the Western Ghats coast and in Malabar, south of Goa. Cashewnut cultivation is usually limited to small plantations in Kerala; the crop is mainly exported.

Fiber Crops

Cotton holds a premier position among fibers and occupies a large cultivation area: 7.5 million ha. With an annual output of over 7 million tons, India ranks high among the world's major producers. The quality of lint is poor, and yields are low. Cotton is a demanding crop: moisture restricted to a limited growing period within the 60 to 86 cm rainfall zone, warm temperature and rich clayey loam soils. Indian production is, therefore, limited to a few areas: the ideal Deccan Lava region of Maharashtra and Gujarat where rich moisture-retentive lava soils, warm temperatures, and regulated irrigation combine to create the leading producing area and the alluvial, irrigated Haryana-Punjab area where cotton occupies 30 percent of all cropland. Elsewhere, areas of significant production are Karnataka and Tamil Nadu with 6 to 15 percent of cultivated area under it. Yields, low by world standards, are highest in the Punjab-Haryana area and in Tamil Nadu, a condition made possible by excellent irrigation facilities, rich alluvial soils and the introduction of better strains (Figure 6.9).

Jute, a minor crop in terms of cultivated area, is an important cash crop and a foreign-exchange earner. Despite expansion of cultivation outside the traditional area in the Ganga Delta, the crop shows marked regional concentration. Partition of the subcontinent in 1947 deprived India of its major source-area in Bangladesh for the mills around Hooghlyside near Calcutta. Rapid expansion of cultivation followed by the Mahanadi Delta in Orissa, in the Assam Valley and in *tarai* areas of Uttar Pradesh and Bihar. Diffusion of a newly-developed *mesta* variety in *tarai* helped meet

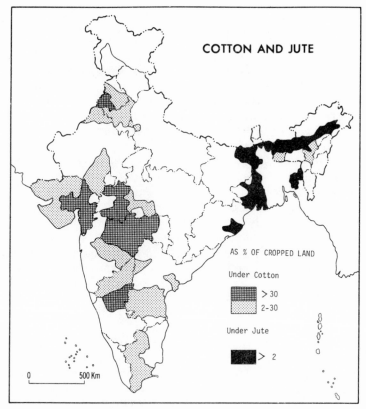

FIGURE 6.9

requirements of the Hooghlyside jute industry, leaving a small surplus for exports. India is now nearly self-sufficient in its needs, importing only a modest amount of very refined varieties from Bangladesh (Figure 6.9).

Plantation Crops

Tea, coffee, rubber, and cashewnuts are the principle plantation crops, grown in widely separated areas. The tea tree grows best in areas of abundant moisture, gravely soils, well-drained hill slopes (usually between 3,000 to 4,000 feet of altitude), in Assam, in Darjeeling district of West Bengal, and in the Nilgiri Hills. Plantations were first established during British rule in Assam (and still retain substantial

British management and capital) and spread to the Darjeeling Hills at higher elevations (7,000 feet altitude). Plantation size generally varies between 200 and 250 ha, while India's total area of tea gardens amounts to less than half a million hectares. Sixty percent of the output comes from West Bengal (Darjeeling Hills) and Assam, the remainder comes from the Nilgiri Hills (Tamil Nadu and Karnataka). A very small amount is grown in the hilly areas of Himachal Pradesh and Uttar Pradesh. After China, India is the largest producer in the world. Most production is exported.

Coffee plantations lie exclusively in the warmer tropical south on the Nilgiri Hills and on the eastern slopes of Western Ghats in Karnataka. The estates are small and the total cultivated area is modest. Most production is consumed at home, mostly in South India. Only one-third of the 45 million kilogram total production is exported.

Rubber plantations are confined to the lower elevations of the Nilgiri Hills and the Western Ghats, in areas of more abundant rainfall, a shorter dry period and warmer temperatures. Production is very small, but is steadily growing in response to increasing domestic demand created by industrialization.

Other major cash crops grown are tobacco, spices, and coconuts. *Tobacco* occupies 500,000 hectares of cropland and production is 500,000 tons annually. Nearly one-third of its cropland lies in Tamil Nadu. In the north it is grown widely in the silty, alluvial Ganga Plains. Smoking is widely practiced in the country; thus most production is consumed at home, although some is exported to Britain. Several varieties of spices are grown in various parts of the country. Chillies are widely used and are grown primarily in south India, with the states of Tamil Nadu, Andhra Pradesh and Maharashtra accounting for 60 percent of the production. Pepper production is concentrated along the moist slopes of Western Ghats. India is the world's largest exporter of pepper. Ginger-root and cardamon are grown mostly in Kerala and large quantities are exported. Coriander and tumeric are more widely grown, although South India retains supremacy in their production. The most favored area of coconut production is the Kerala coast. Spices and coconuts are grown on small holdings. Unlike rubber, tea and coffee, these two are non-plantation crops.

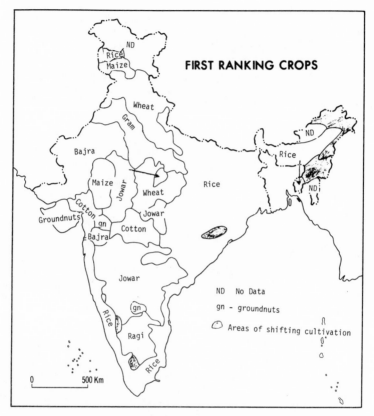

FIGURE 6.10

Crop Associations

Figure 6.10 identifies areas of leading (first-ranking) crops and reveals several characteristic crop patterns. Apparent is the predominance of food crops which occupy over 70 percent of the cropland. Cash crops (jute, tea, coffee) occupy a secondary position. This map could well be called a Crop Regions Map. Major crop divisions conform to environmental-cultural controls. In most instances the leading or the first ranking crop occupies a major portion, sometimes well over 50 percent of the cultivated area of the district. In well-watered, alluvial parts such as the Lower Ganga Plains, double or multiple-cropping is practiced chiefly of the rice crop. Given local variations in topography, soils and moisture conditions, several crops supplement the first ranking one. Only in the coastal plains, the Lower Ganga Plains, the Assam Valley, Tripura and the Kaveri Delta, where ideal environmental conditions exist, is rice a monocultural crop occupying over 85 percent of the cultivated area. Another region of monoculture is west Rajasthan, ecologically a counterpart of the rice-dominant region, where "dry crop" *bajra* predominates.

In areas where grain is not a leading (first ranking) crop, a leguminous crop like gram or oilseeds usually predominates. Gram is a first-ranking crop in north-central India, north Rajasthan, south Punjab, Haryana, southwest Uttar Pradesh. White groundnuts lead all crops in Gujarat. Cotton, a non-food crop attains first rank in a few districts in the Deccan Lava Region in Gujarat and north Maharashtra. Even where non-food crops predominate, food crops occupy an important position.

The predominant trait of Indian agriculture is subsistence farming. Most production is raised for immediate family consumption; only a fraction is sold off the farm to landholders or in nearby markets. Exportable quantities entering world trade are limited to a few plantation crops (tea, coffee, rubber) or fiber crops (cotton, jute). Cash crops meant for nearby or distant markets occupy only a secondary place in the crop regions. Crop associations within the crop regions often have complex distributional patterns. Usually four and eight crops may compete for cropland and may be termed as secondary crops in a crop region, but still tend to have widespread distribution. Pulses, oilseeds and fodder crops are examples of secondary crops with extensive distribution. Cotton, groundnuts, maize, bajra and barley are more widely distributed. Unlike rice, these do not exhibit a single area of regional concentration.

Secondary crops in the rice region are jute, oilseeds, pulses, and tea, all of which — excepting tea — are associated with low-lying alluvial plains. Tea is important in the hills adjoining the Assam Valley and in Darjeeling and Jalpaiguri districts of West Bengal. A rice-coffee combination is restricted to the plantations in the hills of Coorg and Karnataka. The pulse-jowar-rice combination is particularly noteworthy in the Krishna Delta, where rainfall is deficient (less than 125 cm annually). Tobacco is also locally important there. Oilseeds are widely grown as a second or third ranking crop in the rice region of southern Bihar and the Mahanadi Delta. Maize and wheat association with rice occupy a major proportion of cropland in the Kashmir Valley and the *tarai* region in Uttar Pradesh. Cotton is a second crop in Meghalaya and along the northern coast of Maharashtra. Gram is important in the Lower Ganga Plains and in western Uttar Pradesh.

Within the wheat region, maize and barley are second crops in the hills of Himachal Pradesh, while cotton is significant in areas of irrigation in western and central districts of Punjab as a *kharif* crop. Bajra holds a secondary position in the drier districts of south Punjab and south Haryana. Wheat is an important second crop in the jowar region which extends from east Rajasthan and the Malwa Plateau to the drier, central parts of the Deccan Plateau, and as far south as north Karnataka. Jowar and cotton are important rain-fed *kharif* crops in the Deccan Lava Region, whereas oilseeds and groundnuts occupy drier portions of the jowar region. Cotton is a leading crop in north Maharashtra and southern Madhya Pradesh. Groundnuts lead in Gujarat and one district in Andhra Pradesh; maize in the Aravalli Hills of southeastern Rajasthan with barley as a second crop. The second area of maize concentration is the Kashmir Valley, where wheat and rice are the secondary crops. In the southern part of the Deccan Peninsula, major crops are *ragi* on the uplands of south Karnataka and north Tamil Nadu. Oilseeds and groundnuts are secondary crops in the *ragi* region.

CURRENT TRENDS
IN AGRICULTURAL DEVELOPMENT

Given the magnitude of agriculture in the Indian economy and the complexity of its underlying problems, the overall record of its achievements since Independence appears promising. Future directions would depend on how effectively past experience is utilized to maximize real and potential gains. A major initial disappointment was in the area of foodgrain production, the growth rates of which ranged from slow to fluctuating to generally bleak during the first three Five Year Plans (1950-1966). Performance has been satisfactory since then, a result primarily of break-thoughs in productivity made possible by the introduction of high-yielding varieties of foodgrain crops.

Until the Third Plan (1961-65) growth performance of most crops remained weak; but major acceleration occurred during and since the Fourth Plan (1965-71). The watershed of 1966 in agricultural production is coincident with the diffusion of agricultural modernization (introduction of HYV, mechanization, and chemical fertilization) in selected parts of the country. Since then growth in the areas utilizing HYV has increased dramatically.

Contrary to the prevailing stereotypes, Indian farmers demonstrated willingness to work and accepted challenges and opportunities to improve their conditions. This was particularly true in regions where Intensive Agricultural Area Programme of 1965 (IAAP) and high yielding varieties programme (HYVP) of 1966 were launched by the government. These two programmes were initially concentrated in those geographic areas where these were most likely to succeed rapidly. Dramatic results were obtained in Punjab, Haryana, and western Uttar Pradesh where dwarf Mexican wheat varieties were introduced and in Tamil Nadu, Andhra Pradesh, Kashmir and Kerala by the use of new strains of rice. Since 1970 these programs have been gradually diffused to other sections of the country. A new HYV of wheat as a dry *rabi* crop was also diffused to the predominantly rice producing areas of West Bengal, Assam, Orissa and Andhra Pradesh with promising results. For example, little wheat was grown in West Bengal before 1972, but 1 million tons of wheat was produced almost entirely of the high-yielding varieties in 1972.

FOODGRAIN REVOLUTION

For several years prior to Independence, the growth of foodgrain production stood at near stagnation, averaging only 0.11 percent annually, whereas population had been growing at about 1.4 percent. Colonial policy primarily emphasized the production of export-oriented crops with the result that the country's capacity to feed itself had steadily deteriorated as population pressure mounted. Since Independence, despite substantial gains made in food produc-

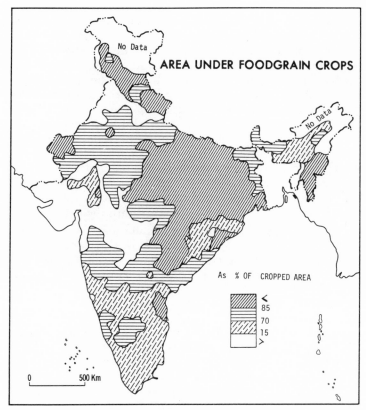

FIGURE 6.11

tion, the tempo of population pressure increased, posing a major threat to foodgrain self-sufficiency.

Since 1951, when the First Five Year Plan was launched, the country has been importing foodgrains. The volume of imports fluctuated from less than 1 million tons in 1955 to over 10.4 million tons in 1966. Since then these have oscillated between 3 to 4 million tons annually, fluctuations responding to oscillations in monsoon behavior and resulting harvests. In 1976 a near self-sufficiency was reached, but attainment of food self-sufficiency became a major objective of the planned development.

In view of the central role of food crops in Indian agriculture (Figure 6.11) and the country's dependence on foodgrain imports, an analysis of past trends and future potentials of foodgrain production may be made. Comparisons with China, another large and developing country, may be interesting. Compared to China, India's record has not been poor. China, like India, has been importing foodgrains. China's foodgrain production since 1950 until 1975 grew at about 2 percent a year as compared with the 2.8 percent annual rate for India. Both countries experienced population pressure. Precise comparisons of imports are difficult to make, but China has been importing foodgrains at a higher level than India, although its population has been growing at a somewhat slower rate. India has nearly attained self-sufficiency in foodgrain production; China continued to import substantial amounts until the early 1970's.

India's foodgrain production has fluctuated widely from year to year since 1947, but four distinct patterns are discernible. During the pre-Independence period (1947-1950) foodgrain production ranged between 55 to 60 million tons annually, growing at about 2 percent a year, barely keeping up with population increase. The second period, synchronized with the First Plan (1951-1956), experienced foodgrain production increase at a rate of 4 percent a year, thus outpacing population growth. This was made possible by the huge investments in irrigation projects and the Community Development Programs. Considerable gains both in area and in production of foodcrops resulted in a decline of food imports, from over 3 million tons in 1951 to 700,000 tons in 1955. Production during the First Plan period peaked at 63 million tons. The third period coincided roughly with the decade of 1955-65 (Second and Third Plans). Production initially grew at 3.4 percent a year, then slackened to nearly 2 percent annually in 1965 and 1966, the years of disastrous droughts. Population growth averaged over 2.6 percent annually during the period. In output, production of foodgrains had declined to a level at 65 million tons in 1966 (the level of 1955), after having risen to 70 to 71 million tons in the early 1960's. Consequently, foodgrain imports rose substantially, from 700,000 tons in 1955 to over 10.4 million tons in 1966 (Figure 6.12).

It became clear that by the end of the Third Plan the government had not succeeded in its stated objective of reaching self-sufficiency. In fact, during the late 60's there

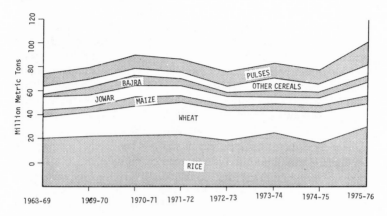

FOODGRAIN PRODUCTION, 1968—1976

FIGURE 6.12

were serious food shortages, while the foreign exchange situation had also reached a crisis level in view of large food imports. Nearly 30 million people in the major cities lived under mandatory rationing; another 200 million, or one-third of the entire population, was under partial rationing. Failure of the monsoons in 1965-66 further aggravated the shortfalls in production and drastic, revolutionary efforts were clearly needed to improve the foodgrain situation.

The traditional approach to agricultural development had relied heavily on such methods as expansion of cultivable area and efficient utilization of the underemployed farm labor. These had failed to produce results during the first three Five Year Plans. During the 1960's some policy changes were elaborated which rested on two basic principles; first, that the farmer has a larger role in transforming environment than prescribed by the age-old belief that he must always adhere to the environmental controls; and second, there are greater regional variations in agricultural productivity than traditionally recognized. The second principle was demonstrated by a joint Indo-American study, known as the Intensive Agricultural District Programs (IADP) which emphasized the need for a fresh approach to agricultural development. The IADP used a package program of raising foodgrain production by an intensive effort concentrated in 17 selected districts which were most likely to yield good results. The results of this experiment were mixed, but it led to the development of a new strategy based on the recognition of the need for provision of technological inputs into agriculture particularly in areas which can yield optimal results. In a sense, then, the "Green Revolution" was not an overnight phenomenon but was based, in part, on the experience of the IADP study.

In 1965 the administration shifted its focus from traditional methodology to technological applications for agricultural development. The goal of the new strategy was to take India to self-sufficiency in foodgrains by 1971 by raising production from 89 million tons in 1964 to 125 million tons by 1977. The approach was three-pronged: introduction of new seeds and modern agricultural techniques, concentration of these new inputs in the irrigated areas, and the provision of price and cheap-credit incentives to the farmers so as to draw them into the participation process of the development program.

Indian government announced a "New Strategy" in 1965 with its basic objective of maximizing agricultural production by directing state effort in the first instance to those areas which were best endowed for food production. The key element of this maximizing process was the injection of large capital and technological inputs, first in the selected areas and to subsequently enlarge its coverage to other parts of the country. The introduction of high yielding varieties (HYV) of foodgrain crops and mechanization were to be the primary inputs; inputs of chemical fertilizers and regulated water supply formed the remainder of the new package.

This bold, new strategy was based on three major assumptions. First, the new varieties of crops to be introduced would nearly double per hectare productivity for the major food crops; second, maximum potentials are attainable by concentrating high yielding varieties of seeds and modern inputs in irrigated lands, and finally, cultivators respond to scientific practices if price and credit incentives are provided. The IADP program of 17 districts was extended later on to include 114 districts (approximately one-third of all the districts), and its name changed to IAAP (Intensive Agricultural Area Programme).

A major element in increased foodgrain production was

the introduction in 1966 of the HYV of wheat and rice developed in Mexico by Norman Borlaug for the Rockefeller Foundation. Dwarf strains of these crops were introduced in areas of favorable environmental conditions, particularly in Punjab, Haryana, and western Uttar Pradesh, and became an instant success. Between 1966 and 1971 wheat production rose by over 90 percent, recording a growth rate of 19 percent a year. Nearly 60 percent of all foodgrain production between 1966 and 1971 was attributed to the new HYV of wheat. The foodgrain situation became so promising that by 1966 analysts proclaimed that the "Foodgrain Revolution" or the "Green Revolution" had arrived in India.

Yields increased phenomonally in the initial stages in favored areas. For example, in 1968 farmers who had adopted the new technology in Ludhiana district of Punjab increased their average yields in wheat from 2,100 lbs to over 4,200 lbs per hectare. Nationally one-fifth of wheatland was switched to the new Mexican strains, which produced in 1971 about 35 percent of the total wheat crop. Yields did not rise as dramatically elsewhere as in the Punjab and Haryana districts since the new technological innovations were not accompanied by adequate supporting facilities for irrigation, fertilization, and mechanization.

Regionally, the diffusion of HYV was spotty. From the "core" area of Punjab-Haryana, where about 80 percent of the area was devoted to it, the HYV of "miracle wheat" quickly spread to other parts of the North Indian Plains in west Uttar Pradesh to districts as far east as Bihar, and to Rajasthan and Gujarat-Maharashtra in the south. Between 1965 and 1972, the area given to HYV of miracle wheat increased by 120 percent nationally. Initial growth was rapid in the "core" area, its diffusion to east Uttar Pradesh, Bihar, West Bengal, the Brahmaputra Valley and Orissa as a second *rabi* crop followed.

High-yielding varieties of rice were simultaneously introduced in several parts of the country: in Bihar, West Bengal in the north and Tamil Nadu, Kerala and Karnataka in the south. Yields of rice rose appreciably after the introduction of these new varieties but not as dramatically as in the case of high-yielding varieties of wheat. Areas of notable success with rice yields showing gains of over 30 percent between 1965 and 1970 were limited to Malabar, Tamil Nadu and

West Bengal. New rice strains were particularly susceptible to damage by pests and diseases. Rice farmers were generally poor and could ill afford the expenses of chemical fertilizers and pesticides used for new seeds and unlike the Punjabi farmers they did not possess reliable irrigation and drainage facilities. Futhermore, new rice strains were short-grained, tasted unfamiliar and lumped together in cooking. Public acceptance was weak. Rice, therefore, remained the "orphan" of the "Foodgrain Revolution."

As regards other foodgrain crops, substantial success has been achieved in developing high-yielding strains of maize which are responsive to good irrigation facilities as well as in millets for the dry regions. But actual production in both cases has remained insubstantial primarily on account of the limited area originally devoted to these crops, but also because of ineffectual irrigation facilities, lack of fertilization and weak enthusiasm among maize and millet growers.

In a nutshell, the accomplishments of the Foodgrain Revolution have been highly selective among farmers and unevenly distributed in space. Its backbone has been the phenomenal success in dwarf Mexican wheat strains. Performance of new rice strains has been somewhat short of satisfactory. Its continuing success would depend on how effectively the remaining serious problems of diffusion and management are overcome. A major challenge is, of course, the expansion of its benefits to cover remaining sections of the country and the farming community.

Most gains have been achieved where farmers possessed economic larger landholdings, had access to improved farm equipment and good irrigation facilities and could muster a reserve of capital through savings or credit loans. Studies in Ludhiana, a typical district in Punjab where new dwarf wheat varieties were introduced in relatively larger land-holdings and where farmers had access to irrigation facilities, gains produced through diffusion of HYV have been truly remarkable. But Ludhiana is not typical of large sections of the country or even typical for the wheat-growing belt. In Bihar and Uttar Pradesh, both wheat growing areas, over 80 percent of all cultivating holders have farms of less than 3 ha. In the rice-growing regions, the average farm size is even smaller, between 1 and 2 ha. On such small holdings, the impact of new technology has been proved to be inadequate for future investments in agricultural development.

In general, big farmers maintaining cultivating households of 15 ha or over were the largest beneficiaries. They were able to muster capital reserves for the purchase of farm machinery and equipment, install electric wells and utilize chemical fertilization. The inevitable result was that economic disparities widened between large farmers and the majority of small farmers, or owner-cum-tenant cultivators. This process of widening economic disparities was clearly counter-productive to the objectives of the Five Year Plans of enabling the small marginal farmer and agricultural laborer to "participate in the process of development." A Small Farmers Development Agency (SFDA) was set up during the Fifth Plan to help bring 3.5 million small farmers into the orbit of participation process of growing HYV of foodgrains. This agency was responsible for the provision of irrigation facilities and technical advice to small farmers through existing institutional and administrative channels of credit and cooperative societies. Yet there was always an element of risk for the small farmer in obtaining loans, and he feared loss of his land to repay heavy debt in the event of a bad monsoon. As a result, agricultural modernization failed to have any serious impact on smaller farmers, and might even have intensified polarization among farming classes.

Crucial to the dramatic rise in foodgrain production have been the two pillars of Green Revolution: an adequate and controlled supply of irrigation and the application of chemical fertilizers to the crops during the growing season. Recent studies (Frankel, 1971; Mellor, 1976) have demonstrated that the big farmer was the major and quick beneficiary of the Green Revolution because he could make capital investments in irrigation and chemical fertilizers. A quarter of India's cultivated land currently enjoys an assured water supply from irrigation; most of this is held by big farmers. "In consequence, insofar as the majority of the small farmers adopt the new practices, they can be expected to do so slowly, cautiously and partially" (Frankel, 1976).

The infrastructural and marketing facilities created during the Third and Fourth Plans, however meager these were, also tended to help the big farmer. Big farmers could afford to maintain their own transport or buy new tractors through credit loans; the small farmer was considered a poor credit risk and left without adequate facility. Moreover, his crop would be too small to warrant provision of credit or other facilities. Inevitably he would be left to use a more expensive mode of transporting his crop to the market or even sell it.

The legislative record of land-redistribution has been adequate, but implementation has flagged. Big landowners have ways to evade the land ceiling orders. One interesting method is to assign portions of their land among relatives on legal documents thus evading the "land to the tiller" and land-ceiling orders which enjoin each cultivating household to adhere to a fixed ceiling on their farming landholdings. This indeed has bred discontent among the small farmers, and expressed itself in political turmoil, particularly among the traditionally deprived landless scheduled castes (*Harijans*) who generally work as hired cultivators. No wonder *Harijans* have been behind recent political unrest and violence in Bihar and Tamil Nadu.

Indian planners are currently faced with the challenge of meeting fertilizer and new-strain seed needs incumbent on the introduction of HYV of foodcrops. To serve 40 million ha of irrigated area placed under new strains of foodgrain crops, the country would require 2.4 million tons of chemical fertilizers and 144,000 tons of high-quality foodgrain seeds (combined wheat, paddy, maize, bajra, jowar). Over 100,000 ha of additional cultivated land will be needed to produce the required amount of seeds. This can only be achieved by elimination of cultivable wastelands or encroachment on existing cropland; both propositions have remote possibilities of realization. Potentials for augmenting fertilizer production also appear restricted particularly since the escalation of world prices since 1973 of imported oil has resulted in oil shortages. Pesticide, another key input in Green Revolution, is in critically short supply.

Despite setbacks and shortcomings, outlook for foodgrain production appreciably improved in 1974 when a record production of 104 million tons were produced. Production reached the level of 120 million tons in 1978 (129 million tons in 1979). Since 1973 the country had virtually attained foodgrain self-sufficiency, and imports of foodgrain crops were reduced to a trickle. On the average, foodgrain production grew at a rate of a little over 4 percent annually during the Fourth Plan. To run a winning battle with population, a sustained growth rate of 4.5 percent a year in foodgrain production is required. Prospects for such increases for some years appear promising. Long range projections are hard to make; whether India wins in this foodgrain-population race, it is difficult to predict.

In sum, the introduction of HYV of foodgrains have brought foodgrain revolution in the country by stimulating agricultural modernization and commercialization and production. Its accomplishments, however, have been uneven over areas and among farming classes. The future of the Green Revolution faces several institutional, economic and political challenges. What is needed is a carefully designed and vigorously implemented strategy of overall agricultural modernization encompassing institutional, economic and political bases of the agricultural problem within the framework of development programs applied universally and over all agricultural classes.

TOWARD A NEW
RURAL DEVELOPMENT STRATEGY

There are two major inter-related problems of agrarian society facing Indian planners. First, how to bring a massive landless peasantry into the participation process of the "Green Revolution," and second, how to eliminate or reduce agricultural unemployment formed by a huge cadre of poor landless peasantry. Mellor has advocated the formulation of a broad integrated development strategy as one of the prescriptions dealing with the twin problems. Such a development strategy centers around the concept of "employment oriented" growth which could draw the landless and poor cultivators into its orbit. It is suggested that such a strategy would be instrumental in overall economic growth of the country. Such a growth would be possible if increased demand for labor is created which in turn will raise incomes and living standards of the poor.

Raising labor productivity is the key to this process. The initially displaced surplus labor on the farms, consequent upon agricultural mechanization, could amply be absorbed in a newly-created agro-based service industries (secondary and tertiary sectors of economy).

Mellor develops his thesis in this way. Increased food supply would increase a vigorous rural industrial and service sector of rural development. Increased food production would raise the standards and incomes of the poor. However, necessary increases in food supply could occur only through technological innovations of the "Green Revolution." The creation of agro-based rural industries would enhance the importance of consumer-oriented goods of small industries such as canning of food, dairy farming, cottage industries, small-scale fertilizer plants, repair and servicing of new agricultural machines (tractors, bicycles, electric pumps, etc.). The focus would be on the development of small labor-intensive industries as opposed to the development of large capital-intensive industries pursued by the government of India. Mellor concludes that "as an alternative to capital-intensive strategy, this employment oriented approach has potential growth in total incomes (of the rural agrarian society) as for greater participation of the poor in the benefits of production" (Mellor, 1976).

Three necessary steps for the development of such a strategy have been suggested. First, priority is to be given to achieving increased agricultural production through technological inputs (new HYV of crops, seeds, chemical fertilization, electric wells, mechanization, etc.). Second, labor-intensive small-scale agro-based industries are to be created. Third, administrative and institutional environments are to be improved by enacting legislation favoring land redistribution and credit-marketing institutions, but more importantly such legislation is to be effectively implemented.

Two basic pillars of such a strategy are stepping up foodgrain production and the creation of rural agro-based industries. Foodgrains account for a large portion of the expenditure of the poor; its increased supply would raise their living standard, provide raw materials to produce goods to support increased employment in such industries as dairy farming, food canning, cottage industries production of fertilizers and also raise wages for the agricultural labor. The traditional failure of agricultural to provide employment for the rural population could be fruitfully changed to a more fulfilling role of absorbing rural, idle manpower. Emphasis could be shifted to the production of cash crops (cotton, jute, tea, sugar cane) made possible by increasing yields of foodgrain crops through introduction of technological innovations. Foodcrops would continue to dominate the cultivable area, but increased foodgrain production would release land to be devoted to export-oriented cash crops. A greater variety of crops would generate raw materials for the development of labor-intensive rather than capital-intensive small-scale industries. Cash crops and export-oriented cottage industry could also bring more foreign exchange and pay for short term shortfalls in foodgrains in times of erratic monsoons.

Technological inputs into agriculture demand a well-developed infrastructural base-rural communications, an irrigation system, banking and marketing facilities—all entailing large expenditures. Large investments in infrastructural improvements must either come from foreign aid or through accumulation of a domestic capital reserve through greater agricultural productions.

Finally, the ultimate success of any strategy depends on how well it is implemented. Stable political conditions may significantly improve its chances.

CITATIONS AND BIBLIOGRAPHY

Alexander, P. C., *Industrial Estates in India*. Bombay, 1963.

Bhardwaj, R., *Structural Basis of India's Foreign Trade*. Bombay, 1970.

Blyn, G., *Agricultural Trends in India, 1891-1947*. Philadelphia, 1966

Brown, D. D., *Agricultural Development in India's Districts*. Cambridge, Mass., 1971.

Chakravarti, A. K., "Green Revolution in India," *Annals of the A.A.G.* Vol. 63, 1973, pp. 319-330.

Chakravarti, A. K., "India's Agriculture," *Focus*. Vol. 23 (5), 1973.

Chandrasekhar, S., *Population and Planned Parenthood in India*. London, 1955.

Chatterjee, S. P., *National Atlas of India*. (Hindi Edition), Calcutta, 1957.

Day, R. H., *et. al.*, *Economic Development as an Adaptive Process: The Green Revolution in the Indian Punjab.* New York, 1977.

Dayal, E., "A Measure of Cropping Intensity," *Professional Geographer.* Vol. 30 (3), 1978, pp. 289-96.

Dutt, A., *et. al.*, "Dimensions of India's Foreign Trade," *International Geography, 1972.* Vol. 1, Toronto, 1972.

Etienne, G., *Studies in Indian Agriculture.* Bombay, 1968.

Farmer, B. H., *Agricultural Colonization in India Since Independence.* Oxford, 1974.

Frankel, F. R., *India's Political Economy, 1947-77.* Princeton, 1979.

Frankel, F. R., *India's Green Revolution: Economic Gains and Political Costs.* Princeton, 1971.

Jannuzi, F. T., *Agrarian Crisis in India.* Austin, 1974.

Khusro, A. M., *Economics of Land Reform and Farm Size in India.* Madras, 1973.

Ladejinsky, W., "Ironies of India's Green Revolution," *Foreign Affairs.* Vol. 48, 1970, pp. 758-768.

Lewis, J. P., *Quiet Crisis in India.* Washington D.C., 1962.

Mellor, J. W., *Developing Rural India.* Ithaca, N.Y., 1968.

Mellor, J. W., *The New Economics of Growth.* Ithaca, N.Y., 1976.

Merillat, H. C. L., *Land and the Constitution in India.* New York, 1970.

Poleman, T. T., *et. al.*, *Food, Population and Employment.* New York, 1973.

Rao, C. R., *Data Base of Indian Economy.* Calcutta, 1972.

Rao, K. L., *India's Water Wealth.* New Delhi. 1975.

Sengupta, P., (ed.), *Census Altas,* Vol. 1 (IX). Delhi, 1970.

Singh, J., *An Agricultural Atlas of India: A Geographical Analysis.* Kurukshetra, 1974.

Singh, S. K., *The Indian Famine of 1967.* New Delhi, 1975.

Streeten, P. L., (ed.), *The Crisis of Indian Planning.* London, 1968.

Thorner, D., *et. al.*, *Land and Labor in India.* New York, 1962.

Wilber, C. O., (ed.), *The Political Economy of Developmemt.* New York, 1973.

CHAPTER 7

SETTLEMENT, CITIES,
AND URBANIZATION

As in most developing countries, spatial distribution of settlements in India is skewed. A majority of the people (80.1 percent in 1971) live in small villages, 90 percent of which contain less than 1000 inhabitants. Universally dotting the landscape, except where topographic, soil and climatic conditions are unfavorable, these villages are interspersed with a relatively few large cities. According to the 1971 Census, there were only 3,119 urban places in India, 2,097 of which contained less than 20,000 inhabitants. Table 7.1, showing the number and size-categories of rural towns and urban settlements, indicates that there is an inadequate development of graded hierarchy of settlement sizes in the country.

INADEQUATE DEVELOPMENT
OF CENTRAL PLACE HIERARCHY

A functionally integrated and graded spatial system of settlements acting as central places, i.e., serving area around them has yet to evolve in the country. Most villages have grown self-sufficient, isolated, and not effectively linked with higher level settlements even within their travel range and are inaccessible to the larger market centers. Large market centers — centers for the exchange of goods and services — are only sparsely scattered along a few linearly developed railroads or paved roads. Spatial dispersion of small villages was dictated in ancient times by such historical factors as the movement of caste and religious groups as well as by local variations in soil fertility or availability of water.

243

TABLE 7.1

DISTRIBUTION OF SETTLEMENTS, RURAL AND URBAN, 1961 AND 1971

	1961		1971	
Size of settlements	Number of Settlements	Population (in millions)	Number of Settlements	Population (in millions)
URBAN				
One million & above	7	14.2	8	20.7
100,000-999,999	100	20.9	143	32.6
50,000-99,999	139	9.5	219	14.7
20,000-49,999	518	15.7	652	19.9
10,000-19,999	820	11.3	987	14.0
Below 10,000	1,116	7.2	1,110	7.1
Total	2,700	79.3	3,119	109.1
RURAL				
10,000 & above	776	12.3	1,358	22.3
5,000-9,999	3,421	22.3	4,974	32.7
1,000-4,999	91,948	166.3	117,978	217.7
500-999	119,167	83.9	132,990	94.4
Below 500	352,023	75.5	318,633	71.9
Total	567,335	360.29	575,933	439.1

Source: Bose, A. *India's Urbanization, 1901-2001,* Tata McGraw-Hill, Publishing Co. Ltd., New Delhi, 1978, p. 347.

Villages emerged as self-contained socio-economic units, and their functional linkage with higher ranking settlements, therefore, lagged. Commercial and industrial enterprises were concentrated in the few, larger urban nuclei, which developed at places where the local chieftains established their administrative headquarters. A pyramidal centralization of administrative and commerical functions (and in some instances of religious activities) in a few urban centers was thus established in ancient and medieval times. Under British rule (19th and early 20th centuries) a linear pattern of railroads linking these urban centers was established, especially in the north Indian plains, without a similar development of transverse feeding sub-branches to feed the smaller towns away from the linear axis. With the passage of time, ancient and medieval central places such as Patna, Allahabad, Delhi, Agra, Madurai and Thanjavur greatly increased in size as a result of railroad linkage and enlargement of their market functions. As modern highways were built, they tended to parallel the railroads and further polarized the settlement pattern. During this extension of the railroad and road network by the British great amounts of funds were spent to link the large cities and the hinterland with the ports, and "entirely too little allocated to build a network of roads" that would have helped to commercialize the rural landscape (Johnson, 157). A systematic, spatially graded central place development, containing interconnected transport and communication facilities, thus failed to evolve.

The movement of goods, capital, people, and entrepreneurship to cities, rather than their allocation in various size-categories of central places which are spatially dispersed in a regulated manner, has resulted in a further increase in the size of larger cities. Thus a structural dichotomy of dualistic economies has taken place which is represented by the tradition-bound, relatively inaccessible, self-contained village of small size on the one hand and a large, overcrowded, urban center in which trade, industry and professions are concentrated, on the other (Johnson, 152). Such a dualistic society with concentration of industry, trade and professions only in large urban centers and leaving rural subsistence economy in traditional socioeconomic order has divided society into two distinctive worlds—urban and rural. Between these two worlds, there is a striking deficiency of various size-categories of central places. Johnson calls it "central place deficiency," which is measured in terms of the ratio between villages on one hand and the urban centers on the other (Johnson, 174). Developed countries contain low ratios, suggestive of a lower "central place deficiency." India's high ratio indicates a highly deficient development of central places.

The pattern of central places in the north Indian plains around Kanpur is a representative illustration of the inadequate development of graded central places. Kanpur serves as a regional center for over 11,000 villages in an area of

17,000 square miles inhabited by over 10 million people. This entire area is served by only 30 medium-sized (10,000-20,000 population) market towns, dispersed in space, each serving an average of about 340,000 persons (mostly farmers). Only a few villages, located close to the communication routes (roads), are linked with the market centers. A government conducted survey of 1966 indicates that in this area virtually no produce (including such items as milk, poultry, fruits, vegetables and grain products) is transported further than 15 miles. Marketing is seriously limited by inefficient transport facilities. Over 4,000 villages with a combined population of 300,000 are not served by any road. About 5,500 villages are located more than 5 miles from any market. Only 30 percent of the villages are linked by a surfaced road with any market; 34 percent have the benefit of unsurfaced roads which become impassible in the rainy season (Johnson, 193-196).

Government planning has largely neglected development of a central place hierarchy of settlements, and has allocated only meager funds for this purpose in the Five Year Plans (1951-1983). The establishment of medium-sized and smaller cities acting as market for the countryside has not aroused sufficient enthusiasm, and the virtues of the village as a self-contained unit have been traditionally extolled. Most new development has been located in the proximity of an existing large city. Of the 397 new industrial estates established in India during the first three Five Year Plans (1951-1966), only a few were located near the medium-sized cities. This policy of developing large cities and locating most new industry close to them has only accentuated the regional differences. What is needed is the development of a network of coordinated and graded market places between the villages and the large cities which could commercialize the stagnant agrarian society and relieve the unplanned migration of surplus rural labor to the cities. Industries also need to be dispersed in the countryside in the form of a well-planned spatial clustering of related industrial enterprise in or near small cities that "will supply the necessary frame for the whole network of development sequence, linkages, and feedbacks upon which the successful transformation of . . . the countryside largely depends." (Johnson, 169). However, Johnson's controversial ideas have been criticized, par-

been criticized, particularly on grounds of initial heavy investments and the time-lag between investments and anticipated returns.

RURAL SETTLEMENT PATTERNS

The size, spacing and functions of settlements have been described in the previous section. This section deals with the spatial dispersion, site and morphological plan of the rural settlement forms. While the sites of Indian villages have generally been influenced by a number of physical factors (relief, geology, drainage, exposure to wind, rainfall and sun rays, etc.), their internal forms and house-plans have mostly been affected by a number of cultural factors, e.g., customs, caste and ethnic distributions, and cropping patterns. The great variety of Indian landscapes and their rich historical heritage means that settlement patterns range from the most nucleated (compact) to the highly dispersed (scattered). In general, settlements tend to be nucleated or compact in the dry farming areas of Punjab, western Uttar Pradesh, Rajasthan, northwest Maharashtra, Gujarat and relatively dispersed in areas of higher rainfall and wet farming in Bengal, Assam, Bihar, and Orissa. Highly dispersed settlements are also characteristic of the coastal areas of Kerala, the Ganga delta and in the Himalaya. Four variations of these two broad categories may be identified as major rural settlement types in the country: nucleated, clustered-and-hamlet mixed, fragmented and dispersed (Ahmed, 139).

Nucleated settlements characteristic of the western parts of the Indo-Gangetic plains, central India, northwestern Maharashtra, Gujarat and Rajasthan consist of a compact village surrounded by agricultural fields. Dry farming in areas of comparative aridity (rainfall less than 40 inches annual) imposes conservation of water in the village (2 or 3 wells or tanks) at selected points for efficient distribution to residences and irrigation channels for fields. Residences belonging to the lowest caste (untouchables) are often located in a separate section of the village or are not contiguous to the main village. A small street or vacant land usually separates their residences from those of the other castes. A combination of several factors has contributed to the nucleation of rural settlements in these areas: uniformity of relief, soil fertility, deep water-table, relative insecurity due to recurrent invasions during medieval times, and caste interdependence. Nucleated settlements also reflect the characteristic caste or clannish solidarity among the villagers. In the *tarai* areas of the Himalaya in the north Indian plains where rainfall is comparatively higher, nucleated villages have grown on safe and higher sites in response to regular seasonal inundations.

Cluster-and-hamlets, the second settlement type, is common in the transitional zone between the nucleated and dispersed types in eastern Uttar Pradesh and western Bihar, areas of adequate rainfall. Village buildings are generally located in one main nucleation, containing the main caste groups. This is surrounded by a few scattered hamlets belonging to minor caste groups of the village.

The third type, that of fragmented settlements consisting of clusters of residence spatially scattered in the village, is characteristic in regions where a number of lower castes predominate. Villages in this case do not, as a rule, contain any caste group with a clear majority. Such settlements predominate in western Bihar, northern parts of West Bengal, and Orissa.

The fourth type, the dispersed settlement, is common in the Himalaya (Himachal Pradesh, mountainous areas of northwestern Uttar Pradesh), and Kerala state in south India. An abundance of surface water, a multiplicity of castes and relative security from invaders during medieval and modern times have contributed to this pattern of settlements.

In the Himalaya, disposition of physical features, such as slope, soils and exposure to sun and wind, have inhibited nucleation of settlements. A variation of the dispersed type, a linear arrangement of dispersed residences, is common in Kerala, where residents are generally strung along a street backed by fields of paddy and other crops. In the Ganga delta region of West Bengal, residences are scattered in the fields, resulting in an extreme dispersal of settlement. The main reason for this is a plentiful water supply.

While there are many variations in the internal structure of rural settlements, two representative examples, one of a nucleated village in the dry farming area of Gujarat and the other of a dispersed village in the paddy farming area of West Bengal may be usefully selected for study.

The village of *Smiala* (population 1,400) is located 13 kms southwest of the commerical and industrial city of Baroda (population 300,000) in the dry farming area of Gujarat State. It is connected by a paved road with Baroda and with Padra, a small city located 3 kms away. There is regular bus service between Smiala and Padra. A narrow guage railroad line also links the village with Baroda. Because of its proximity to a large city and good interconnections with the surrounding area, a commercial economy has been slowly penetrating the village. In the last twenty years there has been a gradual decline of village handicrafts. People now commute to Baroda for the purchase of such manufactured items as cloth, sugar, kerosene, oil, and other daily provisions, most of which were previously obtained in the village.

Within the village there is strict residential segregation of the various castes (Figure 7.1). Brahmans (3 households), the higher castes, occupy the best location near the temple, *Panchayat* (village government headquarters) and the village well. Predominant Hindu castes are few: Patidars (cultivating proprietors), 32 households; Barias (agricultural laborers), 128 households; Banias (merchants), 4 households; and Vankars (weavers), 26 households. There are also 39 households of the Muslim community which form a class of tenant cultivators. Patidars live in the central location. Chamars (shoemakers), the lowest caste (untouchables), live in a small agglomeration divided from the rest of the village by a small gully. Caste hierarchy is revealed in the residential segregation as well as by the size and quality of houses. Better housing belongs to the upper castes of Brahmans and Patidars. Caste solidarity is strong. *Chamars* (an untouchable caste) are not allowed to use the main well of the village, despite legal sanctions against untouchability. The untouchables are also denied participation in the village festivals. They have their own well and a religious shrine. The landless laborers' lot is altogether miserable, and they are increasingly seeking jobs in Baroda (Fukutake, 102-5).

Supur village (population 580) lies in West Bengal, and is an example of a dispersed village characteristic of a wet farming area. The village is 6-1/2 kms from the nearest

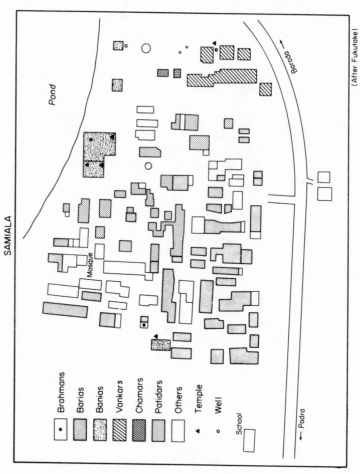

FIGURE 7.1

SUPUR

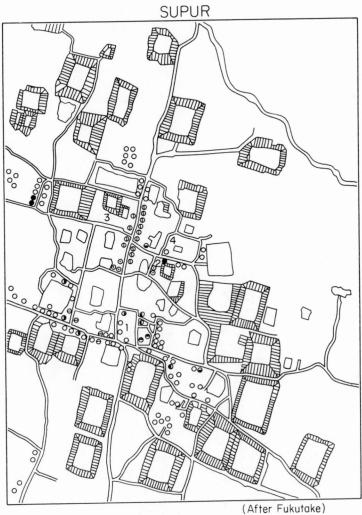

(After Fukutake)

- ● Brahmin
- ⊙ Baidya
- ◑ Kayastha
- ◐ Vaisha Saha
- ⊕ Dhopa
- ⊖ Suri
- ◓ Goala
- ◒ Baishnab
- ○ Others

1 - Panchayat Office, 2 - Zamindar Office, 3 - Goswami Temple
4 - Zamindar Temple

FIGURE 7.2

railroad station at Shantiniketan, and is connected with Bolpur by an uneven dirt track. Residences (117 households) are dispersed over a large area, lying close to the several ponds and tanks which are surrounded by the fields (Figure 7.2). Wide spaces between one house lot and the other are occupied by palm trees, brushes and grasses. Rainfall is over 70 inches annually and there is plenty of surface water, which is utilized in paddy fields and by the houses around the ponds. There is a greater diversity of caste groups (about 30) than in Smiala, in addition to the Muslim community and the tribal elements (Kora, Santal). Within the village, housing distribution suggests the existence of a line of social demarcation separating the untouchables (basketmakers, cobblers, fishermen) and tribal communities from the upper castes (Brahmans: 3 households and Kayastha: 4 households). Three households of landlord families own most of the village land. Land reforms since 1952 have transformed the peasantry into cultivating proprietors. There is, however, little desire for any change or improvement in agricultural technology on the part of the rich farmers who own most of the land and wealth, and who utilize the abundant supply of cheap labor formed by the lower castes. They are disinclined to invest capital in improvements, and are content with the current output from the land which supplies most of their needs. They are also content at their control over the exploited cultivating castes (Fukutake, 164-169).

INTERNAL URBAN FORMS

In internal forms, the urban settlement pattern of India occasionally is an intensified replica of the rural settlements, as for example, the urban duplication of village residential segregation patterns. Urban settlements, however, contain several additional features acquired during British rule.

Indian cities present a striking contrast to the American urban landscape. American cities are younger, exhibit an essential planning in their gridiron layout and the segregation of functional areas, and a basic internal morphological unity. Well-planned cities in India, on the other hand, are very few and of recent origin. The planned cities of Chandigarh and Bhubaneshwar and the industrial townships of

Bhilainagar, Durg, and Rourkela belong to this category and were developed in the last twenty years. Among the few notable exceptions to this general rule are the well laid-out, romantic capital city of Jaipur (built by Jai Singh, A.D. 1699-1743), old Delhi (Shahjahanabad), and the capital city of New Delhi, built by the British between 1911 and 1931.

The rich, almost chaotic cultural, economic and architectural diversities of the Indian urban landscapes are a product of a variety of influences, including different religions, languages, and caste groups; and finally of the impact of British colonial rule. Through the medieval ages, Indian cities grew into amorphous assemblages of "period" pieces (historical remnants belonging to various periods) and juxtaposed areas of diverse communities, without any basic unit of layout and function (Brush, in Turner's citation, 57-58). During the British occupation, the Anglicized sections (known as "Civil Lines") were added to the old, indigenous parts of the cities, producing a dichotomous situation of contrasting patterns of the juxtaposition of the old, congested, unplanned parts of the city with the spacious and laid-out new sections.

The Indigenous City

The older indigenous sections of the city (known in most cases as the "old city") are packed into a small space, usually a mile or less in diameter, but housing a majority of the city's total population. Streets are winding, irregular and narrow, made narrower by the protruding open shop fronts on the ground floor. The old city contains mostly one or two-story brick structures and is not uncommonly surrounded by walls and an outer moat, broken by a few gates (c.f., Delhi, Agra, Lucknow). The street pattern reflects the original defense consideration of containing residences, administrative offices, and religious shrines within the wall. Though essentially residential in character, the old city shares its limited space with commercial and industrial uses. Thus, "a melange of convoluted streets, cul-de-sacs, alleys and byways gives access to residences and commercial uses and much small industry encroaching . . . on the public right of way" (Breese, 64). Outside the wall and the "old city" street patterns are more regular. Only in the Peninsula are these patterns of the indigenous city absent.

Population densities are very high in the old city. Some parts of Calcutta contain about 1/2 million persons per square mile. Old Delhi has 350,000 persons per square mile and in parts of Bombay there are over 250,000 persons to a square mile. Under heavy population pressures the original land uses of residences have often disappeared. Dwelling units are often converted to shops or small factories, or subdivided to house more families. Thus, the high density of residences is compounded by a mixture of land uses: residential, commercial and industrial. Generally, the lower story contains commercial uses, whereas residences occupy the upper story. Service industry and in some instances small-scale industry are also interspersed in the residential areas. In general, residential areas are lacking in shopping facilities, open space, and such amenities as water supply and sewage.

Within residential areas, various communities are segregated into areal groups (neighborhoods known as *mohallas*) by caste, religion, occupations and regional associations, resulting in an essential lack of social cohesiveness. Brahmans and high castes are usually located in the best-built areas near the center of the old city. Mulsims live in separate *mohallas* and so do the "labor" castes. Menial outcasts or "untouchables" reside outside the walled portion of the city.

The hub of the retail merchandise activity, however, is the centrally located *chauk* (the main shopping area) or the *bazar*. It is crowded with countless small retail stores dealing in food, cloth, hardware, jewelry and other consumer goods. Bankers, moneylenders, health practitioners, dentists and public letterwriters all congregate here. Upper rooms of the buildings in the *chauk* are used as dwelling units. In larger cities, specialized services and goods tend to congregate into specific areas around the *chauk* and to develop into shopping subcenters or small bazars such as a cloth market, a grain exchange, a street of brassware, a bazar of goldsmiths or silversmiths or potterymakers. In these small bazars craftsmen perform their work and display their wares in an open front shop. There is also the ubiquitous cart peddler, who does his work (ranging from corn-roasting to fixing your eyeglasses) in the customer's presence, giving them a chance to supervise.

The density of streets and a functional mix in the old city is further complicated by a diversity of transportation in large urban areas. Pedestrian traffic is generally dense, although it fluctuates at different times of the day. Goods in the *chauk* are also in constant movement. Modes of transportation are many and varied — human, animal and vehicular. Between the sluggish donkey and the rapid commuter train (as in Bombay) are: tongacart, pedicab, motorcycle rickshaw, bicycle, oxcart, taxi, private automobile, handcart, trucks of several kinds, bus, and streetcar (as important modes of transportation of men and goods). The chaotic mixture of land uses produced by such diverse transportation facilities has been thus described by Breese, "The melange of facilities, sharing the right-of-way in generally uncontrolled fashion, is both the product and the creator of a high mix of land uses in Indian urban areas, especially in the old city sections" (Breese, 57). The old and the new, the bullock cart and the taxis jostle each other in chaotic complexity and the *chauk* is always humming with life.

Modern European Sections

In contrast to the hodgepodge settlement patterns of the old city are the modern well laid-out European sections of the cities. These were built mainly during the 20th century to house the British officers and civil administrators, the Christian missionary community and the growing elite community of Indian businessmen. Such sections are usually juxtaposed to the "old city" and contain such settlements as Civil Lines, Railway Colonies, Military cantonments, and new residential colonies. These modern sections present an aspect of comparative spaciousness, comfort, greenery, peace and functional zonation. The tree-lined streets are broad and well-surfaced, and follow a gridiron pattern. Buildings are constructed of brick and are frequently surrounded by large fences and landscaped lawns. House lots are distinctly marked and land use zonation is generally enforced.

The Civil Lines section typically is separated from the old city by a railroad and a transitional zone outside the old city walls. Originally designed during British rule to house offices and residences of non-military (civil) branches of the government at the district or province (now state) level, civil lines persist in most of their original functions. Public offices such as the district magistrate's (administrator) head-quarters, the tax collector's office, law courts, police bar-racks, the jail, the government printing press, a public li-brary, hospitals, and post and telegraph office are located here. In addition, hotels, cinema-houses, colleges, Euro-pean style clubs and stores, previously serving the needs of the British ruling class and the Indian elite groups all tend to be congregated in the Civil Lines, thus creating a second-ary "central business district" away from the old city *chauk*. Residences follow the Anglicized bungalow pattern of large houses containing spacious high-ceilinged rooms and a big verandah or porch in the front, admirably suited to the hot climate. During the post-Independence period densities in-creased within the Civil Lines with a concomitant growth of middle-class "colonies" along the fringes of the Civil Lines. These new "colonies" are intermediate in density and plan-ning between the old city and the Civil Lines.

The cantonments or the military stations are located far-ther apart in space, only occasionally merging with the civil lines. After the Indian Rebellion of 1857 large military establishments were set up in all parts of the country with regional headquarters in urban cantonments in order to quell any future national uprising. Cantonments are spa-ciously laid out in geometric street formations containing barrack-blocks with rows of residences for soldiers, separate officer bungalows, hospitals, churches, officers' clubs, pa-rade grounds, rifle ranges, ammunition depots and military supply warehouses. Cantonments are "the single most vora-cious land eaters in Indian urban areas" (Breese, 66). Usual-ly there is a small market area (*bazar*) mainly catering to the needs of the military personnel, although civilians from the nearby villages are also allowed to shop in the cantonment *bazar*. The entire cantonment complex is developed as a self-contained unit.

During and since the construction of the railroad net-work beginning in the later part of the 19th century, a large number of workers were engaged by the Indian railways. Large, sprawling colonies containing special subsidized quarters to house the railroad employees were constructed, usually along the railroad lines. These Railway Colonies ex-hibit a regularity of layout, a monotonous uniformity of structures and a graded hierarchy of housing amenities in direct relation to the wage scale and official status. Unlike the Indian tradition of the caste- and religion-based settlement pattern of the neighborhoods (*mohallas*), the residential plans of the colonies transcend considerations of castes, religions, and languages. In them a Punjabi Sikh occupies quarters beside a Tamil Brahman or a Malayali Christian. The commercial and industrial sections of the Railway Colonies are less crowded than their counterparts in the old city.

Since Independence, the federal government has constructed several colonies for employees working in its various civilian branches in New Delhi, Bhopal, Hyderabad and several other cities. These colonies resemble the Railway Colonies in their gridiron street pattern and residential segregation of employees according to their wages and official status, although housing amenities tend to be generally superior. Such government housing is frequently located at some distance from the place of work of the residents and the old city. Residents therefore must commute to work or shopping on bicycles or by city transit.

Despite the close justaposition of the old city and the newer European style colonies, there is usually a transitional zone containing a railroad station, bus depot and cinema theater, and a residential spillover from the old city. This transitional zone of commercial-cum-residential functions catering to the needs of the old and new sections of the city represents a fusion of the European and Indian mores.

Bustees

A special feature of most Indian cities in the last twenty years has been the mushrooming growth of *bustees* or shanty towns. These are composed of cells of makeshift hovels which house thousands of squatters created by the large and continuing stream of in-migrants from the rural areas. Unable to find housing in the old city, migrants to the cities have spread out into *bustees* which are usually strung along the perimeters of the built-up areas, but are occasionally found well within the municipal areas of the city. The resident squatters (illegal occupants) generally choose vacant or underdeveloped areas of the city, such as parks, abandoned quarry sites, railroad plazas, railroad sidings or even the vacant portions of new colonies or the civil lines. Squatters' housing usually consists of tin-roofed tenements or one-roomed structures of mud walls. These appear in clusters of a few to several thousand units and house one to several families, thereby producing very high density areas with few public amenities. Shanty towns have added to the existing urban problems of congestion, poor transportation, inadequate public services, and an absence of proper functional zonation, and they impede official efforts toward rational urban planning. Furthermore, as a result of the prevailing unhygienic conditions in the shanty towns, they have become the breeding grounds of several diseases which may spread into neighboring areas. Municipal authorities constantly attempt, albeit futilely, to contain or eliminate the *bustees* by dismantling them, only to discover their reappearance soon after.

Urban Fringes

With the expansion of the city, the nearby villages are usually incorporated into its fold as "rural enclaves." These "enclaves" are generally deficient in such civic amenities as sewage disposal, water supply and electricity, and offer low-cost housing especially for those engaged in small-scale industrial operations such as furniture making and yarn weaving and dyeing.

Since Independence several private residential colonies have also sprung up in spaces between the "rural enclaves" and the vacant areas close to the new city (civil lines, government colonies), although these colonies still represent a fraction of the construction of government colonies. Private colonies usually contain small suburban neighborhoods designed for the requirements of the middle-class and high-income groups. In format, these private colonies range from ill-planned imitations of the government colonies to well-designed versions of the foreign suburban development patterns. In general, such colonies are spaciously laid out and contain single-family, one or two-story structures on wide streets with a modified gridiron pattern. However, they suffer the great disadvantage of having inadequate public transit facilities to the rest of the city. Since high class shopping centers are still lacking in these colonies, the residents must usually commute to the old city *bazar* or civil lines district for shopping. As a result, most suburban growth has sought locations along the few established lines of movement leading to the city core. Deficient siting and planning, and uncontrolled growth of these colonies have created new problems of transport bottlenecks, and further taxed the provision of muncipal services.

URBAN GROWTH PATTERNS

As in other developing countries, the urbanization process represents growing modernization and economic progress. Indian cities have been acting as diffusion centers of culture and economic advancement.

A few admininstrative, religious and military centers were established during ancient and medieval times. In addition to their administrative and religious functions, these cities have acted as foci of economic, commercial, industrial and artistic activities. For centuries Pataliputra (Patna), Varanasi, Allahabad, Agra, Ujjain, Lahore and Madurai were well-developed cities. Several cities grew up as centers of pilgrimage (Hardwar, Gaya, Rameshvaram, Madurai) and have long been renowned for their shrines and temples. With these notable exceptions, large industrial-commercial cities belonging to pre-British times were few in number and generally archaic. Once established as religious or administrative centers, these cities acquired commercial and industrial functions as well. Their fortunes rose and fell with the frequent movement of the seat of government from one place to another during different dynastic rules.

Modern cities based on industry and trade were essentially developed as market centers during British occupation when the Indian ports were connected by paved roads and railroads with the inland areas of agricultural production and raw materials. Some old cities languished as a result of competition with these newly emerged cities, but several adjusted to the need for a changing functional role, and acquired a modern industrial and commercial base, shaking off their traditional handicraft industries. The establishment of modernized marketing facilities for the collection and distribution of agricultural materials, and the development of railroad transport helped quicken the growth of

TABLE 7.2

URBAN POPULATION 1901-1971

Year	Total Urban Population (Millions)	Percent Urban	Increase in Preceding Decade (Millions)	Increase in Preceding Decade (Percent)
1901	25.8	10.8	— — —	— — —
1911	25.9	10.3	0.1	0.4
1921	28.1	11.2	2.1	8.3
1931	33.5	12.0	5.4	19.1
1941	44.1	13.9	10.7	32.0
1951	62.4	17.3	18.3	41.4
1961	78.9	17.9	16.5	26.4
1971	109.1	19.9	29.9	37.8

Source: *Census of India,* 1961, 1971.

their commercial activities. By a process of accretion of functions throughout historical times, most cities became functionally diversified, combining commercial, industrial, administrative and religious functions. Single function cities, specializing in commerce, transport, recreation, public administration, or manufacturing activities were very few. Some notable exceptions were: Jamshedpur (iron and steel center in South Bihar); Ahmadabad (cotton textile manufacturing center in Gujarat); Bhilainagar, Durg, Rourkela (the three steel manufacturing cities developed since Independence); and Nangal and Sindri (fertilizer industry). New Delhi and Chandigarh were established as centers of public administration. Many of these also served as centers of wholesale trade, transport and services.

The British also established a unique set of secondary or summer capital cities in the hills, where most civil branches of the federal and state administration would move during the hot season (mid-April to mid-September) to escape the heat of the plains. Most "summer capitals" were connected with the plains by railroads or roads. Simla (federal summer capital until 1947), Darjeeling, and Ootacumund are some examples. During British rule, a number of single function hill-resort cities also grew up, such as Nainital, Dalhousie, Mussoorie, and Mt. Abu and Mahabaleshwar.

Until 1931 urbanization was slow and halting, suggesting a relatively low rate of economic development. India's level of urbanization in 1901 was roughly comparable to that of the United States in 1830. Since 1931 the rate of urbaniza-tion has quickened (Table 7.2). At the time of the 1971 Cen-sus, about 109 million persons lived in India's nearly 3,000 urban centers, an urban population outranked only by those of the United States, the Soviet Union and the People's Republic of China. Urban population is defined in Indian Census as that contained in places of 5,000 population with municipal status with three-fourths of its labor-force engag-ed in non-agricultural occupations. In addition, places with a population of less than 5,000, a density exceeding 1,000 persons per square mile, and a dominant non-agricultural base are classified as urban. In 1901 only 26 million persons (11.8 percent of the country's population) were classified as urban dwellers. By 1971 urban population had increased to about 109 million or 19.9 percent of the country's popula-tion. Three noteworthy trends of urban growth during the 20th century may be observed. First, urban population has been growing at a faster rate than the country's population during the five decades since 1921 (Tables 3.1 and 7.2). A faster rate of urban population growth indicates a net in-migration to the cities. Between 1951 and 1971, 17 million persons from rural areas moved to the cities. A second trend is the remarkably higher growth rate of the cities (popula-tion 100,000 and over). Not only have the cities been grow-ing rapidly, their share of the urban population has been progressively increasing. In 1901 there were 25 cities con-taining 23 percent of urban population. In 1971 their number increased to 151 absorbing 53.3 percent of the ur-ban population of the country. The growth of "millionaire" cities also shows a parallel trend. Their number rose from 2 to 8 during the same period, and they registered over eight-fold increase in their population. Thirdly, small towns with populations less than 10,000 remained nearly constant in their absolute population (7 million in 1901, 7.5 million in 1931, 6.6 million in 1971), partly resulting from a changed definition in 1961. Their share in urban population has been declining. During the five year plans most large public industrial undertakings (metallurgical, transport equip-

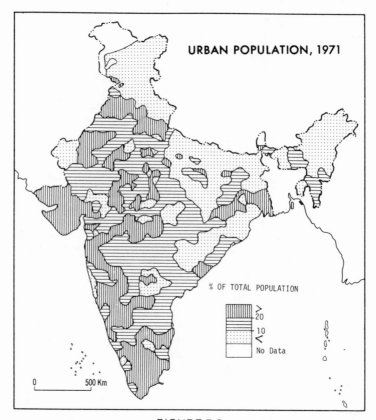

URBAN POPULATION, 1971

% OF TOTAL POPULATION

> 20

10

< No Data

0   500 Km

FIGURE 7.3

ment, manufacturing and chemical plants) have been located near the large cities. Small towns and medium-size towns
(10,000-100,000 population) have been growing at lower
rates than the cities (population over 100,000).

Regional Patterns of Urbanization

Until 1931 the main urban concentrations (over 40 percent of their population as urban) were Calcutta, Bombay,
Madras (the three major ports), and a few nuclei of modern
manufacturing, commerce and services. Areas of lesser urbanization (25 to 40 percent population as urban) were also
limited and were associated with those inland districts (civil
divisions) which contained large commercial, industrial and

administrative cities such as Lucknow, Delhi, Amritsar, Ajmer, Nagpur, Indore and Ahmadabad. By 1971 the urbanization patterns of 1931 had become intensified. Urbanization had extended along the main railroad and road links in the north Indian plains, the industrial area around Calcutta and the heavy industrial zones around Bangalore-Mysore, Madurai-Coimbatore, Ahmadabad-Surat, Kanpur, and in the Punjab as "urban corridors" (Figures 7.3 and 9.2). In 1971 districts in which large cities are located figured prominently as those containing a high rate of urbanization (over 50 percent of population as urban). Most districts in the country were at least 10 percent urbanized by 1971, and only a few districts with urbanization status less than 10 percent were found in the agriculturally stagnant parts of the middle, and lower Ganga Plains, non-irrigated sections of west Rajasthan, remote hilly tribal areas in the northeast frontier, the flood-prone Mahanadi Delta an southern Bihar.

Growth of urbanized population for the decade of 1961-1971 was 38 percent. Within the states growth of urbanization ranged from a high of 166 percent in Nagaland (an area very low in urbanization) to a low of about 24 percent in Punjab between 1961-1971. The regional patterns of urban growth during this period are presented in Table 7.3. These are at the state level and are of limited value, since Indian states are very large in size and display a wide diversity of development levels. Broad regional trends may, however, be noted.

One, states with a low level of urbanization experienced high growth rates. The backward states of Nagaland, Manipur, Orissa, and Assam, each containing less than 10 percent urban population saw this figure grow at faster than average rates. With the exception of Orissa, their high rates can be attributed to the emergence of new administrative cities in predominantly rural territories, and a continuing influx of refugees from Bangladesh and West Bengal to the urban centers. High growth rates in Orissa are associated with the growth of mining and industrial activity. Above average urban growth rates were also recorded in Bihar, Madhya Pradesh and Jammu and Kashmir showing evidence of change resulting from the new development plans, the building of transport links, exploitation of minerals and establishment of heavy industry.

TABLE 7.3

URBAN POPULATION OF STATES, 1961, 1971
(Percent of Urban Population to Total Population)

	1961	1971	Percent Growth 1961-1971
India:	18.0	19.9	37.8
Andhra Pradesh	17.4	19.3	33.8
Assam	7.4	8.4	*51.5
Bihar	8.4	10.0	44.4
Gujarat	25.7	28.1	41.2
Haryana	17.2	17.8	35.6
Himachal Pradesh	6.3	7.1	35.5
Jammu & Kashmir	16.7	18.3	42.0
Kerala	15.1	16.3	35.6
Madhya Pradesh	14.3	16.3	46.3
Maharashtra	28.2	31.2	40.6
Mysore	22.3	24.3	35.1
Nagaland	5.2	9.9	166.6
Orissa	6.3	8.3	63.5
Punjab	23.1	23.8	24.9
Rajasthan	16.3	17.6	38.0
Tamil Nadu	26.7	30.3	38.4
Uttar Pradesh	12.9	14.0	30.5
West Bengal	24.4	24.6	27.6
Territories:			
Chandigarh	82.8	90.6	134.7
Delhi	88.7	89.7	53.8
Manipur	8.7	13.2	109.2
Meghalaya	12.5	13.0	———
Tripura	9.0	7.8	18.2

*Includes Meghalaya

All figures are rounded off to one decimal.

Source: *Census of India, 1971,* Paper 1, pp.5, 12.

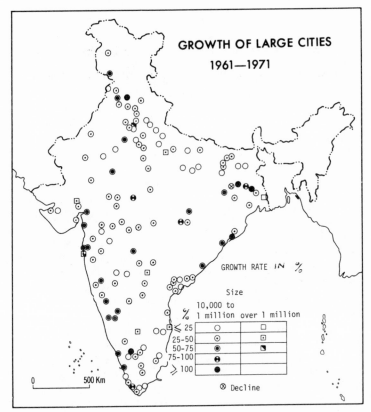

FIGURE 7.4

A second trend is the continuation of high growth rates for large cities, a trend which started in 1921. Figure 7.4 gives the location and growth of cities (over 100,000 population) between 1961 and 1971. As noted earlier, high growth rates for the cities are attributable to heavy in-migration. Since 1951, however, there has been a slackening in the growth rates as compared to the previous decades. This recent slowing in the acceleration of the growth of large cities suggests a slowing of in-migration, a situation perhaps resulting from rising unemployment in the large cities and a slight improvement of economic conditions in smaller cities and the countryside.

Thirdly, there has been an uneven spatial distribution of

the degree of growth rates (Figure 7.4), resulting largely from the development of selected locations of heavy industry established during the Third and Fourth five year plans (1961-1971). These industrial centers registered phenomenal increases: Dhanbad, 121.8 percent; Bhopal, 83 percent; Durgapur, 72 percent; Durg, 124 percent in the decade 1961-1971. Some administrative centers, such as Chandigarh and Bhopal (capitals of states) also grew over 75 percent.

The Role of Cities

Cities in India, as elsewhere, have been the centers of artistic and cultural diffusion. Patronized by the princes and feudal lords during ancient and medieval times, these centers attracted artists and artisans from far and near. In modern times, in addition to their cultural role, these centers have become the foci of manufacturing, trade and transport, thereby acting as reservoirs of varied employment opportunities. Thus, in the midst of a vast countryside still steeped in economic and cultural backwardness and apathy, urban centers propagate modern economic, social and political ideas. The cities are the places where social change originates and where the talent and organization necessary for the origin and execution of new ideas are available. Many cities function as administrative centers. They are also the loci of political and economic power for the propagation of administrative programs. Industrial and commercial enterprises are generally located in them. The combination of all these forces means that they are likely to play an influential role in the future development of the country.

Indian cities lead in the growth of literacy, in female education and in the fight against tradition and backwardness, and therefore help diffuse progressive modern ideas into the countryside. The census of 1971 reported 52.5 percent of India's urban population as literate, a figure well over twice that of the rural population (23.6 percent of rural persons are literate). Most centers of specialized learning in such fields as medical sciences, engineering, vocational education, commerce and law are concentrated in the cities.

Modernizing influences generated by theaters, cinema houses and libraries are largely urban phenomena. Recent sociological studies report that several progressive tendencies are gradually taking root in Indian cities: the growing functional inoperability of caste distinctions, the breakdown of traditional *jajmani* system (a client-patron relationship based on service rather than cash payments (discussed in Chapter 4), a more positive response to family planning programs, and the development of political consciousness. In sum, cities are acting as great tradition breakers and playing an innovating and stimulating role in the country.

Nor is the role of cities wholly confined to their municipal limits or areas in their immediate proximity. As the spatial connections between cities and villages are developed by new roads, feeder lines and railroads, rural life is increasingly being transformed. The traditional rural economy, based on the *jajmani* principle, is gradually being replaced by the monetized transaction and the goods and services produced by traditional handicrafts are being displaced by imports of machine-manufactured goods from the cities. As urbanization accelerates, the stationary subsistence rural economy will undoubtedly be inexorably drawn into a wider, expanding and capitalistic circle. On the social front, the power of the Brahmans, the landlords and the village elites, already loosening, will further decline as a consequence of the diffusion of democratic ideas originating in the cities.

One consequence of the growing rural-urban links has been the cityward migration of rural population. Cities continue to absorb the courageous, and perhaps the more talented of the rural in-migrants. This represents a new loss of rural leadership, for in-migrants to cities often fail to return to the countryside. Despite greater urban employment, job opportunities are more numerous in cities and wages are also higher. Incomes of immigrants rise appreciably after they move to cities (Ginsburg, 13).

Cities, especially the larger ones, have become major reservoirs for massive investment funds available through government planning and foreign aid programs. They thus tend to become the scene of most national development activity, new construction, industrial endeavor, commercial enterprise and educational opportunity. Since Independence, Indian cities have assumed a heightened role of economic power and responsibility.

PROBLEMS OF URBANIZATION

If urbanization has been an instrument of economic, social, and political progress, it has also been accompanied by serious socioeconomic problems. Indian urban growth during the last four decades has mostly proceeded without proper planning. Physical expansion of the cities has not kept pace with the rapid increases in their population and economic activities. This has resulted in excessively high population densities, substandard living conditions and the growth of slums. The average densities of population in large metropolises are extremely high. Delhi contains 22,000 persons per square mile, Greater Calcutta 36,000 and Madras 28,000. High urban densities, especially in central parts of the cities, have resulted from a large and continuing stream of rural immigrants. The first large flow of migrants to the cities was in the "depression" of the late 1930's, as men moved in search of jobs. Later, during 1941-51, another 9 million persons moved to cities in response to wartime industrialization and partitioning of the country in 1947. In-migration to the cities has now stabilized at about 1-1/2 to 2 million persons per year. The decade of 1961-1971 thus registered a movement of 15 to 20 million persons. This in-migration has been strongly felt in the central districts of the city (the "old city"), where the in-migrants flock to their relatives and old friends before they look around for housing. Population densities beyond the "old city" decline sharply. Brush refers to this situation of high density in the central parts of the cities as "urban implosion," which results from the concentration of people in the center of the city close to their work and shopping (Brush, 369).

One of the grave problems facing the rapidly growing urban areas is housing. Chronic overcrowding has led to enormous housing deficits. An Indian National Sample Survey in 1959 indicated that 44 percent of urban families (as compared to 34 percent of rural families) occupied one room or less. In larger cities the figure of families occupying one room or less rose to 67 percent (Turner, 280). Moreover, the current rate of housing construction is very slow. Indian cities require annually about 2 million new dwellings but less than 10 percent of the requirement is being constructed. Major factors responsible for slow construction are: a shortage of building materials and capital, inadequate expansion of public utilities into suburban areas, the extreme poverty of urban immigrants, strong caste and family ties with ancestral dwellings and places of work in old sections of the city, and the lack of adequate transportation to suburban areas where most vacant land for new construction is located. The situation regarding the building needs of non-residential development is equally depressing. Old buildings are grossly inadequate and obsolete for the spatial requirements of manufacturing, commerce, transport and service activities. In the absence of effective planning, this has led to a haphazard distribution of factories, warehouses, workshops, transport terminals, etc. This lack of zonation, along with the restricted availability of open spaces and inadequate public utilities, has made living conditions in several cities harsh and has jeopardized the smooth functioning of the economy. Without massive government aid there does not appear to be any immediate or long-range solution to the housing problem.

Problems of unemployment, poverty and destitution are no less serious. Urban unemployment, nation-wide, is estimated at 10 to 20 percent of the labor force, and is even higher among the educated population. About one-half of all the educated unemployed in the country are concentrated in the four largest cities. Furthermore, urban incomes, although higher than those in rural areas, are nonetheless appallingly low. Twenty percent of the urban families surveyed in the early 60's reported incomes below Rs. 130 ($16) per month. Nearly one-third of the urban population lived in poverty.

The task of Indian urban development is undoubtedly a difficult one and is linked with the broad question of economic health of the country. It has been pointed out that "the prospects for India's urban future will remain clouded until employment opportunities increase, ·production in non-agricultural sectors of economy is accelerated, and a substantial rise in incomes makes available the savings and investment necessary for urban expansion. . . . Urban development is merely a piece of the whole fabric of (the country's) economic development" (John Brush in: Zelinsky, 300-310).

How and in what regions should India's future economic development take place? Two opposing views with regard to

the future locational strategy in Indian economic development have been expressed. Spearheaded by Lewis and
Johnson, a strong plea has been made for a planned decentralization of India's industrial development and its reloca-
tion in medium-sized and small cities (population 20,000-
30,000) (Lewis, 197-199; Johnson, 157-177). Harris has
advocated a contrary view favoring the expansion of large
cities and centralizing future small-scale industries in them
in order to maximize the returns from a smaller resource
being invested at the on-going centers of activities (Britton
Harris in: Zelinsky, 271-274). Both views, however, highlight the urgent need for urban and regional planning. In
view of the acute and chronic problems of urban congestion,
high unemployment and scarcity of available funds, there
appears a need for development of small-scale industry in
medium-sized cities within the broader framework of regional planning. Currently, there is a lack of such a focus
in the location strategy of urban and regional economic
development. Persuasive arguments have been advanced
favoring replacement of the existing polarized development
concentrated in large metropolitan and rural areas by a
"technologically progressive, . . . geographically decentralized society organized along town-centered . . . lines along
with the development of villages" (Lewis, 173-200). This
plan envisages the location of new or expanded industrial
enterprises in different size-categories of settlements: (1)
villages, (2) medium sized cities and satellite towns proximal
to large cities. According to the plan the location of small
agro-industries in villages and medium-sized cities will maximize the proximity of agriculture to concentrations of industrial and commerical activity. A dispersed industrialization would help provide the kind of market environment
that Indian agriculture needs, supplying the necessary network of development sequence and linkage between the
polarized worlds of large cities and villages. In such a
scheme, within these intermediate level cities, an integrated
development of small local processing and fabricating enterprises, with the promotion of agro-industrial markets, has
been proposed. It is further suggested that such a development of intermediate level cities would absorb a part of the
migration stream which now crowds the larger Indian cities.
This migration stream could fruitfully be utilized in new ac-

tivities in the villages and in new agro-industries of the medium sized cities. The development of a graded hierarchy of settlements thus envisaged would be comprised of villages, medium-sized cities and large cities, which can become centers for production, trade and services offering employment opportunities for the young people who now are migrating to the metropolitan areas (Johnson, 167-171).

CITATIONS AND SELECT BIBLIOGRAPHY

Ahmad, E., "Rural Settlement Types in the Uttar Pradesh," *Annals of the A.A.G.* Vol 42, 1952, pp. 223-246.

Area Handbook for India. Washington, D.C., 1970.

Berry, B. J. L., and Spodek, H., "Comparative Ecologies of Large Indian Cities," *Economic Geography.* Vol. 47 (suppl.), pp. 266-285.

Brush, J. E., "The Spatial Patterns of Population in Indian Cities," *Geographical Review.* Vol. 58, 1968, pp. 362-391.

Breese, G., *Urbanization in Newly Developing Countries.* Prentice Hall, Inc., 1966.

Chandra Sekhar, A., *Census of India.* 1971, Paper 1 of 1971.

Das Gupta, J., *Language Conflict and National Development.* Berkeley, 1970.

Fukutake, T., *Asian Rural Society.* Seattle, 1967.

Ginsburg, N., "From Colonialism to National Development: Geographical Perspectives on Patterns and Policies," *Annals of the Association of American Geographers.* Vol. 63, 1973, pp. 1-22.

India: A Reference Annual. New Delhi, 1973, 1977-78.

India: Town and Country Planning Organization, "Land Use Pattern of India's Cities and Towns," *Urban and Rural Planning Thought.* Vol. 11, 1965, pp. 188-190.

Johnson, E. A. J., *The Organization of Space in Developing Countries.* Cambridge, Mass., 1970.

King, A. D., *Colonial Urban Development.* London, 1976.

Lall, A. and Tirtha, R., "Spatial Analysis of Urbanization in India," *Tijdschrift voor Economische en Sociale Geografie.* Vol. 62, 1971, pp. 234-248.

Lewis, J. P., *Quiet Crisis in India.* Washington, D.C., 1962.

Market Towns and Spatial Development in India. New Delhi
     National Council of Applied Research, 1965.
Mitra, Asok, *Delhi, Capital City.* New Delhi, 1970.
Mookherjee, D., *et. al., Urbanization in a Developing Eco-
     nomy, Indian Perspectives and Patterns.* Berkeley,
     1973.
Murphy, Rhoads, "Traditionalism and Colonialism: Chang-
     ing Urban Roles in Asia," *Journal of Asian Studies.* Vol.
     29, 1969, pp. 67-84.
Owen, W., *Distance and Development: Transport and Com-
     munications in India.* Washington, D.C., 1968.
Singh, R. L., (ed.), *India: Regional Studies.* International
     Geographical Congress, India, 1968.
Singh, R. L., (ed.), *India: A Regional Geography.* Varanasi,
     1971.
Spate, O. H. K. and Ahmad, E., "Five Cities of the Gangetic
     Plain," *Geographical Review.* Vol. 40, 1950, pp. 260-
     278.
Turner, R., (ed.), *India's Urban Future.* Berkeley, 1962,
     especially chapter by John E. Brush.
Zelinsky, W., *et. al., Geography and A Crowding World.*
     New York, 1970, particularly John E. Brush's article:
     "Some Dimensions of Urban Population Pressure in
     India," pp. 279-304.

CHAPTER 8

INDUSTRIALIZATION: BASES, DEVELOPMENT AND DISTRIBUTION

India has been the traditional home of refined consumer-oriented manufactured items since pre-Christian times, although its modern large scale industry is of recent growth. A base for industry had been laid during the pre-Independence period, but the colonial authority did not push vigorously for industrial modernization. Despite its potentially large market and resource endowment, industrial development of the country remained limited. The railroad established by the British was geared to administrative convenience and exploitation of raw materials with export potential. Industrial growth remained spotty and limited.

At the present time (of a labor force of 220 million) only 5.5 million are employed in about 64,000 factories, of which 14,000 are registered and regulated. Additionally, about 20 million work in cottage industries of handloom spinning or village crafts. The latter have a long and distinguished heritage in Indian economy.

In general, Indian industry is labor-intensive. Nearly 85 percent of the establishments are small units employing less than 10 workers. Capital-intensive, power based, efficient scale of operation has been generally limited to the public sector. A relatively under-developed technological-managerial base, comparative capital deficiency, dependence on imported machines (much reduced since the 60's) have resulted in low per-worker production.

These shortcomings apart, industrial production has nearly tripled since Independence, the largest expansion being in the manufacturing of heavy machinery, engineering goods and chemicals. Textiles, heavy metallurgical and engineering products dominate industrial production, others

273

TABLE 8.1

INDUSTRIAL EMPLOYMENT AND OUTPUT
(Percentage Distribution)

	Persons Employed	Value Added by Manufacturing
Textiles	27.8	21.2
Iron and Steel	8.6	10.6
Chemicals	4.6	10.8
Non-electrical machinery	5.1	5.2
Electrical machinery	3.9	4.7
Sugar	3.0	3.6
Paper	1.6	1.8
Rubber	1.3	2.5
Cement	1.0	1.6
Food processing	5.8	3.0
All other industries	37.3	35.0

Source: *India, Pocketbook of Economic Information,* Government of India, New Delhi, 1972, p. 79.

occupying a minor position. Table 8.1 indicates the relative significance of various industries (as of 1968).

Industry in the private sector accounts for over 70 percent of the industrial labor force. The government announced its Industrial Policy in 1956, demarcating areas of jurisdiction with some overlaps. Heavy metallurgical and engineering, petrochemical, pharmaceutical, aircraft, defense, nuclear and shipbuilding industries were placed in the public sector. Manufacturing of sugar, textiles, paper, cement, and light-engineering goods were to be developed in the private sector.

GROWTH OF MANUFACTURING

Indian manufactured goods ranked with those produced in China and the Byzantine Empire during ancient and medieval times. The 4th century A.D. wrought-iron pillar near Delhi and the "sheer" Dacca "muslins" are testimonials to the quality of products manufactured in India. Industrial decline, however, set in by the latter part of the 19th century in the face of competition from cheap British goods. Colonial policy of the British favored the development of "home" industries in England, and kept India merely as a provider of raw-materials or as a consumer of British products.

As early as the 4th century B.C. North India was dotted with flourishing manufacturing centers. Kashi (Varanasi), Mathura, Vanga (Bengal), Kalinga (Orissa), Ujjain were important cotton textile centers. Magadh (Bihar) and Pundra (Bangladesh) were famous for the woolen fabrics. Silverware, gold ornaments, furs, skins and perfumes were other important products. Smelting technology was well advanced. Brisk domestic and intercontinental trade in gold, silverware and iron products existed. An efficient and elaborate economic organization dealing with the production and trade of crafts and mining was in operation.

Contemporary Greek historians chronicle the flourishing status of trade and manufacturing during the first four centuries of the Christian era. Both Ptolemy's *Geography* and the *Periplus* (of anonymous authorship) mention that the coasts of India were studded with trading ports, chief among these were Bargaza, (Bhroach) and Muziris (Cochin), all carried on trade with the Greek and Roman ports. Major items of export were cotton, silk, pepper, ivory, aromatics and precious stones. Imports consisted of wines, clothing, glass and coins.

Manufacturing continued to flourish, but trade had declined during the medieval times as India became more self-centered. During the period of Mughal rule (16th-17th centuries) Indian art, culture and crafts had reached their zenith. New manufacturing techniques were developed by artisans and craftsmen.

By the middle of the 18th century, the Europeans had developed commercial contacts with India and had established trading posts or factories along the coasts. By the early 18th century they had consolidated themselves as traders-rulers not only along the coasts, but in the North Indian plains as well. The European posts were heavily fortified and wereself-sufficient. Their commercial and manufacturing activities consisted mainly of the production of ornaments and textiles. These fortified posts, in due course, became foci for inland commerce and military penetration. Principal among the manufactured items during the 18th and 19th centuries were textiles whose production had become a highly specialized activity. Fabrics such as taffeta, muslin, percale, gingham and satin were produced for the domestic market. Other items produced were brassware, carpets, silk, silverware and pottery.

By 1850 manufacturing, however, remained in the craft state and in the rural areas. Initially the urban centers along the railroad lines (established by the British) became collection and transit points for domestic trade. As communication links were improved, for example, paving the roads, supply lines were facilitated. Government establishments mainly produced gunpowder, ammunitions, arms and military uniforms. Major manufacturing centers during the early 20th century using factory techniques and modern machines were confined to a few locations (Calcutta, Varanasi, Lucknow, Agra, Delhi, Jaipur, Bombay, Madras, Pune, Hyderabad and Jamshedpur).

Even as these commercial industrial centers were developing, the focus of economic, social and political organization was the village-centered craft manufacturing based on the traditional *jajmani* system. In a typical self-sufficient rural organization, craftsmen, carpenters, smiths, tailors, oilcrushers, potters, weavers and others were supported by a fixed annual payment in kind by the landlords or clients. The producers belonged to certain castes and depended on the client-castes for livelihood. Little was produced beyond local demand. Luxury items (silk fabrics, jewelry, ivory carving) were manufactured in urban centers and the capitals of the princely states. The village-produced artifacts were immune to the price-mechanism of the cash-structured urban society.

With increased urbanization and commercialization, village-produced goods slowly became unable to cope with the increased demands from the growing cities, nor could these compete in price with the urban-made goods. Urban factories began to pour forth large quantities of cheap products. Rural crafts soon became uneconomic. The *jajmani* system was weakened, resulting in the flight of craftsmen to agricultural activities and newly developing industries.

Most of the railroad system was laid between 1840 and 1880. This facilitated the movement of such raw materials as tea, cotton and jute to the ports for processing. British colonial policy particularly favored the import of manufactured cloth from Britain to boost the Lancashire textile industry. Between 1860 and 1880 Indian exports of raw cotton increased from £25 to £55 million, which accounted for 50 percent of Indian exports. Finished cloth imports from Britain surged from £7 million to £25 million during the same period.

As domestic demand for textiles increased, cotton mills were opened in Sholapur, Bombay, Nagpur and Ahmadabad, in the country's major cotton-producing region. With the exception of iron and steel manufacturing, cotton textiles remained the only large scale industry in the country. In 1900 it employed nearly one-third of all factory workers (of a total of about 1 million).

In the intervening years between World War I and World War II, factory employment increased to 1.5 million, reflecting the textile industry's expansion and also the expansion of war-based industries (gunpowder, arms, ammunition). Other industries were growing slowly. In 1939 India's steel production was 1 million tons, and coal production 28 million tons. Industrial employment had risen to 1.8 million.

Recent Industrial Growth

In addition to the traditional industries of sugar, leather products and rural crafts, at least two modern industries: textiles and iron and steel, had been established during British rule. The foundations of industrial institutions had also been laid, and there existed a small class of experienced entrepreneurs. As of 1950 the industrial sector, however, was a very small one. Registered and regulated industries utilized a mere 2 percent of the labor force, and contributed only 6 percent to the net domestic product. Textiles continued to dominate the industrial sector.

Since Independence, Indian planners have always considered industrial growth to be a catalyst for the rapid economic transformation of the country, and accorded the development of the industrial base a central place in the Five Year Plans. Central to the creation of a sound industrial base were two premises: first, the development of heavy industry would lay a foundation for the development of other industries, second, (related to the first) only sound development of the industrial sector would make the country economically independent of foreign sources for capital goods and machinery production. For such an industrial development, government planning rested on three basic assumptions. First, the country, with its vast market base, would provide an adequate level of effective demand. Secondly, the complex industrial structures demanding technical knowledge would be domestically available. Assured domestic demand was altogether lacking in the 1950's and 1960's, and grew at a much slower pace than anticipated. In technical base, the country was obliged to depend on imports. Thirdly, Indian planners were confident of building adequate domestic capital formation required for developmental programmes. Such was not the case. The creation of domestic capital continued to lag and had to be replenished by large foreign aid infusions. Large imports of heavy machinery and food crops during the 1960's undoubtedly aggravated the foreign aid situation. Moreover, domestic production of such exportable goods as tea, jute, iron-ore, mica, coir, cotton goods and sugar did not experience the targeted phenomenal expansion which would have created a surplus balance of trade. Despite restrictive import policy, substitution and export stimulation, negative trade balances during the Second and Third Plans (1951-1956 and 1956-1961) continued to create problems of foreign aid and hard currency.

Industrial production was slow during the early 1950's, growth rates oscillating between 3 and 6 percent per year. It rose to 8 percent between 1953 and 1956, reverted to a little over 4 percent in the late 50's. Development picked up after that, averaging a healthy 10 percent a year during the early mid 60's. Index numbers of most manufacturing items jumped substantially particularly in the production of heavy machinery and electric machinery. Industrial employment rose at an annual rate of 6 percent. Production of consumer goods and light engineering items, however, registered poor growth performance. Only the tea and sugar industries showed some advancement, but domestic demand for these items had been rising faster. Meanwhile, foodgrain imports had been fast rising, particularly after the serious droughts of 1966 and 1967. Recurrence of droughts in 1972, and the wars with China and Pakistan during the 60's led to industrial stagnation. By 1973, it had become quite clear that emphasis on heavy industry had to be relaxed, and that a reorientation toward the development of a diversified and integrated system of graded industry broadly-based to cover rural-urban needs and capable of mobilizing a vast, idle rural-urban labor force was required. This reorientation was reflected in the policy statements of the Fourth, Fifth and Sixth Plans (1969-1974, 1974-1979 and 1978-1983).

The need to create an industrial base for the rural and mid-sized urban centers recognized by the Fourth and Fifth Plans was largely obscured by the emphatic importance given to heavy industry (heavy metallurgical products, locomotives, heavy machine manufacture, etc.) in the earlier Plans. All these items are capital-intensive, rather than labor-intensive. Although the Fourth Plan did not entirely forsake the development of petro-chemicals (new plants set up at Bombay and Koyali near Baroda), steel manufacture, and the production of cement, paper and fertilizer, all of which recorded moderate growth. Emphasis on these was relaxed to further the growth of chemicals, fertilizer and light engineering goods, with greater private-sector participation. Domestic demand for these items was rising fast in response to the modernization process which accompanied the "Green Revolution." While these industries were not directly labor-intensive, they did create a base for the development of ancillary, small-scale agro-industries which created additional employment opportunities. An example of the growth of small-scale engineering and metal industry is the development of an industrial-urban corridor (Figure 9.2) between Delhi and Amritsar in Haryana and Punjab states to include the industrial centers of Karnal, Ambala, Ludhiana, Jullundur and Amritsar, oriented to the production of such items as bicycles, sewing machines, tractors and automobile parts.

In an effort to diversify and decentralize the industrial base several industrial estates were set up during the 50's and 60's. These were located close to cities in order to make use of the existing infrastructure. Industrial estates contain small-scale industries and produce diverse goods ranging from consumer products such as textiles, light engineering goods and small machines, watches, bicycles and handicrafts. These public sector, low-capital enterprises were occasionally housed in shed-like structures and made use of the local semi-skilled labor force. In 1962, there were 71 estates containing 138 factories located in different parts of the country. These employed 19,000 persons, and producing 20 million dollars worth of goods. By 1972 the number had gone up to 40 estates employing 23,350 persons. The Fifth Plan's outlay for expansion of estates amounted to 18 million dollars.

The policy of industrial decentralization was mainly limited to setting up industrial estates. It hardly affected the spatial pattern of industry which was concentrated in a few foci. Some spatial dispersal has recently started, especially in sugar, textiles, cement and paper industries. A special feature of the Fifth and Sixth Plans was the development of industrially backward areas. 229 districts out of a total 355 were identified as backward and eligible for grant loans. No effort is made, however, to draw a coherent, national plan of industrial decentralization based on the policy of a spatially-integrated development of industrial expansion bridging the rural-urban dichotomy.

DISTRIBUTION OF INDUSTRY

At the close of colonial rule, industrialization was localized in a few major ports and scattered inland urban-commercial nuclei. The post-Independence period, particularly since the mid-1950's witnessed a process of intensification of industrial growth in the existing areas and the emergence of a few new industrial-urban nuclei. Large, uninterrupted stretches of manufacturing units covering the landscape and profoundly affecting the economy, transport and life-styles of the inhabitants, were only beginning to be formed. In scale, degree of manufacturing activity and the impact on landscape, such areas could be termed "nascent industrial regions." These could hardly be compared to the manufacturing regions of the U.S.A. or Britain where industrialization overwhelmingly affects large tracts of land. In India, within the nascent regions, large stretches of rural countryside remain virtually unaffected by the industries of

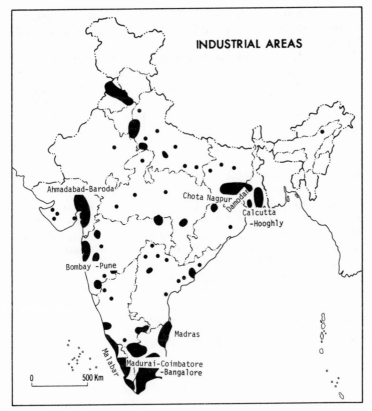

FIGURE 8.1

urban centers. Six major industrial areas or nascent regions which come closest to a typically Western analogue of an industrial region can be discerned in Figure 8.1. Calcutta-Hooghly side employs about 750,000 workers, Bombay-Pune some 670,000 and Ahmadabad-Baroda 330,000 while the Chota Nagpur region in South Bihar, Madurai-Coimbatore-Bangalore and the southern Kerala coast manufacturing region are also significant. In all, these six areas account for one-half or 2 million of the country's industrial labor force of the country.

Calcutta-Hooghly side area is a sprawling 50-mile industrial conurbation along the Hooghly river (a tributary of the River Ganga). Besides Calcutta, other major industrial centers located in this area are: Kanchanpura, Bhatpara, Chandernagore, Naihati, Barrackpur, Titagarh, Serampur, Dumdum, Bally, Alipur and Howrah. Jute textile manufacturing is the main industry, absorbing nearly 40 percent of the industrial workers, followed by engineering, chemical, food processing and paper industries. The English and the French selected Calcutta as a convenient site of access from the Bay of Bengal to the North Indian Plain at the mouth of River Hooghly in the 17th century. Soon it became a focal point of Indo-British trade, although it lost a part of its hinterland to Bombay after the opening of Suez Canal in 1869. In 1912 it further lost some additional industrial functions when the capital of India was moved inland to New Delhi. Its primary functions as the premier jute manufacturing center persisted, however, based on its location in the world's leading jute producing region. The development of railroads across the Ganga Plains as the British administration fanned out across North India during the early 20th century enhanced Calcutta's connections and commerce.

Partition struck hard at the jute industry by removing its major source of raw jute in the Ganga-Brahmaputra Delta. Problems of refugees from East Bengal further aggravated the economic situation. Problems multiplied as the original site became prone to innundation and constant silting. Population congestion, poor communications with the industrial units, power and water supply breakdowns and political turmoil all contributed to its industrial stagnation in the early 1950's. Recent improvements in port facilities include channel deepening and the construction of a deep water access port at Haldia near the mouth of the Hooghly River, both designed to allow access by oil tankers. An oil refinery for processing imported oil has been constructed near Haldia. In 1976 an up-stream dam was built at Farakka to relieve the problems of silting and water shortages. Recovery since the 1950's has also been a result of its inherent locational advantages, such as proximity to India's chief mineral belt of Chota Nagpur, and to the power and navigation resources of the Damodar Valley Corporation (D.V.C.). The country's three major foreign exchange earners—tea, jute, and jute textiles, accounting for 40 percent of country's total export earnings—pass through the port.

Bombay-Pune (Poona) area includes the industrial centers of Bombay, Pune, Ambarnath, Pimpri, Trombay, Nasik and Tarapore. Textile industries long-time dominant, account now for forty-one percent of the manufacturing labor force. Diversification since 1945 has led to the growth of other industries, particularly engineering, chemicals, pharmaceuticals and petroleum-based products. Shipbuilding, electrical, automobile, film and food-processing are also important. Coal hauling from the distant Damodar Valley fields in South Bihar has been a major problem, but is now largely offset by the development of hydroelectricity in the nearby power plants located on the steep western edge of the Western Ghats. India's first major nuclear plant is close by at Trombay. Oil refining is located in the nearby Cambay region where oil has been recently discovered.

Bombay's initial advantages as a port closest to Europe have gained added importance as being nearest to the Middle Eastern oil and for the exports of finished textile and electrical goods to the Middle East and African market. The entreprenurial experience and skill of the Parsi houses (Tatas being one of these) have transformed the area into a leading manufacturing region of the country.

The industrial area of *Ahmadabad-Baroda* lies north of the Bombay-Pune industries and specializes primarily in cotton textile manufacturing, which consumes over 75 percent of the industrial labor force. Chief centers are Ahmadabad, Jamnagar, Surat, Baroda, Rajkot and Kaira. Lying in the heart of the cotton-growing region, the textile industry enjoys a decided locational advantage. Entrepreneurial experience is amply provided by India's traditional business community of the Gujaratis. Surat is an important silk manufacturing center as well. Non-textile industries include the manufacture of chemicals and light engineering goods. Baroda is an important center of chemicals and pottery manufacture. The development of Kandla as a new port has significantly contributed to the recent expansion of industry.

Chota-Nagpur-Damodar Valley industries owe their location chiefly to their proximity to India's major coalfields of Jharia, Raniganj, Bokaro and Burnpur. The major iron and steel centers of Durgapur and Asansol are located in the

Damodar Valley, as are also the plants of Kulti, Burnpur, and Bokaro. Sindri has a major fertilizer plant. The country's oldest and largest ironsteel plants (Tata Iron and Steel Works) of Jamshedpur and that at Rourkela developed during the Five-Year Plans are in the Chota Nagpur Plateau.

The Damodar Valley Corporation (D.V.C.) supplements coal-based power to the industry by provision of hydroelectric and thermal energy. A variety of minerals; bauxite, iron-ore, copper, manganese, are found in this India's leading mineral-belt and are utilized by the industry. As a result, the Chota Nagpur and the Damodar Valley area has become a leading region of heavy iron and steel manufacture. Other industries include the manufacture of chemicals, fertilizers, and light engineering goods. Calcutta's commercial and port facilities are nearby, within a radius of 200 miles.

In South India *Madurai-Coimbatore-Bangalore* form an important manufacturing zone. Nearly one-half of the manufacturing labor force is engaged in cotton textile industries. Bangalore has diversified industries: aircraft, automobile, telephone and locomotive manufactures, all primarily in the public sector. High grade coal is hauled from the distant Chota Nagpur Plateau, but hydroelectric power is accessible within easy distance in the Nilgiri Hills. Iron-ore is available nearby. Industrial location is favored by relatively mild climate at about 3,000 ft. altitude. Most production is consumed at home, but exports to the Middle East and African countries are steadily growing. Madras acts as a major port for the goods.

Malabar Coast contains several industrial centers: Cochin, Ernakulam, Alwaye, Kozhikod, Quilon, Trichur and Kalamasary. Food processing industries based on the local products of the plantations and fishing areas predominate, such as rice-milling, coconut oil extraction, soap-making and shrimp canning. Oil refining and fertilizer manufacturing are other industries. Cochin is a major port.

Figure 8.1 also shows all urban centers of 100,000 and over which contain a large industrial component.

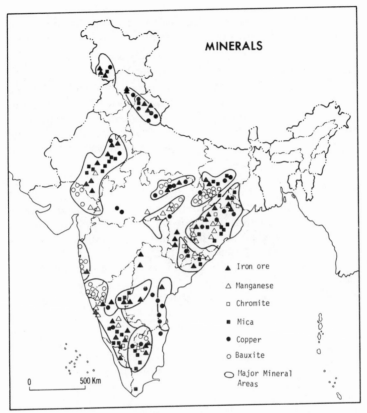

FIGURE 8.2

MINERAL RESOURCE BASE

India is well-endowed with major minerals basic to the development of industrialization. It ranks high among world producers of iron-ore, coal, mica and manganese. Its high-grade iron-ore (*Fe* content over 55 percent) reserves are the largest in the world; manganese reserves are extensive and production of mica provides nearly 75 percent of the world's output. Reserves of chromite, bauxite, kyanite and lime-stone are also considerable. A major deficiency is that of petroleum which must be imported in substantial amounts particularly to meet with its rising demand created by fer-tilizer manufacture. Discovery of off-shore oil along the

Gujarat-Cambay coast, with seemingly large potentials is likely to ease the situation.

Major mineral-bearing areas (Figure 8.2) are dispersed primarily south of the North Plains in the Deccan Plateau; a few lie in the Himalaya. The northeastern section of the Deccan Plateau is country's major mineral belt. Principal mineral concentrations lie in close association with rocks of the Palaeozoic Era. Mineral areas outside the Chota Nagpur Plateau are in Karnataka and in East Rajasthan-Madhya-Pradesh.

India ranks seventh in the world (after the U.S.A., the Soviet Union, China, the United Kingdom, Poland and West Germany) in the production of coal. The production is nearly 80 million tons annually or 3.5 percent of the world production. Production has gone up rapidly since Independence (nearly two-and-a-half times), and so have requirements which, by the end of the Fifth Plan in 1979 are estimated to rise to 135 million tons annually. To achieve self-sufficiency an annual growth rate of 13 percent is targeted during the Plan. Proven reserves are large, placed at 24 billion tons by the Geological Survey of India in 1972, but about a quarter of these lie outside easy reach below the surface. Quality is also poor. High-quality near-surface coking coal, suitable for the metallurgical industry is obtained in small quantities from the coalfields of Bihar in Jharia. At the present rate of consumption India's near-surface coke could last only for 30 years. The reserves of non-metallurgical coal are larger, currently estimated at 115,000 million tons, but their production costs are high.

Electricity generating stations, steel mills and railroads consume 65 percent of the total coal production. The two states of Bihar and West Bengal supply nearly three-fourths of the total production. Major fields are Raniganj, Jharia, Bokaro and Giridih in the Damodar Valley. Mines have thick, near-the-surface, easily extractable seams of moderate quality. Fields of Madhya Pradesh, Godavari Valley and at Singreni in Andhra Pradesh, together contribute 15 percent of India's production. Minor fields are Umaria and Talchar in Madhya Pradesh and in lower Mahanadi Valley.

Some coal of tertiary age is mined in Assam and utilized in tea factories. Lignite is also extracted from Neyveli mine near Madras and is used for the production of electricity and in the fertilizer industry. The Fifth Plan aims at raising lignite production to six million tons by 1979.

The location of major fields in the Chota Magpur Plateau has helped the growth of Jamshedpur as a major iron and steel center, but it is distant from such other industrial areas as Bombay, Hyderabad, Madras, and the growing light engineering industries in Punjab and Haryana. Nearly 40 percent of the coal demand of the states of Punjab and Tamil Nadu remain unmet largely because of the shortage of the hopper cars and the inability of the railroads to make the necessary transfers.

Indian reserves of high-grade iron-ore are estimated to be over 880 million tons or nearly 4 percent of the world's total. Four other countries, the Soviet Union, Canada, Brazil and Australia have larger reserves. Current production is 38 million tons annually which is twice that of 1960 level. 24 million tons is mined by private companies, the remainder is state-controlled. Fields are scattered in the Deccan Plateau; many are located in the relatively inaccessible interior. The major producing region extends from Singhbhum in Bihar to Mayurbhanj, Keonjhar in Madhya Pradesh and Orissa. Large reserves occur in the Damodar Valley and the Raniganj areas, in close proximity to the coalfields and the iron and steel manufacturing centers. Other areas of reserves lie in more inaccessible locations in Karnataka. Large scale exploitation has so far been hindered by inadequate transport system. Figure 8.3 charts the growth of major minerals between 1951 and 1976.

Domestic demand of coal is weak; nearly two-thirds of the production (25 million tons) is exported. 80 percent of the exports go to Japan and the remainder to the East European countries, West Germany and the United Kingdom. Ore is exported through Vishakhapatanam and the newly developed port of Pradeep near Cuttak north of Vishakhapatnam.

Petroleum reserves are limited. Production is 7.5 million tons annually, capable of satisfying only one-fifth of the nation's demand. Consumption has been rising at a faster rate than production during the last two decades. In 1961 production was less than 1/2 million tons but could meet a quarter of India's requirements. The Fifth Plan estimates

MINERAL PRODUCTION, 1951-1976

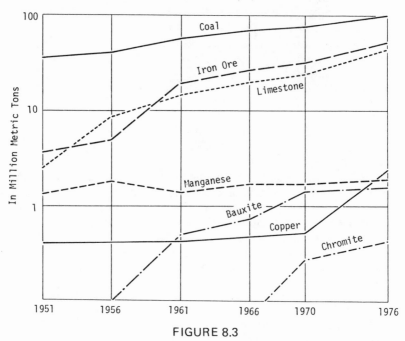

FIGURE 8.3

that by the end of 1979 domestic demand will escalate to 36 million tons annually and that increased imports will place an "excessive burden" on the economy.

Oil bearing areas are located in Assam, West Bengal, the Ganga Valley, Punjab, Himachal Pradesh, Kutch and the West Coast. Structurally, the most promising region is the Indo-Ganga-Brahmaputra foredeep to the Himalaya and the synclinal tracts marginal to the Peninsula. Recent exploitation has been limited to the off-shore Gujarat-Kutch-Cambay coast. The Cambay field, developed since 1965 with Russian-Rumannia technical collaboration, is currently yielding 4 million tons annually. The inland fields of Kalol and Ankleshwar in Gujarat are being now developed. Reserves of this region are estimated at 60 million tons. Refineries are located at Trombay near Bombay, and Koyali in Gujarat. Production in Assam started in 1892 in the upper Brahmaputra Valley. Major fields are at Digboi and Sib-

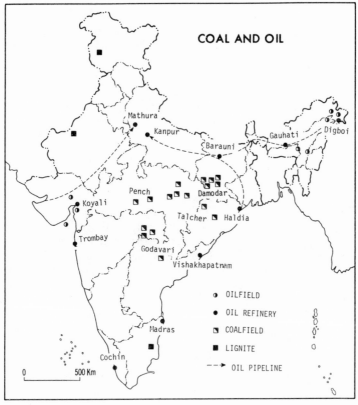

FIGURE 8.4

sagar. Reserves are probably as large as those of the Gujarat fields, current production is a little larger. Refineries are located at Tintinsukia and Nunmati, both close to the producing fields.

Refineries are also set up along the Gujarat coast, at Haldia near Calcutta, at Vishakhapatnam, Madras and Cochin, each with capacities ranging between 2 and 3 million tons annually, and close to the major importation points or close enough to the producing fields. Inland, the Barauni refinery has a capacity of refining nearly 3 million tons annually, and is located close to the industrial region of South Bihar-West Bengal. The Barauni refinery serves the industrial centers in the north Indian plains and the industries of Kanpur, and is connected with Haldia port. In all, the current capacity of the Indian refineries are in the neighborhood of 35 million tons (Figure 8.4).

Estimates of the reserves of natural gas yet remain to be determined, its usage is very limited, ranging between 925 and 1,000 million cubic feet annually. Production is closely associated with the two major petroleum areas of Assam and Cambay Coast, from where it is piped to the consuming centers in the country.

Other Minerals

Manganese, extensively used in the iron and steel industry, has been produced in exportable quantities since 1891. Among minerals, it is second to iron-ore as a foreign exchange earner. Production is nearly 2 million tons annually or roughly 9 percent of the world's output. India ranks after the Soviet Union, Union of South Africa and Brazil in production. Price fluctuations in the world market and increasing competition from South Africa have affected adversely India's position. Mining centers are widely distributed in the states of Madhya Pradesh, Orissa, Karnataka, Maharashtra and Rajasthan. The principal producing area lies in the Keonjhar hills of Orissa, which is close to Vishakhapatnam, its export outlet. Total reserves are estimated to range between 165 and 175 million tons of which 25 percent are of high grade.

Among the metals used in the engineering industries (nickel, lead, zinc, copper, chromite, and kyanite) only chromite and kyanite are abundantly found in the country, the remainder are imported or are inaccessible for extraction. Lead and zinc are found in Rajasthan in small quantities, the former is refined in Bihar and the latter processed in Udaipur (Rajasthan). Production is limited to 700,000 tons each annually. Annual production of chromite, which is largely used in chemical industries has risen from 107,000 tons in 1960 to over 300,000 tons, and it is exported. Major fields are near Cuttack and Keonjhar in Orissa; other fields lie in Singhbhum in Bihar, Bandara in Maharashtra and Hassan in Karnataka. Magnesite is also produced in exportable amounts from the fields near Salem in Tamil Nadu and Karnataka. Asbestos is, however, imported. India's kyanite deposits are probably the largest in the world. Annual production has increased from 20,000 tons in 1960 to four times since. The major producing area lies near Jamshedpur.

Bauxite, mica, uranium, thorium and graphite, the chief minerals used in the production of electricity are produced in fair to abundant quantities. Producing three-fourths of the world's mica, India retains its monopoly, but faces competition from the Soviet Union and Brazil which have recently stepped up their production. Production has declined from 30,000 tons in 1960 to 14,000 tons in 1974. The country's major mica-belt lies in Hazaribag area of the Chota Nagpur Plateau which accounts for about one-half the production, the remainder comes from Nellor in Andhra Pradesh, and Bhilwara in Rajasthan. Bauxite production has nearly leaped five-fold since 1960, from 387,000 tons to over 1.7 million tons in 1974, most of which is exported to Japan, Australia and the European countries. Domestic demand is meager but growing fast. West Bihar, Orissa, Madhya Pradesh, Maharashtra, and Tamil Nadu contain the major fields. Ore is processed and aluminum is produced at places near the hydro and thermal electricity installations at Hirakud in Orissa, Asansol in West Bengal and Alwaye in Kerala. Alumina content of Indian bauxite ranges between 50 and 80 percent.

Minerals used for the production of atomic energy exist in relatively large quantities. Thorium reserves, estimated at 500,000 tons, are among the largest in the world, and are located in the littoral sands of the Kerala Coast. The uranium-bearing formations have been found in Singhbhum and Rajasthan.

Minerals used in the glass, ceramic, and fertilizer industries are limited. Rock salt production is about 4,300 tons annually. Ninety percent of the annual output is, however, derived from evaporated saltwater along the Kutch, Maharashtra, and Tamil Nadu coasts. A small amount is exported to Japan. Gypsum is obtained in adequate amounts, one million tons annually, chiefly from Rajasthan. Sindri fertilizer utilizes most of the output.

Building materials such as sandstone, slate, limestone, and marble are in adequate amounts. The Deccan Peninsula is a rich storehouse of several of these. The Himalaya also yields slates, and limestones; the slate quarries of Himachal Pradesh being particularly noteworthy.

Gold is traditionally an important metal in Indian literature and mythology. Gold holdings, considered essential in
Indian homes, are substantial, although estimates are hard
to make. Seventy percent of the annual production of 4,000
kilograms comes from the Kolar goldfield in Mysore.

DEVELOPMENT OF ELECTRICITY

Basic to India's economic modernization is the development of an adequate supply of energy. Such traditional
energy sources as wood, dried cattle dung, and vegetable
wastes are not only primitive, and uneconomic, but also
scarce and unsuited to modernization. The use of coal,
hydro-electric power, petroleum and nuclear energy, started
essentially in the twentieth century and remains underdeveloped. Presently, ninety percent of the domestic fuel used in
the rural sector and 75 percent in the cities is derived from
the traditional sources with fuel wood accounting for 70 percent of all the sources and the remainder from dried cattle
dung and vegetable wastes. Fuelwood has become very
scarce, as the forest cover had been removed steadily since
medieval times, while demand for wood has grown unabat-
ed.

Roughly 55 percent of country's installed capacity of
power generated (19 million KW) is derived from thermal,
forty-four percent from hydro and only one percent from
nuclear sources. Thermally derived energy is focused primarily on the coal-rich section, particularly in the D.V.C.
region. Potentially, the hydro-based energy is large and fairly well distributed. The Central Water and Power Commission estimated it to be about 41 million KW at 60 percent
load factor of which only 3.6 percent had been developed
by 1961. By the end of the Fifth Plan 9 percent of the potential would have been developed generating about 46 million
KWh in 1979. Consumption, however, has been rising,
more rapidly. For example, per capita annual consumption
rose from 18 KWh to 110 KWh between 1951 and 1974. This
has resulted in a large shortfall in hydro-electric power, and
occasional power failures and shortages. The Fifth Plan envisaged the addition of 17 million KWh of new installed
capacity of hydroelectric power between 1974-1979.

Potentially, several areas are well-endowed for the

development of hydroelectric power: (A) a belt along the Himalaya from the Sutlej to the Brahmaputra Valley, which is estimated to account for about 60 percent of India's total potential; (B) the hills in the southern part of the Deccan, the area of Nilgiri Hills; (C) the region of Western Ghats' eastern slopes in Maharashtra and Karnataka. The Himalayan region is coal-deficient whereas the southern one has access to limited amount of lignite. Demand is minimal in the Assam section of the Himalaya, where potential for development is greatest (30 percent of Indian potential), but little development has taken place. In general, actual development has been hampered by seasonal and annual fluctuations in rainfall, lack of perennial rivers and problems of reservoir construction in hard rocks in the Deccan Plateau. Inter-state rivalries and water disputes have occasionally prevented the exploitation of hydro-resources for power generation. In the Himalaya region, where rainfall, terrain and water storage conditions are ideal, problems of inaccessibility, construction and distance from demand areas here caused hydroelectric development to lag.

Tamil Nadu and Maharashtra lead in actual production with over 2 million KW each in development of installed generating capacity, followed by Uttar Pradesh, West Bengal, Karnataka, Gujarat, Punjab and Orissa, and the D.V.C. region as a unit, each with over 1.5 million KW developed installed capacity of hydro-energy. In per capita consumption, however, Punjab leads, followed by Maharashtra, Tamil Nadu and Gujarat. Currently there are 99 operating power stations, of which 43 are hydro-electric and the remaining mostly thermal. Figure 8.5 shows the location of the major power plants in the country.

A nuclear power plant is located at Trombay near Bombay, two are located in Rajasthan at Rana Partap Sagar. Two nuclear breeder reactors, one at Kalapakkam in Tamil Nadu and the other in Uttar Pradesh, are scheduled for commissioning in the Fifth and Sixth Plans. Plans for extension of transmission lines to serve the industrial areas distant from the coalfields and hydroelectric power stations form a part of the Fifth Plan. The immediate beneficiaries of nuclear power will be the industrial corridors of Ahmadabad-Baroda-Bombay, and Madras-Bangalore. The construction of new nuclear plants appears limited mainly because of prohibitive installation costs.

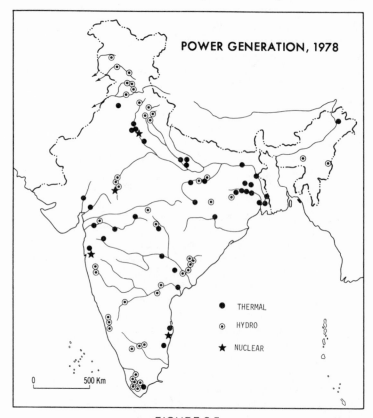

FIGURE 8.5

In sum, power utilized in Bihar, West Bengal and Gujarat is primarily thermal, urban-industrial market oriented,
and close to the coal fields. In Punjab, Jammu-Kashmir,
Karnataka, Kerala and Tamil Nadu it is both thermal and
hydro. In Gujarat, Assam and Maharashtra gas turbines
and diesel are also used for power generation in addition to
hydro and thermal sources.

Both industrial progress and the success of the Green
Revolution have been accomplished through the utilization
of electric power. Demand for it is likely to accelerate
despite current shortfalls. The principal users are: industry
(68 percent), irrigation electric pumps (10 percent, up from
4 percent in 1950), domestic household consumption (9 per-

cent) and railroads (3 percent). Electrical power utilization for irrigation pumps has dramatically increased in Tamil Nadu, Punjab, Harayana and Western Uttar Pradesh, areas where high-yielding varieties of food crops have been introduced. Between 1951-1974 nearly 2.4 million electric pumps were installed and during the Fifth Plan an additional 1.5 million would be energized.

Electricity has been an instrument of industrial decentralization. It has helped push the agro-based small industries into the rural sector in the Haryana-Punjab-Delhi industrial corridor. The Fourth and Fifth Plans envisage extension of electricity to the backward and rural sections under the Minimum Needs Programme (MNP) by the provision of electric power to health centers, irrigation pump sets, drinking water and construction of roads. By the end of 1974, 148,000 of the 567,000 villages (India's total number of Census villages) were provided with electricity. The Fifth Plan has targeted to cover more than 258,000 or 40 percent of the villages. At present all the villages of Haryana and Tamil Nadu have electricity. Punjab and Karnataka are close to reaching 100 percent rural electrification. Areas poor in rural electrification are the hilly states of Himachal Pradesh, Manipur, Meghalaya, Tripura, Arunchal Pradesh, Nagaland, Jammu-Kashmir, Assam and Orissa.

The Fourth Plan recognized the need for the development of an integrated regional network of electric grid lines (Regional Grid) in order to provide an economic and efficient flow of power to the places of need. So far integrated grids were limited to a few industrial areas like the D.V.C. region, the Hooghly-side, the Greater Bombay Industrial Complex, and in localized sections in Kerala and Tamil Nadu. The D.V.C. grid is the only large integrated system of transmission of power utilizing both thermal and hydroelectric energy. By 1972 the total length of the integrated grid of transmission lines was 11,800 kms. The Fifth Plan aims at extension of high voltage lines and standardization of power transmissions.

MAJOR INDUSTRIES

Iron and Steel Industry
Prior to Independence, the colonial administration had

practically ignored the creation of a strong industrial sector
in India despite its adequate resource-base for the development of modern metallurgical and chemical industry. The
British authorities generally maintained that India was
never likely to develop a large scale industrial base, and that
its minerals (iron ore, coal, manganese and bauxite) could
be more profitably exported, whereas finished iron and steel
goods and machinery could be more competitively imported
than produced at home. At the turn of the 20th century the
total production of pig iron in the country amounted to a
mere 75,000 tons, produced by a company started in 1874.
The Tatas established the first, large-scale plant to manufacture iron and steel at Jamshedpur in Bihar in 1907.
Backed by the Tata entreprenurial skill, financing and
determination, and favored by a set of ideal geographic circumstances, the plant rapidly prospered.

At the time of Independence in 1947, there existed only
three large, modern plants in the country, two in the private
sector, Tata Iron and Steel Company at Jamshedpur and Indian Iron and Steel Company at Kulti-Burnpur in West
Bengal. The third was government-owned at Bhadravati in
Mysore. Total production was a little over one million tons
of crude steel and one million tons of pig iron. During the
First and Second Plans, emphasis on heavy industry led to a
rapid growth of the iron and steel industry. Three new
plants were set up in the public sector with an initial capacity of one million tons production of iron and steel ingots
each at Rourkela in Orissa, Bhilai in Madhya Pradesh and
Durgapur in West Bengal. Expansion resulting from these
plants pushed the production of crude steel to 6.5 million
tons by 1965-1966.

The concentration of all major plants, with the exception of the one at Bhadravati in Chota Nagpur in the northeastern section of the Deccan Plateau, primarily reflects the
constellation of ideal circumstances in this region which is
known as the coal-steel belt of the country. The industry
tends to be raw-material oriented. Studies in 1962 revealed
that transport costs in raw material assembly for the steel
plants was the lowest for Jamshedpur and highest for Bhadravati. The iron-ore fields of Singhbhum in Orissa are
within 75 miles, and the Damodar Valley coal 125 miles, the
molding sand from the Subarnarekha River and the alloys

within 50-60 miles of Jamshedpur and within easy reach of Durgapur, Burnpur-Kulti areas. The engineering works at the Hooghly side near Calcutta offering the largest market for steel ingots, are only 150 miles by a connecting railway link with Jamshedpur and closer for the Durgapur and Kulti-Burnpur industries. Limestone and manganese come from the nearby fields in Orissa. The Bhilai industry is a little closer to the manganese and limestone supply base. These centers are conveniently connected by a railroad with Vishakhapatnam shipyard on the east coast and also lie on the main railroad link between Calcutta and Bombay. The three public sector plants set up during the Second Plan were established with foreign aid and collaboration: Durgapur with the United Kingdom, Rourkela with West Germany and Bhilai with the U.S.S.R. Public sector undertakings were subsequently expanded at Bokaro during the Fourth Plan with Soviet assistance. The Bokaro factory is blessed with advantages of location, including proximity to mineral resources and transport connections with the existing foci of the iron steel industry in Chota Nagpur and was targeted to develop a production capacity of 10 million tons by 1979.

The Bhadravati plant in Southern India is located within 25-35 miles of iron-ore, manganese, limestone and timber areas, but is remote from coalfields. Timber is used as a fuel in the industry but is being rapidly depleted. The transport cost of hauling coal by rail from the distant Domodar area are the highest among major plants. The nearby Bangalore industry utilizes its production in metallurgical, engineering and ancillary industries of the Hindustan Machine Tools Factory.

To remove regional imbalances, the government planned to set up three new steel plants during the Fifth Plan in South India, at Vijyanagar, Salem and Vishakhapatnam, each with a production capacity of 2 million tons annually. Only feasibility studies have so far been completed.

Steel production, which recorded substantial progress during the 1960's flagged later on for a number of reasons. Emphasis on the development of heavy industry which was capital-intensive but low in employment content was shifted in favor of employment-oriented industries. It was widely feared that India could not afford capital-intensive enterprises as these tended to create foreign exchange pressures and did little to aid the unemployment situation. Furthermore, it was estimated that "investment of capital in larger firms from 1957 to 1965 may have led to a net loss of 2.9 million potential jobs" (Bhagwati, 1970). Analysis of Indian industrialization generally favored the creation of an industrial base of smaller, consumer-oriented, employment-rich manufacturing units capable of utilizing idle segment of the rural labor force in agro-based agricultural machinery industry and agricultural goods.

Several developmental problems have also plagued the growth of industry, notably inadequate transport linkages, underutilization of mill capacities, shortages of coal supply, and inefficient power supply. The Sixth Plan (1979-1984) has set up a production target of 15 million tons of steel ingots, and nearly 12 million tons of finished steel (more than twice the figure of 1975). Those favoring the development of an employment-oriented, capital-conserving, small consumer-based steel industry are of the view that these targets can be reached easier by the creation of a rural agro-based sector of the industry (e.g., by manufacture of agricultural implements, engines, small machinery, etc.).

Engineering Industries

Insignificant and confined to a few large industrial centers such as Calcutta, Jamshedpur, Bombay and Madras before Independence, engineering industries have recently acquired special significance. The country is now self-sufficient in such engineering goods as bicycles, diesel locomotives, light electrical and electronic goods. Despite substantial progess made in the last 20 years, engineering manufactures form 25 percent of the import bill, a major portion of which is paid by foreign-aid receipts.

During the last two decades substantial progress has been gained in the manufacture of machinery for sugar, tea, cement, jute, cotton, paper. Printing, rice milling and machine tools manufactured also became significantly mechanized. Calcutta, Bombay, and Madras are the leading centers. Calcutta specializes in the production of machinery for textiles, tea, chemicals, sugar and paper; and Bombay in the machinery for cotton textiles, chemicals and paper. Madras is more diversified in manufacturing. Light electrical machines and electronic instrumentation and machine tool manufacturing area was also located in all these centers. During the post-Independence period, Coimbatore in Karnataka, Ahmadabad and Baroda in Gujarat have emerged as centers producing electrical, textile and chemical machinery.

The Indian government has recently been encouraging decentralization of industry with a view to achieving a more balanced regional development. In 1970, the Hindustan Machine Tools Ltd., a public sector undertaking, located five of its major plants at Bangalore, Pinjore (Haryana), Hyderabad, and Kalamasary (Kerala). Bangalore is the largest machine-building center in the south and has attracted a concentration of industries like watch-making, telephone equipment and aircraft manufacture in the public sector. Its private sector industries include ceramics, electric goods, and the manufacture of soap and textile machinery. Pleasant climate, planned urban development and government-encouragement have been important factors in the growth of these industries here. Elsewhere, public sector machine-tool plants are located at Ajmer (Rajasthan), a machine plant for the production of weapons for the Defense Services at Secunderabad (Andhra Pradesh) and a precision-instrument plant at Kota in Rajasthan.

The manufacture of heavy metallurgical engineering machines during the last two decades also progressed substantially since 1961, particularly in the production of mine-pumps, conveyors, shuttle cars, and haulers, paid for largely through foreign aid. Production of these items is nearly three-fourths of a million tons annually making the country practically self-sufficient in coal mining machinery requirements. Major plants are located in the Chota Nagpur Plateau area in Ranchi where the Heavy Engineering Corporation (H.E.C.) is located, at Dhanbad in Bihar and at Durgapur. Private sector heavy-machinery plants are located at Naini (near Allahabad, set up in 1965) and in the south at Tungabhadra, started in 1967 to manufacture transmission power machinery and ancillary items.

The public sector heavy electrical equipment production has also made good progress during the 1960's and 70's. Major plants are located at Bhopal (Madhya Pradesh), New Delhi, Hardwar (Uttar Pradesh), Tiruchirapalli (Tamil Nadu), Hyderabad and Rupnarainagar (West Bengal). These plants manufacture electric transformers, steam turbines, boilers and tele-communication equipment. Shipbuilding is chiefly in the public sector and is located at Vishakhapatnam, Cochin and Malgaon.

Light industries are regionally dispersed, but are concentrated close to the centers of heavy industry and have a larger public sector participation. Manufactured items include bicycles, watches, typewriters, sewing machines, diesel engines and electric pumps. Production is growing rapidly, in pace with the increasing domestic demand and has even shown recently a healthy export performance. Indian manufacturers have established contacts with the Middle East, Africa and Southeast Asia to assist them in setting up these industries in their countries. Although small industrial units specializing in light industry have sprung up near the major industrial cities all over the country, particularly noteworthy is the emergence of a light-industries urban corridor (Figure 9.2) along a 200 km urban-railroad belt in Punjab-Haryana-Delhi-West Uttar Pradesh including the urban centers of Ludhiana-Ambala-Rohtak-Panipat-Delhi-Ghaziabad-Meerut-Bareilly which contains numerous small private-sector industrial units producing agricultural machinery, motor scooters, bicycles and sewing machines.

Jameshedpur industries also manufacture a wide variety of light engineering goods. Lakhnau (Uttar Pradesh) and Jabalpur (Madhya Pradesh) are the important centers of automobile equipment and parts; Delhi, Calcutta, Bombay and Madras are the other centers. Production of commercial vehicles has steadily grown since 1960, but domestic demand has been rising faster and is now 40,000 units per year.

Metal-based Industries

With the growth of heavy industry, domestic demand for such metals as copper, nickel, zinc and lead has risen. Although current production is still small, 3000 tons of lead, 28,000 tons of zinc, and 18,000 tons of copper, the Fifth Plan has ambitious targets for stepping up their production. While the production of copper, lead and nickel would be developed exclusively in the public sector, aluminum and zinc would also be encouraged in the private sector. The non-ferrous metals have been allocated 55.6 million dollars for their development in the Fifth Plan, a figure well over 6 percent of all industrial development programs.

Major aluminum plants are located at Jaykaynagar (West Bengal) close to the bauxite fields of the Chota Nagpur plateau, in Salem (Tamil Nadu) and near Goa, also proximal to bauxite areas. These plants make use of the thermal power obtained from nearby generating stations. Another plant is located in Alwaye (Kerala). New smelters are planned at Korba and Ratnagiri. Copper melting is located close to the mines at Khetri in Rajasthan and Gharla in Bihar. Zinc smelters are located at Debri (Rajasthan) near the mines and at Vishakhapatnam and Alwaye, based on the imported concentrates. Lead and nickel smelting plants are also located near mines in Rajasthan, Orissa and Andhra Pradesh.

Textile Industries

Producing between 9 and 10 percent of the world's raw cotton, India ranks behind the United States, the Soviet Union and China in the production of raw cotton. In jute it rivals Bangladesh as the leading producer, and in the production of raw silk it is behind Japan, China and the Soviet Union. Textile industry based on raw cotton and raw silk has ancient roots in the country. India was renowned in the western world for the production of fine silks and sheer "Dacca" muslins in ancient and medieval times. Textiles formed its leading exports even before the Christian era. This fame remained uneclipsed until the latter 19th century when the imported, cheap and plentiful cloth manufactured by the Lancashire industry virtually wiped away the domestic production.

Both in terms of employment and output, however, the cotton textile industry still occupies a pre-eminent position among industries. It employs over 1.2 million persons, or nearly 27 percent of the total industrial labor force, in its nearly 700 registered factories and contributes over 20 percent of the value added by manufacture. The first organized cotton textile factory was established in Calcutta in 1818, whereas the first jute mill was set up in 1854 also near Calcutta. The modern industry picked up momentum much later, during the 1930's and 1940's after the grant of government protection to appease the *Swadeshi* (nationalistic) movement. In 1939 there were 389 registered cotton textile mills. Since then growth has been steady. Between 1950-51 and 1974-75 the production of cotton yarn nearly doubled, commensurate with increased domestic requirements. The peak was reached in 1961 when exports to Third World countries became an essential part of foreign trade.

The early start of the cotton textile manufacturing in 1850 in Bombay was undoubtedly favored by its geographic location in the heart of the cotton growing region, its accessibility to a wide variety of cotton grades and by its superior transport facilities. Industry was initially spurred by its nearness to British industrial centers for the import of machinery and export of yarn. Besides Britain, early importers included China and Japan, but the Chinese market dried up as Japan and China experienced the manufacturing revolution by the early 20th century. Meanwhile, the home market was expanding particularly for the urban elite. The *Swadeshi* movement launched against the imported British manufactured cloth helped the growth of the fabric manufacturing industry substantially. Bombay, and later nearby locations such as Ahmadabad, became important centers, followed by numerous smaller urban constellations surrounding the two foci. Freight costs of cotton lint hauling were competitive at these places as was the case also at some inland locations such as Nagpur and Sholapur. Nagpur benefited from fuel supplied by either the Damodar coalfields, whereas Sholapur was close to hydro power produced in the Western Ghats.

In the North Indian Plains, good transport facilities, a growing home market and nearness to the cotton-growing region of the Ganga Plains, all contributed to the emergence of such centers as Kanpur, midway between Calcutta and Delhi on the important railroad route and others farther west at Delhi and beyond it in the Punjab. Cotton being a non-perishable commodity, the location of manufacturing centers were determined on the basis of demand, transport facilities and availability of power. Calcutta's cotton industry started in 1905 by which time the jute industry had already been well-established. Despite competition from the jute industry such advantages as proximity to the Damodar Valley coal, port facilities and a large local market fostered the rapid development of cotton textiles. Industrial centers in Punjab (Ludhiana, Amritsar) grew up following the development of Mandi hydro-electricity.

In South India, industry came later, around 1870, first at Madras and then at Coimbatore, Bangalore and Madurai. Major development occurred since the 1930's, following the arrival of hydroelectric power from Pykara. Although the industry is regionally well-distributed in areas of consumption, the heart of the cotton-mill industry is a pentagon formed by the cities of Bombay, Ahmadabad, Sholapur, Nagpur and Ujjain. These five centers account for over one-half of the mill consumption of raw cotton, and three-fourths of the number of looms in the industry. In addition to the initial advantages which led to the industry's location here, a number of factors helped sustain and expand the industry. The Gujarati and Parsi entrepreneurial experience, well-regulated markets for collecting and distributing raw cotton and excellent internal transport facilities all helped in maintaining the pre-eminence of this region.

In addition to the mill sector (registered factories) discussed thus far, a much larger cottage-industry sector of decentralized hand-loom cloth-making has traditionally flourished in the country. This has recently expanded more rapidly than the "organized" sector because of the administration's special encouragement provided through funding under Five-Year Plans. Expansion of this sector has been rapid largely because of the handwoven cloth is inexpensive and oriented toward local, rural markets. There are thousands of small handlooms spread throughout the country. The total production of cotton cloth in 1973-74 was 7,800 million meters; the Fifth Plan aimed at increasing it up to 10,000 million meters by 1978-79, mainly by expanding the decentralized handloom sector.

India is now second only to Japan as an exporter of cotton fabrics to the world markets. In value, cotton yarn and goods rank after tea and jute manufactures among Indian exports. Southeast Asia, the Middle East and Africa are the major markets. Trade statistics of the last two decades, however, indicate that the industry has suffered in its relative contribution to the country's earnings. Government policy since the First Plan has been favoring capital-intensive heavy industry, particularly iron and steel. In

1951, cotton textiles produced 41 percent of the nation's value-added through manufacturing, and nearly one-third of the textile output was sent abroad, representing 38 percent of India's exports. Since that year foreign shipments have been continually declining. In 1974, textiles' share of manufacturing value-added was 21 percent (about one-half of the 1951 level), and in export value, cotton fabrics represented 25 percent of the total. The administration is now considering a more rapid expansion of the decentralized sector.

Jute manufacturing is one of the foremost of industries, accounting for 12 to 16 percent of all exports, making it the largest foreign exchange earner. Before 1947 India held a pre-eminent position as a producer of jute manufactures as all the industrial units (70,000 looms) were concentrated along the Hooghlyside near Calcutta. Partition in 1947 robbed India's jute industry of a major supply area of raw jute. In order to retain its supremacy as the largest jute manufacturing country, India had to extend its jute growing area outside the traditional jute heartland of the Ganga-Brahmaputra delta, a major portin of which became East Pakistan. Jute cultivation was, therefore, extended to Orissa, West Bihar and the Tarai region of the Ganga Plains, thus restoring the supply base to the industry. Raw jute supply is now nearly self-sufficient; only small quantities are imported form Bangladesh.

The highly localized distribution of the industry along a belt 60 miles by 3 miles adjacent to the Hooghly developed, beginning in 1859, under ideal geographic conditions. The Ganga-Brahmaputra delta supply region of jute cultivation was connected by excellent river-borne and railway links. The Hooghlyside lay roughly midway between the Damodar Valley coalfields and the jute cultivation region. Transportation economy dictated the selection of a Hooghlyside location, for if the mills were to be located in East Bengal transhipment costs would have been prohibitive, first in carrying coal and mill stores, and to the mills, and again in transhipping the finished goods to Calcutta for export. Following the emergence of Bangladesh in 1972, Indo-Bangladesh negotiated to import Bangladeshi jute by Indian mills since Bangladesh lacked mills to process all of its raw jute.

Current production of jute manufacture is 1.2 million tons of which 75 percent is exported. Production has remained nearly steady or has declined slightly in view of competition from Bangladesh industry and the growth of synthetic fabric industry.

India's woolen industry is relatively small. It received a setback in 1947 when the major supply base fell to West Pakistan's share after partition. Production of yarn is about 200,000 tons, and that of fabric 125,000 meters annually. Domestic demand is large. Major manufacturing centers are Kanpur (Uttar Pradesh), Dhariwal (near Amritsar in Punjab) and Srinagar in Kashmir. Elsewhere, handloom cottage woolen industry is well established in the hills of Himachal Pradesh and Kashmir based on the local, fine sheep-wool.

The *silk industry* is even smaller in terms of total employment, although it has traditionally held a pride of place among Indian textiles. Karnataka, Tamil Nadu, West Bengal and Kashmir are the major producers. The cottage industry sector has expanded more rapidly in the last 20 years under government encouragement. *Rayon, and the synthetic fabric industry* has grown since 1950 with annual production jumping from 2,000 tons of yarn to 12,000 tons. The industry is located at the large cotton-textile centers, principally at Bombay, Ahmadabad and Amritsar.

Sugar Industry

India produces roughly 4.5 million metric tons or 10 percent of the world's sugar cane. It is also world's leading producer of unrefined country-sugar or jaggery. Next to textile manufacturing, sugar is the country's major agro-industry.

At the time of Independence it was one of the well-established industries. There were over 100 factories producing about one million tons of sugar annually. By 1940 it had become the world's largest sugar producer. It had then 145 factories and produced a little less than one million tons of cane-sugar per year. This was an eight-fold increase since 1932. It had also emerged as a modest exporter by the early 1940's. Cuba and Brazil, however, soon took over as the largest producers and world's principal sugar exporters. During the 1960's despite a remarkable increase in domestic production, export was meager, roughly 2 to 5 percent of domestic production. Since then, export has averaged between 10 and 15 percent of the production, made possible by almost tripling the domestic output (3.5 million tons in

1965). The Fifth Plan has projected a production of 5.7 million tons for 1979.

The traditional "heartland" of the industry has been the middle Ganga Plains, which accounted for over 80 percent of the production until 1930, when a dramatic shift to the South began to take place. In 1959-60 the Ganga Plains (mainly the States of Uttar Pradesh and Bihar) contributed 65 percent of the country's production. Current production of the region is about 50 percent. The dispersal was oriented toward the tropical region in the Peninsula where the four states of Maharashtra, Andhra Pradesh, Tamil Nadu and Karnataka now account for about 45 percent of the total production. Between 1950 and 1965 twenty new factories were set up in Maharashtra, 11 in Andhra Pradesh, 8 in Tamil Nadu and 4 in Karnataka.

The middle Ganga Plains stil remain a major region of the industry. Factories in western Uttar Pradesh, parts of eastern Uttar Pradesh and the adjoining north Bihar districts, collectively produce about one-half of the country's production. Mills are raw material oriented and lie close to the sugarcane areas. There are generally small, clinging to the railroad or roads for easy hauling of the bulky raw material. The Peninsula, west coastal areas and the delta districts of the east coast contain most of the factories, utilizing the good transport facilities of the areas.

In the northern states cane quality suffers from low sucrose-content, a shorter crushing season and lower productivity per hectare. The tropical southern states are ideally suited for cane production from the climate standpoint, capable of producing cane with higher sucrose-content. Extension of irrigation facilities, growth of cooperatives and administrative regulatory incentives and improvements in transport, both for cane production and for the sugar manufacturing industry helped the growth of industry during the 1960's in the southern states. This process of decentralization of the industry is likely to continue. Factories in the south also enjoy a comparative cost-advantage in respect of the sugar-cane supply. The sugar-cane Inquiry Commission of 1965 after examining the comparative cost-benefits of sugarcane cultivation in the various parts of the country concluded that Maharashtra ranked first in cost-benefit advantages (one measure was gross value of sugarcane per unit area).

A problem which the industry has chronically faced is the recurring cycles of international pricing and demand fluctuation affecting the domestic production and its exportable amounts. Domestic demand has risen appreciably, however, during the last two decades which has met partly by the production of unrefined sugar (*gur* and *khandsari*) especially in the rural areas. Statutory controls over refined sugar for domestic consumption have occasionally been applied in order to meet the export demands.

Other Industries

Cement and *paper* are two other major industries. Both were established before Independence. Cement production capacity at the time of Independence was nearly 2.5 million metric tons (in 1975 it was about 15 million metric tons). Paper production also registered similar gains since 1947. As in most developing countries, both products are critically needed in independent India for the construction of dams and buildings, and for the dissemination of news. Both are in short supply despite the remarkable progress already made. The Fifth Plan aims to step up cement production to 25 million tons annually by 1979 in order to cope with the rapidly rising domestic demand in housing, industry and public works. Occasional shortages and black marketing during the 1960's led the government to monitor distribution in the private sector.

Both industries are raw-material oriented, because of the heavy transportation costs. Ideal locations for the industries are nearness to raw materials and fuel supply and proximity to the market since the products are low-cost and bulky. Distance from the market increases the freight-costs substantially. For cement, raw materials used include limestone, gypsum, clay, coal and water; for paper, wood-pulp, grass, coal and water. The cement industry is located in Bihar (close to the coalfields and areas of limestone). Orissa, Gujarat, Madhya Pradesh, Tamil Nadu, and Rajasthan. Since 1950 dispersal has taken place to the coastal locations in Kerala and Gujarat where plants could utilize sea sand, marl and sea shells. The Bombay market is now served by the Gujarat factories, with a grinding and packing plant located in Bombay. Important centers of the industry are Dalmianagar (Bihar), Katni (Madhya Pradesh) and Lakheri (Rajasthan).

Major paper mills were located in Calcutta, Raniganj, Dalmianagar, and Brajrajnagar (Orissa) until 1950. Since then mills in Bellarpur and Nepanagar (for newsprint) in Maharashtra; Sirpur, Kaghaznagar in Andhra Pradesh, Dandeli and Bhadravati in Karnataka, Kaveri in Tamil Nadu have been set up, all dependent on the supply of bamboo from nearby forests. Smaller plants were set up in the Bombay-Pune and Bangalore areas, these centers utilize the nearby available hydroelectric and thermal power. Dalmianagar in Bihar has been recently utilizing sugarcane pulp (bagase) instead of the traditional woodpulp for paper making.

Chemical and Related Industries

Drugs, pharmaceuticals, paints, varnishes, synthetic fibers, D.D.T., and other pesticides, industrial gas and chemical fertilizers were all virtually entirely imported until the early 1960's. Only caustic soda, phosphates, sulphuric acid, soaps and synthetic detergents were produced at home in limited quantities. So phenomenal has been the growth of chemical and related industries during and since the 1960's that these industries rank only after textile manufacturing and iron and steel in value added. Production is still below domestic needs, but the Fifth Plan targets are kept high. Previous achievements during the Third and Fourth Plans fell 20 to 50 percent short of the targets.

Before 1960 sulphuric acid manufacturing plants existed near the textile and steel centers at Asansol, Jamshedpur and Alwaye, whereas caustic soda and soda ash were produced near the areas of availability of limestone and sea salt in Gujarat. Sindri (Bihar) and Alwaye were the two ammonium sulphate manufacturing centers. Demand of chemical fertilizers has increased dramatically following the introduction of HYV in agriculture and shortfalls have been critical since 1965, despite early progress in production. The consumption is still among the lowest in the world, 13 kg/ha of arable land compared to the world average of 43 kh/ha. Production of the working plants in the public sector, located at Sindri (Bihar), Nangal (Punjab), Trombay (Matra), Rourkela (Orissa), Alwaye (Kerala), Neyvelli (Tamil Nadu), Namrup (Assam), Gorakhpur (Uttar Pradesh), and Madras (Tamil Nadu) is estimated to be 2.6 million tons annually. Private sector factories are located at several places in Rajasthan, Uttar Pradesh and Orissa. The Fifth Plan projects include new plants at Durgapur, Cochin, Barauni, Goa and Kota, in an effort to decentralize and expand the fertilizer industry since the transport costs of fertilizers to farmers appears to be a critical factor. Scarcity of raw materials (rock phosphates, sulphur, petroleum) is a stumbling block in the decentralization program. The escalating price of oil in the international market is a limiting factor in raising production. From a long term view it will be necessary to explore the possibility of producing fertilizers from other locally available sources, such as coal. An expected increase in oil production from the Bombay High raises some hope of utilizing domestic oil as well.

The soda ash and caustic soda industry is lcoated in Gujarat, and produces roughly 500,000 tons of soda ash and 1.2 million tons of caustic soda annually. Other producing centers are in Maharashtra, Tamil Nadu, Delhi and Kerala. The cotton and synthetic textile and paper industries utilize caustic soda and the industry tends to be close to those centers.

India's drug and pharmaceutical manufacturing industry in concentrated at three major centers: antibiotics at Rishikesh (Uttar Pradesh), Hyderabad for vitamin manufacturing and sulpha drugs at Madras. Insecticides are manufactured at New Delhi, Bombay, Kolaba, Pimpri near Pune and Alwaye.

The petro-chemical industry is of comparatively recent growth, the first plant being established in 1966. The production of plastics is slightly over one million tons, and of synthetic fibers about 38,000 tons. Potentials for growth appear limited, primarily a result of the paucity of raw materials. The synthetic manufacturing industry tends to be located near the existing textile centers of Bombay, Ahmadabad and Coimbator as are the industries of soap, plastics and cosmetics, all deriving benefits of the established markets, banking and capital resources from those centers. In the south these industries are dispersed in such small and medium-size cities as Ernakulam (Kerala), Bangalore, Ramnathapuram (Tamil Nadu) and Madras, close to the sources of raw materials (Coconut, vegetable oils, rubber, sea salt, soft wood), labor supply and hydroelectricity.

VILLAGE AND SMALL-SCALE INDUSTRIES

A small-scale firm is defined as any enterprise with plant and machinery investment of less than Rs 50,000 or approximately $6250. Village industries are those which cater primarily to local markets. The village industries are also labeled as "traditional." Although Indian planning has been oriented to large-scale industrialization, it has recognized the continuing and special role of small-scale industry in the development process. Between 1950 and 1970 nearly $78 millions were spent for the development of this sector of industry. In addition, a vast unorganized, unregistered segment remains virtually outside the orbit of government planning. Absence of reliable statistics make it difficult to assess the dimensions of small-scale and rural industry.

This industry, as the label suggests, is composed of small firms, often deriving their force from the owner's household, and is primarily based in the villages or small towns. The Five Year Plans sought to encourage these household (cottage) industries by the provision of credit facilities, access to machinery, and technical assistance.

The Fifth Plan allocated an outlay of $75 million for the development of rural and small-scale industries, the largest slice of which was assigned to the development of the handloom industry. With a million persons utilized in it, it currently ranks next only to agriculture in employment, fulfilling about 46 percent of country's domestic needs in cloth and art silk. Processing of cereals, vegetable oils, *gur* and manufacture of soap, pottery, carpets, wood-carvings and iron-smelted objects are some other small-scale (basically rural) industries.

The *coir* industry is primarily export-oriented. Annual production is 140,000 tons of coir yarn, 90 percent of which is produced in Kerala. Coir goods' export earnings average about $2 to 3 million annually and about one-half of a milion persons are engaged in it. India produces nearly 30,000 kg of silk yarn annually, most of which is yielded in small-scale, rural industrial units. Two-thirds are provided by Karnataka alone, the remainder comes from West Bengal, Assam, Jammu-Kashmir, Bihar and Madhya Pradesh. More than 3 million persons are employed in this industry, and exports of silk have been rapidly increasing.

In the Indian context where a large, reservoir of rural labor force exists, the village and small-scale industries (by producing goods and providing services) can play a vital role in the development process. Therefore, the development of a rural employment-oriented strategy of growth based on labor-intensive rather than capital-intensive industries has been advocated by several economists.

PROBLEMS OF INDUSTRIAL DEVELOPMENT

Without doubt industrialization has been an instrument of the country's economic growth. In the last three decades the impact of industrial development has been to increase national income, speed up the modernization process, reduce dependence on imports of several consumer goods and raise labor productivity. The pace of industrial development since Independence has been more rapid than under British colonial rule, but has in general fallen short of the planning targets. A complex set of forces responsible for slow progress of industrialization in the country are reviewed briefly in the following paragraphs.

Industrialization started in India one hundred years later than in the developed countries, and its development coincided with other nations' development when they had reached a mature status of technology. India had not only to integrate the modern means of development but also to catch up with the developed world in establishing the basic structures of industrial development. In other words, it had to tackle greater tasks than other industrial nations at a similar stage of development. To attain world standards of production and labor, India had to develop not only the metallurgical and engineering industries, but also the nuclear, electronic and computer capabilities used by other nations. The pace of Indian industrialization was, therefore, bound to be initially slow. A base of "intermediate goods" (like steel plates, cement, machines, electrical goods) manufactured domestically to help create heavy industry was first to be created.

Given its meager sources of financing and capital accumulation, Indian ruling classes could not muster domestically the large investments needed to create a base for heavy industry. Over a period of planned development large amounts of foreign aid were obtained which resulted in the problems relating to balances of foreign exchange. Heavy reliance on foreign aid and investments constrained domestic initiative and compelled the country to borrow foreign technology and goods at more than competitive prices in the international market. Foreign exchange balances eased off only in the later 1970's when the heavy industry and intermediate goods sector had measurably matured. It also reduced dependence on foreign electric, electronic, engineering and metallurigical goods. During the 1960's foodgrain imports had further aggravated the foreign trade situation and enormously constrained imports of capital-intensive goods.

The Indian economy has had to work under conditions labeled as "economics of scarcity." This scarcity was not entirely in the matter of capital reserves, but in terms of infrastructural deficiencies as well. Shortages of power (electricity, coal, gas), transport facilities, technical knowledge and machinery all impeded industrial growth. An inadequate pace of investment and wide-spread shortages of construction material resulted in the scarcity of buildings needed for modernizing and expanding the industrial base. Scarcity of administrative, management and technical capacities to sustain development processes was particularly critical during the early phases of industrialization. Import substitution and tight industrial licensing as a means of expanding domestic manufacturing resources initially helped to depress the availability of consumer and intermediate goods. The Fifth Plan had to concede that "the initial difficulties experienced in the process of indigenization through reliance on domestic technology became an important factor in impeding the pace of investment" (*Draft Fifth Five Year Plan*. p. 131).

A major development thrust during the Five Year Plans was toward the establishment of a vigorous public sector developed hastily without the creation of a base of administrative machinery adequate to undertake this enormous task. Preparatory work for such tremendous institutional reorganization was poor. High performance was rarely insisted on even after the construction of an administrative base. The result was non-achievement of the targets. During the Fourth and Fifth Plans, achievement levels fell short of targets by 15 to 18 percent.

Political and social agitation, fueled in part by the class caste inequalities, often marred industrial relations. Labor-management relations, never properly nurtured before Independence, remained strained. Factory legislation was slow to take shape. The pace of early industrial growth was inevitably affected.

The quality of labor and of the Indian market has remained notoriously antiquated. The development of skilled, technical manpower for industry has lagged primarily to placate traditional caste prejudices against manual and technical work. Deep-routed prejudices prevail, hampering the creation of an efficient labor force. The domestic market remained chronically underdeveloped through lack of enthusiasm generated by the middle and upper class segment who did not terribly need to raise their standards, and by the poor class who were fatalists, not caring to raise their standards. The result: Indian living standards remained among the lowest in the world. The impact on market: higher standards were sacrificed since these involved manual work.

Among the major geographical problems that faced industrialization was the inadequate infrastructural and locational base of the industries. Industrial locations, in several instances, were established without reference to cost-effective points. Each state clamored for the establishment of major industries in the public sector within its boundaries, and the locational decisions have thus been often politically motivated. The Plans set out to reduce regional inequalities by a process of regionally distributing major public industrial units. This resulted in high transport costs, inefficient operations, power shortages and poor infrastructural amenities for the industries, which in turn led to marketing problems. The Indian railroad system has been working under heavy strain to cope with the increasing industrial demands. Pressure has become so heavy that the movement of raw materials to the industrial sites and of the finished products to the ports and hinterland is uneconomically slow.

Against these shortcomings, it is fair to point out that the country is blessed with a comparatively large resource base, adequate administrative and technical personnel, a large labor force and a wide domestic market. These basic facts contain the potentials for the development of modern industry. What is required is a national industrial policy to turn these potentials into realities.

One approach toward the development of a national, comprehensive industrial policy was suggested by the Planning Commission in 1955. The underlying idea was that industrial development could start at the village and small-town level, progressively building a pyramid of industry with the rural economy as a base. Influenced by this approach rural industrial estates were set up in the various states, using districts as an operational area for developing rural industry. Another approach later advanced by the Commission envisaged the creation of urban-nucleated industrialization in towns of 20,000 to 50,000 population. It was argued that towns of this size would be technologically unfeasible for industrialization. More promising results could be reached if the selected population range varied between 20,000 and 300,000 which could "offer the most congenial physical setting" since these were places likely to maximize the proximity of agriculture to centers of industry and commerce, and to supply the necessary framework for "the whole network of development sequences, linkages and feedbacks upon which the successful transformation of the Indian countryside so largely depends" (Lewis, 169). This approach has been strongly debated in favor of a rural-led employment-oriented strategy which suggests the development of a graded system of market centers from the village level to the larger urban nuclei of the size of 300,000. A graded system of market towns would draw upon the local resources of raw materials and labor force. A prerequisite to development is the creation of spatial integration by the provision of adequate infrastructure, communication linkages and banking-marketing facilities. Implicit in the above approaches is the idea that locational policies of economic growth should be aimed at reducing the rapid migration of people from the farm to urban areas. The creation of employment-oriented agro-based industries in villages and medium-sized towns would provide alternatives for the rural labor force, thus helping reduce its urban-ward migration. Such a policy of industrial decentralization, it is argued, will help restore the regional balance in industrialization.

CITATIONS AND SELECT BIBLIOGRAPHY

Bhagwati, J. N., et. al., *Planning for Industrialization and Trade Policies Since 1951*. London, 1970.
Chaudhuri, M. R., *Indian Industries, Development and Location*. Calcutta, 1970.
Chaudhuri, M. R., *Power Resources of India*. Calcutta, 1970.
Economic and Scientific Research Foundation, *Changes in the Locational Pattern of Select Indian Industries, 1950-1965*. New Delhi, 1969.
Draft Fifth Five Year Plan, 1974-1979. Vol. II, Government of India, New Delhi, 1974.
Gandhi, M. P., *Major Industries of India, 1970-71*. Bombay, 1972.
Karan, P. P., "Indian Industrial Change," *Annals of the A.A.G.* Vol. 54, 1964.
Karan, P. P., et. al., "Geography of Manufacturing in India," *Economic Geography*. Vol. 35, 1959, pp. 269-278.
Lewis, J. P., *Quiet Crisis in India*. Washington, D.C., 1962.
Mellor, J. W., *The New Economics of Growth*. Ithaca, N.Y., 1976.
Noble, A. G., et. al., *Indian Urbanization and Planning*. New Delhi, 1977.
Pattanshetti, C. C., *Dimensions of India's Industrial Economy*. Bombay, 1968.
Rao, K. L., *India's Water Wealth*. New Delhi, 1975.
Shirokov, G. K., *Industrialization of India*. Moscow, 1973.
Sinha, B. N., *Industrial Geography of India*. Calcutta, 1972.
Wilber, C. O., (ed.), *The Political Economy of Development and Underdevelopment*. New York, 1973.

CHAPTER 9

PLANNING, REGIONAL DEVELOPMENT AND INFRASTRUCTURE

Indian spatial development is basically organized around a few metropolitan-manufacturing nodes, which are widely dispersed on coastal and inland locations. These nodes are the major commercial centers and act as collection and distribution points for crops and raw materials for domestic and foreign markets (Friedman, 1964; Berry, 1968; and Reed, 1967). Four such nodes, Calcutta, Bombay, Madras and Delhi dominate Indian economic landscape. These are connected internally with smaller commercial centers by commodity flows and transport systems. Each major metropolitan-node performs the functions of collection, processing, storage, and distribution of regional products. Each developed these functions as inland connections of roads and railroads were established during the 19th and 20th centuries. The few inland commercial foci acquired some of these functions at a later date as tributaries to the four major regional nodes.

Outside the periphery of these nodes lies a comparatively large territory with a rural-based, unorganized and poorly-linked economic system. Space economy thus lacks a graded, integrated socio-economic organization and the rural-urban dichotomy is sharp despite increasing spatial linkages between the several parts of the country, particularly along the major railroads. The "organized" system of city services (banks, offices, companies, municipalities), symbols of "modernization," are scarce outside the urban centers. Rural finance, investments and productive activities are not only unregulated, but are in the hands of the elite castes and landlords. Expansion of productivity chronically suffers from individual monopolies and whims because it is not sub-

316

ject to regulated authority and analysis. Controlled by landlords, or the family heads or village lending-class, lacking in finance and accountability, the economic structure remains disincentive ridden, immune to the influences of outside, urban-based amenities. However, modern technology, an effective transport system, and other infrastructural improvements are steadily advancing. Farmers in the Punjab are now beginning to be organized and are establishing outside links. At the end of the Fourth Plan only two states, Punjab and Tamil Nadu, had completed rural electrification, and Haryana was close to it. The cotton farmers of Gujarat, jute farmers of West Bengal, and tea planters of Assam are now linked to the city-based banking, commercial and marketing facilities, but a national integrated system of economic and institutional linkages has yet to develop.

Recent attempts to integrate the village economies with the city or national economy include the institution of Community Development Programs within the framework of the Five Year Plans. Through these a farmer is encouraged to utilize the organized economic sector by obtaining loans for such farm aids as better seeds, fertilizers, improved farm machinery and electric pumps. Community Development has also been steadily bringing the farmer in contact with the national and state administrative hierarchy, political organizations and political process. All these efforts have, of course, produced increased spatial linkages between the rural areas and the urban centers. Spatial integration is now strong along several railroad tracks where "urban corridors" containing several industrial towns have emerged (Figure 9.2).

NATIONAL PLANNING EXPERIENCE

Following Russia's sudden, if unspectacular, success during the 1920's, the idea of national planning aimed at achieving an overall economic development gained general acceptance among the developing nations, particularly since their attainment of independence after World War II. The major post-Independence question before India was not whether planning was desirable, but rather what type of planning could best be pursued. The Russian example of centralized planning offered a great challenge, but was not in conformity with India's constitutional mandate, ideological tradition or self-prescribed democratic framework. The Western experience of capitalistic planning held promise but its inherent colonial affiliations appeared unsavory. Given the dimensions and complexity of India's problems of demographic pressure, foodgrain shortage, poverty and the general unresponsiveness of society to modern ideas and technology, the issue of economic reconstruction presented a major task for the government at the time of Independence.

Eschewing both the totally state-controlled centralized planning example of the communistic countries and an outright *laissez-faire* economic course, India tried to establish a pattern which combined the socialistic system of state-supervised economic programs with a liberal interblend of private enterprises. Soon it became a pioneer and a model for other developing nations in national planning. Blessed with a functioning bureaucracy, parliamentary tradition, well-considered constitutional guidelines, effective leadership, potentially adequate resource-base and a corps of seasoned economists, it possessed the essential base-structure for the formulation of national plans. The government formed by the Indian National Congress was already committed to economic planning.

Counterbalancing this fortuitous set of circumstances were the reactionary forces. Society was riven by class, caste, religion and regional interests. Centers of authority in the rural society had vested interests making them unresponsive to development. The colonial regime had not aggressively addressed itself to modernization. The existing transport network was geared to the exploitation of raw materials for export rather than toward industrialization. Villages remained relatively closed, and produced little beyond local needs. There were, in addition, problems of the creation of capital needed for all national plans. Investment levels for a country of India's dimensions were exceedingly low, and combined with the proverbially low domestic savings, required huge inflow of foreign aid. The private sector was limited and unorganized.

The idea of planning development did not begin to take root until the 1930's. Although the Russian Five Year Plans had evoked interest among the intelligentsia of the Indian National Congress, the Soviet model aroused much suspicion. Nehru, convinced of the need for planning, was skeptical of Russian-style development. The "big business" interests in the party, vehemently in opposition to any socialistic model, were in fact critical to planning itself. These differences surfaced occasionally during the discussions of the Congress' National Planning Committee (NPC) in 1938. Debate intensified during the 1940's, but the Congress became pledged to a socialistic type of planning.

Even before the discussions of the NPC, Visvesvarayya had suggested a national economic development plan in 1934 which considered rapid industrialization of the country to be a key to planning, and noted that the business community in the private sector has a large role to play in the creation of investment flows necessary for industrialization. Notable among the various planning documents, several of which appeared during the 1940's, was the "Bombay Plan" proposed by eight prominent industrialists. Another plan known as "Gandhian Plan" since it carried the blessings of Mahatma Gandhi, also emphasized the role of rapid industrialization. The "People's Plan" of the Communist Party of India, on the other hand, focused on the desirability of socialistic planning and favored the development of the public sector at the expense of the private.

On the eve of Independence, the administration proposed a document defining the role and scope of future planning in 1946. It was not until 1950, however, that a National Planning Commission was set up with the active support of Prime Minister Nehru, who remained a prime mover in all subsequent plans until 1964.

The First Five Year Plan (1951-1956) thus started with the blessing and support of the Prime Minister. Despite its modest size and goals, it created the foundations for subsequent plans. The basic principles of planning had been set forth; chief among these were: the rejuvenation and expansion of the national economy, the establishment of a healthy private sector within the economy except in the stipulated industries (shipbuilding, fertilizers, large steel plants), creation of an extensive system of government supervision, resource allocation and afforded encouragement to foreign investment in the production of consumer goods and the development of infrastructure (transport, railroads, construction). Thus, planning strongly favored a mixed economy (private-public mix). The major goal of the First Plan was to achieve self-sufficiency of the nation in agricultural and industrial production.

With a brief period of re-examination between 1966 and 1969 (years of "rolling" annual plans), there have been a total of five Five Year Plans since 1951. The most recent, or Sixth Plan, will cover the period 1978-1983 (Table 9.1 details basic statistics related to the Five Year Plans).

Fundamental to any conscious planning effort aimed at transformation of the poor, traditional, and primarily agricultural nation into a prosperous, industrial and modern one, was the tremendous task of human transformation which could only be achieved by changing people's attitudes and lifestyles through a concentrated program of "modernization." From the beginning, high priority was accorded to the betterment of millions in the agricultural sector. Each Plan contained provisions for the agricultural laborers, landless peasants, rural housing and backward classes, as well as for the educated unemployed, the poor and the youth. Economic development was to be attained through expansion of employment and reduction of differences in the distribution of income, wealth and power. Village administration was to be democratized through community participation and *panchayati raj* (local government).

The twin objectives of raising living standards and opening avenues of employment opportunity were considered basic to the formulation of planning and were embodied in all the six Plans. The First Plan aimed at raising national income by 20 percent, and per capita income by 11 percent; these were nearly realized. The Second Plan (1956-1961) sought to achieve an increase of 25 percent in national income and an 11 percent raise in per capita income. Both targets remained unfulfilled, largely as a result of spiralling population growth.

Nearly one-half of the Plan outlays were reserved for construction of the infrastructural base—the building of roads, railroads, power development, educational facilities—and were directed mainly towards modernization of the agricultural sector. Most developmental activity in the expansion

TABLE 9.1
SELECTED STATISTICS, FIVE YEAR PLANS

	First 1951-56	Second 1956-61	Third 1961-66	Fourth 1969-74	Fifth 1974-79 (Draft)	Sixth 1978-83 (Proposed in 1980).
1. Net Investment in millions of rupees	35,000	62,000	104,000	213,500	534,110	Details Lacking
			(As a per cent of total investments)			
Agriculture (and irrigation)	25.0	19.0	20.0	16.0	19.4	
Big Industry (including power generation)	23.0	29.0	35.0	39.0	40.0	
Small industry	5.0	4.0	4.0	3.0	*	
Transportation (and communication)	22.0	17.0	17.0	17.0	17.0	
Other	25.0	26.0	24.0	25.0	21.0	
2. Public/Total Investment Ratio	53.0	61.0	61.0	64.0	66.0	
3. National Income Increase	11.2	25.0	34.0	50.0		
4. Average Net Investment, Ratio of National Income	7.4	10.2	12.8	21.4		
5. Average Domestic Savings as a Ratio of National Income	5.7	8.1	9.8	15.0		
6. Net Imports/Net Investments	21.0	18.0	25.0	32.0		

*No Data.
Sources: *Five Year Plans*, Several Volumes.

of the infrastructural base was to be achieved through public sector investments. In the Fifth Plan the public investment in this area was 60 percent of the total outlays.

Government also moved quickly into investments in "heavy" industries, such as the production of machine tools, telephones, aircrafts, shipbuilding, heavy electric machinery and fertilizers. Imports of heavy machinery an raw materials to build machines were progressively reduced by a strict import-substitution and trade licensing policy aimed clearly at reaching self-sustaining growth through domestic production. While the First Plan (1951-1956) focused primarily on agricultural development, the Second (1956-1961) embarked on a course of rapid industrialization. The public sector's input into industrialization grew from 50 percent in the First Plan to over 70 percent in the Third Plan (1966-1971).

However, the government progressively reduced its share in agricultural investments. Multipurpose installations at Bhakra-Nangal, Damodar Valley and Hirakud, providing irrigation and power and aimed at agricultural development, were started during the First Plan. Planners, however, considered industrialization a panacea for economic development and the planning focus was on industrialization.

The Third Plan's objectives of securing a base for self-sustaining growth and an increase in the national income of over 5 percent annually were not realized. National income, in fact, declined in 1966. To attain foodgrain self-sufficiency was one objective, although the major emphasis was on industrialization. It remained unrealized. Foodgrain imports increased. The course of rapid industrialization entailed large-scale imports of heavy machinery and sophisticated tools, necessitating problems of foreign exchange. War with China in 1962 slowed down all developmental plans. National energy and economy was directed toward war efforts. Harvests were poor between 1965 and 1967. The planning effort had been largely disrupted and its re-evaluation appeared necessary. The Third Year Plan devoted attention to labor-intensive small industries like manufacture of bicycles, sewing machines, metal processing and rural electrification.

Resumption of the 5-year cycle was postponed in 1966 and plans on an annual basis were substituted. The major planning thrust during these interim years (1966-1969) was on agricultural development, to be achieved by increasing the manufacture of such products as fertilizers and agricultural machinery. A "New Strategy for Agricultural Development" was outlined. High priority was given to the introduction of and popularization of high-yielding varieties of foodgrain, the use of power-driven farm equipment and the use of chemical fertilizers. The industrial sector recorded minimal gains, while the agriculture improved, although foodgrain shortages continued to necessitate food imports. The economy was recovering slowly.

Against the unpromising background of a difficult foreign exchange situation and foodgrain imports, the Fourth Plan (1969-1974) was conceived. This plan was designed to produce stability by introducing safeguards against economic fluctuations through a sustained increase in exports by 7 percent annually and through raising domestic production, both calculated to reduce dependence on foreign aid. The cornerstone items of the Plan were agriculture, fertilizer, and steel, development of which were considered essential to achieve major objectives. Reduction of unemployment also was an important objective. This was to be attained by encouraging industry to be labor-intensive, for example by the creation of urban small-scale industry producing bicycles, sewing machines and electric goods. This idea came into direct conflict with the development of heavy industry during the previous Plans. The Fourth Plan reasserted the importance of agricultural development in national economy. Predictably, the agricultural sector advanced satisfactory during the Plan, while performace of the economy in general was below targets.

The Fifth Plan (1974-1979) set before it two broad objectives: the removal of poverty and the attainment of self-reliance. A policy statement detailing processes related to the realization of these broad goals noted that foreign aid was to be drastically reduced and dependence on import oil and steel was to be curtailed. Strict trade licensing was to continue, and mechanization of agriculture received special attention. A feature of the Plan was the scheme for development of backward areas (hills, Rajasthan Desert) and tribal people. Unique to the Plan was the incorporation of a National Programme of Minimum Needs. Such a program envisaged provision of adequate food, elementary education, public health facilities, drinking water, all-weather roads, housing and electrification to at least 30 percent of the rural population within the planning period.

For political reasons not clearly understood, the Sixth Plan (1978-1983) was inaugurated one year ahead of schedule. Its draft outlined "a new strategy of development" which called for giving greater impetus to the goals of "full employment, the eradication of poverty" and the creation of a more egalitarian society. It envisioned doubling of the expenditure ($77.1 billion) of the Fifth Plan, an annual growth rate of nearly 4.5 percent and substantial increases for outlays in agriculture and irrigation, small industry, energy and the Minimum Needs Programme (a carry-over from the Fifth Plan).

The Indian planning experiment has been the object of world-wide scrutiny in view of India's strategic importance in South Asia. The consensus of judgment has pronounced it to be respectable (Neale, 105; Malenbaum, 15), as most achievements reached 80 percent of the targets. The major disappointment was deceleration of the economy during the Third Plan. Inflation, rising foodgrain imports, military involvements with China and Pakistan, shortfall in foreign exchange and undue importance attached to heavy industries without an adequate resource-base, all contributed to the modest performance of the Third Plan. The economy began to move again during the period of rolling plans. National income grew moderately, between 3 to 4 percent annually between 1966 and 1969.

Despite the fluctuating performance during individual Plan periods, the Indian economy made substantial gains during 1951-1974. Foodgrains production rose from 62.7 million to nearly 120 million tons (129 million tons in 1978), production of steel from 1.7 to 4.5 million tons, nitrogenous fertilizers from less than 1 million tons to over 10 million tons, petroleum from 3.9 to 7.2 million tons, and electric power from 11 billion KWh to 65 billion KWh during this period. Installed power capacity increased enormously, although it remained underutilized. Exports made phenomenal gains, particularly during the Fourth and Fifth Plan periods when these averaged a 13 percent increase annually. The area under irrigation nearly doubled. Indian planning was not, then, disappointing. Its three major contributions lay in it rescuing the economy from its traditional stagnation, in raising per capita income (from \$70 to \$160 annually), and in preparing a sound infrastructural base for a self-reliant economy. Yet, the most important objectives of planning were not realized as the drafters of the Sixth Plan concluded, namely the eradication of poverty and the creation of a more equal society. These remained as distant today as when the country embarked upon the course of planned development.

Why then was growth modest and often below the targets? Plans were generally well-structured and articulated, but goals were often over-ambitious. A major bottleneck in implementation and a cause of slow progress was the failure of planning to produce an environment capable of changing the social structures which were inseparably interlinked with economic and political conditions. The social obstacles to Indian economic development were evidently serious. Planners did nothing to undertake the scientific investigations apparently necessary to deal with any social change. No division of the Planning Commission specifically applied itself to social problems, and insofar as research was undertaken, it was not conducted by qualified sociologists. An example of utter disregard of any sociological input into the planning process is that of the Indian caste-system, which according to modern sociologists is regarded as the most formidable obstacle to India's economic progress, but which has scarcely been discussed in the Plans.

The planning process, from its inception, remained under the shadow of the politicians. Although politicians lent it prestige, they also inhibited independent thinking and freedom of action. The bureaucrats produced what the politicians wanted whether it contributed best to planning or not. In order to please the politicians (the Indian National Congress, the party in power at the center) unrealistic targets were established, and in some instances targets were set contrary to planning principles.

The planning machinery has been notoriously slow. Endless steps were required for the process to crystallize. The bureaucratic chain of command through which decisions were finalized consisted of various committees, the National Development Council, the Cabinet and the Parliament. Furthermore, relations between the Commission and the private sector have generally been cool.

Good planning is a function of the statistical assumptions it makes, and the accuracy and relevance of data it collects, analyzes and utilizes. The Commission's statistical bases for planning formulation have been found to be grounded in less than accurate, and perhaps in inadequate data.

Planning problems were aggravated by external factors, such as the scarcity of foreign exchange and restrictive external aid. An unexpected demand generated by private industry drained foreign exchange reserves. During the 1960's imports had to be severly curtailed in the face of dwindling foreign exchange reserves. The situation was further aggravated by the increase of oil prices in 1972. Indian development, which was already working under conditions of scarcity, was hit hard.

Over the years the problem of foreign-aid repayments has assumed staggering proportions. Currently about 20 percent of the projected export earnings go towards debt service payments for foreign aid. Net aid available for investment works out to be a mere 3 percent of the nation's total planned development (Malenbaum, 144). With good reason, the Fifth Plan's major objective was to reduce foreign dependence.

Barring unforeseen circumstances, such as poor monsoons, military involvement, political instability, foreign exchange pressures, inefficient use of modern technology and the failure to create adequate infrastructure, the Indian economy can reasonably grow at a moderate pace. Undoubtedly these constraints are formidable; however, the picture of development appears mildly optimistic.

REGIONAL DEVELOPMENT PLANNING

Indian Five Year Plans are essentially macro-plans. Designed centrally and for the federal level, the regional component is missing. Even policies regarding allocation of resources for development are designed and manipulated through central authority. Major allocations focused on special projects; the plans are merely a loose uncoordinated collection of state and district plans. At the lowest level, the

Community Development Projects are piecemeal efforts to cover selected sections of the country and perhaps come closest to the idea of integrated planning in space. Regional development linking the two spatial levels, the village and the regional, within the overall planning process, has not received much attention from the farmers. Even the two regional projects, the Damodar Valley Corporation and the Dandakaranya Project, are not designed to be comprehensive or spatially integrative.

The Plans recognized the need for development of backward or poor areas. One major planning objective was to achieve a balanced development of the regions. The Second Plan affirmed that no part of the country should remain underdeveloped just as others should not gain lop-sided development. A National Development Council was set up for identification of backward areas where new enterprises could be located. A regional decentralization of major industries was also attempted. New steel plants were located at Rourkela and Bhilai in Orissa and Madhya Pradesh states, partially in view of their relatively low levels of industrial employment. Future sites for steel plants were all planned in South India to restore regional balance in development.

The principle of balanced regional development was applied only toward decentralization of the steel industry and fertilizer factories. Little attention was given to the development and diffusion of agricultural rejuvenation programs, the building of infrastructure linking urban with rural regions, and the expansion of rural electrification and education within an integrated spatial frame in order to achieve a more equitable distribution of regional development. All areas may not be equally suitable for industrialization, so that a wholesale policy of decentralization may not be desirable.

Particularly surprising is the low priority accorded to the development of infrastructure in Indian planning. The need for the creation of a well-designed infrastructure linking India's space economy from the village level to the market towns (acting both as reservoirs and feeders of employment, industry and services to the rural areas) and the larger metropolitan centers, with a view to comprehensive regional development was recognized in the Third and Fourth Plans, and forcefully articulated in the Fifth Plan. Yet allocations for infrastructural development were meager, and allocated for the development of selected backward districts.

The success of the "Green Revolution" could well have become a sufficient motivation for the introduction of more universalized planning efforts. Even the "Green Revolution" efforts were focused on relatively few selected areas. The spatial linkage of this technological advancement with other areas, particularly enhanced by the development of infrastructure, could open up great possibilities of economic regional development in the country. The "Green Revolution" also created a base for the development of agro-based industries in the villages and market centers. The expansion of infrastructural facilities in such centers could well promote economic development in the region.

In practice, regional planning in India was conceived as slicing the federal pie into state and district allocations within which each state/district was to pursue its own projects irrespective of national programs and without concern for other programs. The projects of each state necessarily developed selected areas but a coordinated regional development failed to emerge.

In fund allocations, regional pressures and tension have played an important part. All states displayed tendencies to inflate their demands. Once favorable terms were reached, the states exercised a good measure of control over most projects, especially the ones that related to the lowest level, the level of the village, the Community Development Project, oriented to agricultural development and the *panchayati raj*. Without proper control of the state and national agencies, the two locally-based agencies achieved very little. By the end of the Fourth Plan, it was quite clear that major development in the country had taken place only in a few selected areas under federal jurisdiction (steel plants and industrial development), while a large section of the economy remained underdeveloped.

The Third Plan devoted an entire chapter to policy affirmations regarding balanced regional development. The Fourth and the Fifth Plans identified 229 districts as backward. (This constitutes almost three-fourths of the country.) Underdeveloped areas belonged to two major groups, one containing unfavorable physical features (hilly terrain, harsh climate, forests, deserts) or being culturally backward (largely tribal areas), and the other, economically retarded areas.

Stemming largely from inadequate statistical information and field work, the Fifth Plan encountered special conceptual and methodological problems in the identification of economically backward regions. Once identified, the regions became eligible for concessional finance and special grants. An innovative feature of the Fifth Plan was the development of a National Programme of Minimum Needs, which focused its attention on these backward regions. Implicit in the planning process in India is the view that a balanced regional development can be achieved by identification of backward regions, and by allocation of funds, personnel and administrative machinery to such defined regions. A strategy of economic development unrelated to spatial regional integration could hardly produce results. A truly functioning development process does not mean planning for specified areas or for specific items, but consists of a process which has a focus on spatial integration.

The Damodar Valley Corporation (DVC) project and the Dandakaranya Development Authority (DDA), both designed by federal authority, are perhaps the two examples of spatially integrated regional planning. The DVC is a river-valley, multipurpose project in the states of Bihar and West Bengal. Patterned after the American Tennessee Valley Authority (TVA), the functions of DVC are wide-ranging: promotion of facilities for water-supply, drainage, irrigation, soil-conservation, generation of electric power, flood-control, and navigation, and the promotion of public health and economic well-being of the region. The DVC has been engaged in the construction of dams, canals, and electric transmission lines, afforestation, leaving economic planning in the hands of the states. The DVC is, therefore, not an all-comprehensive regional planning organization. Its functions are focused primarily on water-related problems of the Damodar River Valley, such as river-basin drainage, soil erosion, irrigation and navigation.

The DDA is even more limited in scope. It was established in 1958 with a view to resettling 35,000 Hindu refugees from East Pakistan, and to develop an economic climate suitable for their resettlement. The site for the project was selected in forested, underdeveloped areas within the states of Madhya Pradesh and Orissa. The DDA was also entrusted with the task of over-all development of the area, although agricultural development was the major concern. Following an Israeli model, a hierarchic self-sustaining settlement scheme of villages as basic units within the framework of clustered service-centers was developed. The DDA was, in essence, working on Christaller's well-known Central Place Model. However, in practice, a base for central functions to be sustained by agricultural activities was never created. Actual agricultural productions fell short by more than one-half of the requirements of the settlers. The settlements languished for want of agriculture. Poor development of irrigation facilities and inadequate infrastructure were the primary reasons for agricultural shortfalls. Cottage industries, related to the settlements, proved uneconomic on account of inadequate financing, poor water-supply and lack of power. Problems were compounded because the two districts of the DDA area were never treated administratively as a single regional unit. In fact, comprehensive regional planning in DDA was conspicuously missing.

INFRASTRUCTURAL BASES

Basic to India's economic planning programs is the development of a process which is capable of regenerating the rural economic landscapes which have been stagnating since medieval times. By drawing rural India within the orbit of economic expansion, the process of development can be accelerated. Improvement and extension of the infrastructural base is the key to the rural-urban-linked economic development.

In absolute numbers, the country's infrastructural base appears impressive. The railroad system, with a total track of over 37,000 miles is the fourth largest in the world, ranking after the U.S.A., the Soviet Union, and Canada. It employs about 1.4 million persons, has a fleet of over 1,200 locomotives, and operates 11,000 trains carrying daily over 6 million passengers and one-half million tons of freight. The transcontinental road system dates back to 1,000 B.C., its 100,000 miles of track makes it one of the largest in the world. But these and other infrastructures (airways, inland navigation, shipping, post and telegraph operations, banks, etc.) are, generally speaking, out-moded, inefficient and rudimentary. Despite considerable gains in infrastructural improvements through the Five Year Plans' outlays, the infrastructural base remains deficient. The extent of transport deficiency can be indicated by comparisons with the transport resources in the rest of the world. "India accounts for 16 percent of the world's people but only 4 percent of its improved roads, 2 percent of its rail freight, and 1 percent of its trucks and buses" (Owen, 3).

The railroad system, inherited from the British, reflects the pattern of British advance in the country and its administrative convenience. The track was extended inland starting from the three foci along the coast, Calcutta, Bombay and Madras, where the trading and military posts had been established. In north India, the Ganga Plains, a commercially productive area was suitable for laying railroad tracks. The major British thrust of annexation in the Ganga Plains followed the establishment of a Calcutta-Delhi link between 1757 and the early 19th century. Meanwhile, coastal and inland encroachment resulted in British expansion along the established routes in Central and Southern India. Thus, a skeletal railroad system was developed from the coastal ports, radiating inland to inter-link the ports with the hinterlands. Delhi, a long-time federal capital and economic node in the country, became a major inland focus of internal communications. Gradually, feeder links were attached to the major railroad routes.

The road system, despite its ancient history, has remained underdeveloped. Major roads parallel the railroad system. Feeder links joining the interiors are in poor condition, in places passable only during fair weather. Water transport and navigation has only been regionally significant, especially in the northeast sections of the country and along the coasts. Air traffic was initiated a few years before Independence.

Transport development during British rule was based on two key considerations. First was to facilitate the movement of cash crops such as cotton, tea and jute to the ports for export to Britain or for reimport into the country after processing into finished products (e.g., gunnybags, textiles, tea). Secondly, transport links were developed with an eye on strategic points for effective administrative control and movement of military forces from the several cantonments (garrison towns) established along the railroad line. Transport development did help, however, in a number of ways. In times of famine, foodgrains could be dispatched from surplus areas to the needy regions, while commercial centers sprang up along the railroads.

The Five Year Plans accorded the development of transport facilities a priority status and investments ranged between 20 and 24 percent of total outlays in the public sector. A significant expansion of railroad and road transport took place during the Third and Fourth Plan periods. The volume of passenger and freight traffic increased from 88 to 147 million tons, and 78 to 135 million passenger km between 1961 and 1974. Road traffic increased even faster, registering gains particularly in the volume of freight it carried. In 1974 road transport accounted for nearly one-half (49 percent) of all passenger traffic (up from 41 percent in 1961), and approximately one-third (31 percent, up from 16 percent in 1961) of the freight traffic. Growth of commercialization and increased spatial integration between the rural and urban markets during the period largely accounted for the relatively rapid growth of road transport. Inland navigation and coastal shipping traffic remained underdeveloped. The Fifth Plan aimed at improvement in railroad freight transport of major bulk commodities (coal, iron ore, cement, fertilizers), as well as extension of rural feeder road links. It envisaged linking all villages with a population of 1500 or over by all-weather roads by the end of 1979.

The railroads are nationalized, their operations controlled by the Ministry of Railways. Trucking and buses are handled largely by private firms regulated by state legislation. The surfaced-road-track is estimated to be approximately 300,000 miles, or nearly one-half of the total road length. The National Highway system covering 15,000 miles, is the responsibility of the federal administration. Major highways include: (1) the Grand-Trunk Road from Calcutta to Amristar via Varanasi and Delhi; (2) Kanpur to Agra; (3) Agra to Bombay; (4) Bombay to Madras, via Bangalore; (5) Madras to Calcutta; and (6) Calcutta to Bombay via Nagpur. A major future project is to link the National Highways to an international highway network,

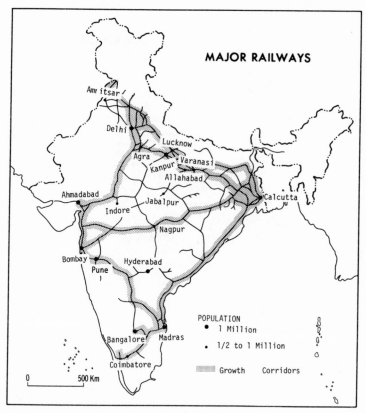

FIGURE 9.1

principally with Pakistan and Burma. In 1960 a Border Roads Development Board was set up for accelerating the development of border transport along the Tibet-Burma-Pakistan borders in the strategic frontier areas.

Despite a steady improvement in transport facilities during the thirty-five years of planning, sections of the country remain inaccessible. Spatial segmentation, particularly of the rural areas, is still a major problem. Great regional disparities in the availability of services both foster spatial segmentation and are a direct outcome of it. Figures 9.1 and 9.2 indicate road and railroad network accessibility in the country. Four major concentrations of railroads are: (1) Calcutta-Dhanbad industrial belt in West Bengal and East

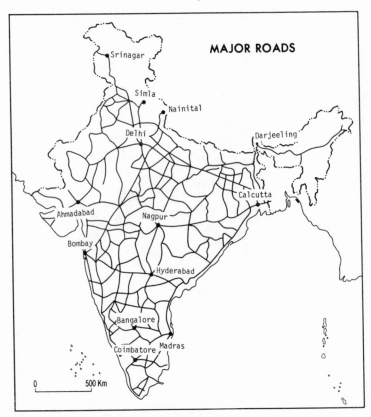

FIGURE 9.2

Bihar; (2) Kanpur-Lucknow commercial belt in eastern Uttar Pradesh; (3) Agra-Mathura commercial belt in western Uttar Pradesh; and (4) Ahmadabad-Baroda industrial region in Gujarat. The Ganga Plains from West Bengal to Punjab contain high railroad concentrations. Elsewhere, in the Peninsula, the distribution is spotty, concentrated around chief commercial industrial centers (Nagpur, Hyderabad, Madras, Bangalore, Bombay, Madura, Vijayawada, and Coimbatore). Road densities generally exhibit similar patterns, but contain several deviations, particularly in South India where road densities are higher than in the North Indian Plains.

Accessibility patterns, i.e., distance from surfaced roads,

Planning and Infrastructure

335

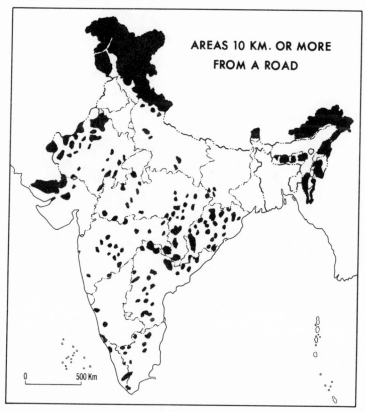

FIGURE 9.3

are essentially similar to the above patterns. The North Indian Plains, Gujarat and Tamil Nadu belong to the highest category containing most areas less than 10 kms from roads. Inaccessible parts (those which lie more than 10 kms from roads) are shown in Figure 9.3. These are the hill regions (Kashmir, Himachal Pradesh, Arunachal Pradesh, Meghalaya, Nagaland, Manipur, Tripura), the western sections of Rajasthan Desert and the forests of Chota Nagpur, Baghelkhand, and Dandakaranya.

Air transport is relatively new and sparse. The major airways and airports are shown in Figure 9.4.

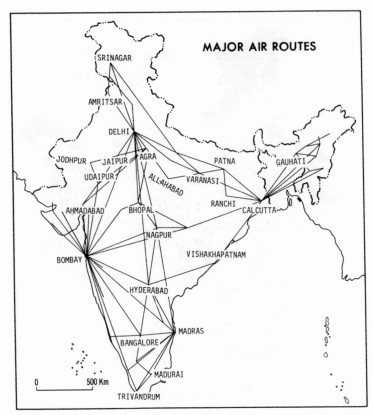

FIGURE 9.4

PROBLEMS AND PROSPECTS
OF INFRASTRUCTURAL DEVELOPMENT

Foremost among infrastructural needs is the extension of surfaced roads to the villages. The total dimension of the problem of the country was vaguely ascertained under the Nagpur Plan. On a state level, a survey conducted for the state of Maharashtra in 1966 indicated that nearly 80 percent of its villages were not connected by a main road, 40 percent were without any approach, only one-third had cart tracks and 65 percent contained only footpaths. Transport conditions in other states are little better. A more recent

study in Uttar Pradesh concluded that such transport inadequacy not only hampered the economy of the area in
general, but led to foodgrain deficits in a potentially rich
farming area. Large sections of Uttar Pradesh (and indeed
all the Middle Ganga Plains) suffer from low productivity
because better seeds and technology cannot be easily supplied to the isolated villages. Crop yields are 75 percent of
those prevailing in other states with better communications.
About one-third of the Uttar Pradesh villages are without
any road connections; one-half are located 5 to 10 miles
from an important market and over 20 percent are located
more than 10 miles from any road. Nearly one-third of the
villages located on a surfaced road are remote from any
market (Owen, 59-60). Problems of transport are compounded where the means of communication are mainly in
the form of bullock-carts, camels or simple human carriers.
Poor transport facilities create difficulty of crop marketing
and of diffusion of technology to the farmers. The first step
toward spatial integration is the provision of a surfaced
rural-road network.

The railway network, like the surfaced roads, is not distributed in proportion to the service area or the population size of the sections of the country. Excepting Tamil
Nadu, Gujarat and parts of the north Indian Plains, one-
half of the country lies more than 10 miles distant from the
railroad track. Furthermore, the effective usage of railway
track is also ill-proportioned, for 15 percent of the track carries 60 percent of the traffic.

Related to road and railway inaccessibility is the question of increasing equipment for such transport carriers as
buses, freight cars, and locomotives. Since World War II
acute shortages of vehicles and freight cars has steadily
grown. Shortages often led to industrial shut-downs and
stoppages of coal movements; road transport and the use of
oil followed such shortages. Near self-sufficiency has now
been claimed in the domestic production of locomotives,
freight cars and other vehicles. But the rise in oil prices since
1973 has aggravated the transportation situation.

Growth of railroads, also of crucial importance to
economic development, is beset with a number of problems.
It depends, at least partially, on the domestic production of
locomotives. Production of rail locomotives, currently

amount to 180 diesel and electric engines annually at Chittaranjan Works, the Diesel Locomotive in Varanasi, the Coach Factories at Madras and Bangalore, are barely sufficient to meet domestic needs. Demand for these is increasing with the attendant strain on the present capacity. In this regard, readjustments in freight rates of road transhipment to competitive levels with those of the railroads can release pressure on railroad freight traffic.

The proverbial low operating efficiency of Indian railroads stems from a combination of several factors: one, the multiple track-gauges, ranging from 2 feet to 5.5 feet in width in different parts of the country impedes the continuous flow of freight shipments of critically needed machinery and food supplies during times of need; two, a poorly-conceived freight rate structure; and three, the uncompetitive edge given to freight rates in comparison with those of passenger traffic. Passenger movement rates have been found at times to be below investment levels, whereas freight rates are unreasonably higher. All this has led to frequent over-utilization of existing facilities and unnecessary congestion on the sections most travelled by passengers, and underutilization of services in other parts, less frequented by passengers. A more judicious rate structure, based on actual costs, distance, freight volume and passenger amenities has yet to be devised. In transhipment of high value commodities, road transport should be encouraged.

Road transport experiences different problems. Truckers complain of a complex group of administrative constraints by local, state and federal authorities. Road maintenance is appallingly poor. Most trucking and passenger busing are in private hands and are prone to complex administrative regulatory hurdles. There has been a phenomenal increase in private trucking and passenger busing in several areas, notably in Punjab, Haryana and Gujarat. During British rule, road transport was practically nonexistent. Railways received major attention at the expense of road transport, because colonial interests lay in the largescale movement of military forces and export-oriented goods for which railroads were most suitable. Such a policy almost strangled road construction. This trend has been reversed since Independence.

Development of surfaced roads is more cost-effective for

movement of passengers and agricultural commodities. Already, in Tamil Nadu, Maharashtra, Haryana and Punjab the rural landscape has begun to undergo transformation since the construction of all-weather roads. New market centers have developed and agricultural technology is being diffused. Farmers have begun to shift their production emphasis from subsistence crops to cash crops, yielding them better investment returns. By promoting the inflow of new technology (fertilizer, high yielding varieties of crops, power driven farm implements) the roads are injecting processes of modernization and progress (schools, banks, medical clinics, credit bureaus) to the rural areas. Studies point out that areas of newly constructed surfaced roads received many economic and social benefits (Economic Benefits, 1961).

A STRATEGY FOR AREA DEVELOPMENT

A major criticism of Indian planning is its neglect of the spatial dimensions of development planning. Despite their formal renunciation of the "piecemeal" or "project-by-project" approach at the beginning of the Second Plan, the later Plans continued to suffer from lack of emphasis, focus and direction in their locational policies. Even the Fifth Plan has made no consistent attempt at integrated spatial planning. There is no central policy and mechanism to coordinate village-level development with that of the medium-sized towns and the larger metropolitan centers. The village-level Community Development Programs are developed internally. This has resulted in spatial and economic "segmentation" of Indian society. Lewis observes that there is a "village fetish" in developmental programs which has further polarized society (Lewis, 169).

The following guidelines outline a framework for the development of a program of achieving spatial integration:

1. Determination of demographic and economic status of the region at different spatial levels (village, district, state). This is a stock-taking stage with a view to finding out growth potentials within the demographic context.

2. Determination of needs and requirements within the context of enunciated planning goals to be achieved.

3. Development of a growth-strategy with a view to establishing a graded system of spatial integration. This

stage would consist of determination of precise facilities in statistical terms at various spatial levels including the following:

(a) a number of various size-group market centers to be established between the villages and large cities. Their size and functions would depend on their distance from the villages. The plan would include provision of the creation of agro-based industries, such as fertilizers, chemicals, cement, woodworking, food processing, bicycles, light engineering and repair and service industries for agro-based industry, keyed to the resource base, talent and training programs of the market centers;

(b) development of surfaced roads between market centers and villages/large urban centers. Transport facilities to villages to be improved. As a first step the devleopment of intermediate-sized market centers (20,000 to 30,000 population) and paved roads linking them with the villages is suggested. Such centers would act as market for the sale of village produce and city-made items;

(c) gradual introduction of mechanization and technology (fertilizers, better seeds and crop varieties) to the villages through market facilities in the newly developed market centers;

(d) absorption of labor released from villages consequent upon mechanization in the new market centers in light industry, banking, or agricultural credit offices. Villagers could be provided with such jobs as clerkships or repair-maintenance jobs and could commute to these "new" towns, and

(e) provision of eacy credit facilities to the commuting rural labor to the "new" market towns.

4. Development of comprehensive planning within the villages and the new towns including a program of technology diffusion, creation of demand for cash crops, infrastructure within the villages (electricity, street paving, drinking water, schools, post offices, banks, community centers).

5. Successful operation of the above strategy would require the creation of a central level (district and/or state) overseeing administrative machinery. It has been pointed out that previous planning was uncoordinated and ineffective because of lack of control by a central coordinating

authority. For example, Community Development Block officers were responsible to the federal government only. They did not coordinate their activities with the states or districts. In matters relating to the development of rural industry, public health, commercial banks and irrigation, different agencies worked independently, and were unresponsive to high-order agencies.

The brief outline above proposes not only the development of "new" market centers, but considers the development of infrastructure on spatially integrated basis. This would necessarily require a large amount of capital and efficient administrative machinery. Creation of a capital and administrative pool within the Five Year Plans is essential. Indeed, shortage of investment outlays for a massive Indiawide spatial planning during the Plans has remained a major bottleneck in Indian planning.

6. Existing urban centers to be spatially integrated with the "new" towns by better communication links. A policy of selected and regulated shifting of the burden of services to new towns is desirable. Smaller industrial units and service components in these centers are to be designed to absorb labor of the larger cities as well.

CITATIONS AND SELECT BIBLIOGRAPHY

Berry, B. J. L., et. al., *Essays on Commodity Flows and the Spatial Structure of the Indian Economy.* Chicago, 1966.

Berliner, J. S., *Soviet Economic Aid.* New York, 1958.

Bhagwati, J. N., *Economics of Underdeveloped Countries.* New York, 1966.

Bhagwati, J. N., et al., *India: Planning for Industrialization and Trade Policies Since 1951.* London, 1970.

Draft Five Year Plan 1974-1979. Vol. II, Government of India Press, Planning Commission, New Delhi, 1974.

Friedmann, J. R. P., et al., *Regional Development and Planning.* Cambridge, Mass., 1964.

Hanson, A. H., *The Process of Planning: A Study of India's Five Year Plans—1950-1964.* London, 1966.

Malenbaum, W., *Modern India's Economy.* Columbus, 1971.

Misra, R. P., et al., *Regional Development Planning in India.* Delhi, 1976.

Noble, A. G., et al., *Indian Urbanization and Planning,* Delhi, 1977.

Owen, W., *Distance and Development, Transport and Communication in India.* Washington D.C., 1968.

Reed, W. E., *Areal Interaction in India.* Chicago, 1967.

Singh, T., *India's Development Experience.* New York, 1974.

Veit, L. A., *India's Second Revolution.* New York, 1976.

CHAPTER 10

FOREIGN TRADE:
CHARACTERISTICS
AND DEVELOPMENT

First among the colonial countries to gain independence after World War II, India possessed large size, a comparatively adequate resource base, a fairly experienced leadership, and a functioning parliamentary democracy when she became free in 1947. Immediately following independence she initiated schemes for socio-economic reconstruction and development.

In foreign trade, efforts were directed mainly toward changing the traditional colonial pattern of agricultural exports (jute, tea, cotton, spices, hides and skins) and imports of manufactured items. She also sought to expand her trading world, which was confined to the United Kingdom and a few other countries. Industrial expansion since independence was below expectation but dependence on the industrial countries for imports of machinery, manufactured items, and foodgrains steadily increased. After 1960 she was able to make inroads into the newer markets of the Soviet Union, the East European countries, and Japan.

In statistical terms (value and number of trading items and countries) her progress since 1947 appears deceptively promising. A significant enlargement of the trading area, and a three-fold increase in dollar amount of trade was achieved. Yet India's share in the world's total trade remained low, less than one percent in 1974, a drop from the figure of 2.4 percent in 1948. More than sixty percent of trade was still conducted with only six countries in 1974. Moveover, the nation's balance of trade steadily deteriorated, because increased imports of foodgrains and machinery were needed

343

for developmental programs. Furthermore, countries such
as Japan and a few newly-developing nations (Hong Kong,
Singapore, and Taiwan and South Korea) posed stiff competition to India's exports. This trend of widening trade deficits was reversed in 1968. Since 1972-73 when she recorded
her first modest surplus in trade balance since Independence,
India has maintained a general trading equilibrium.

Her realignment in trade direction during the 60's was
calculated not only to achieve expansion in her trading territory, but also to relieve dependence on western capital,
which over the years had imposed a severe strain on her
foreign exchange reserves. Agreements with the Eastern
European countries provided for trade transactions in convenient rupee payments. Although the United States and
Britain continued to remain the principal trading partners,
the Soviet Union and Japan became serious challengers.
There was a modest expansion of trade to the Middle East,
African and Asian countries.

PERFORMANCE OF THE ECONOMY,
AND ITS TRADE IMPLICATIONS

The structure and growth of the Indian economy deci-
sively affected her trade. Demographic pressures kept ac-
celerting. Agriculture continued to play a vital role in the
economy, while industrial production and tertiary activity
recorded marginal gains. Economic expansion was only 3.5
to 4 percent a year during the initial years of planning
(1950-61), and then dropped further, to less than 2.5 percent annually during the Third Plan. Serious droughts and
unprecedented declines in agricultural production strained
the economy in the subsequent years.

A notable characteristic of industrial activity was its
shifting structure, from consumer-oriented production to a
growing emphasis on capital goods and intermediaries (fertilizers, petro-chemicals). Emphasis on heavy industry began
with the Second Plan and intensified during the Third Plan.
It has declined since then. Import substitution programs
aimed at development of heavy industry did little to encourage growth of consumer goods' industry. Such a policy
placed stress on specific imports, especially heavy machinery, machine tools and equipment. A state-regulated

system of import licensing became the principle instrument of trade policy. Although licensing waxed and waned within planning parameters, these measures continued to dominate the economy. The State Trading Corporation, set up in 1956, played a decisive role in handling export-import transactions. In order to stimulate public sector industry by importation of heavy machinery, the State Trading Corporation encouraged the development of public sector trade.

Foreign investment was to play a major role in spurring development of indigenous industry. In theory, the government proposed attracting foreign investment precisely for this purpose but it was unwilling to invite foreign investors uncritically. In practice, then, foreign investment shied away from the restrictive atmosphere which the government had created. The minor place it occupied in industrial development hardly made the contribution toward economic development of which it was capable.

Institutionally, India inherited from colonial rule a well structured, experienced administrative machinery, a reserve of skilled entreprenurial talent, and a seasoned cadre within the business community capable of managing projected investments. Economic reconstruction would certainly have flagged still further but for these assets.

Against the background of economic, institutional and political conditions and within the framework of national planning objectives and policies, Indian foreign trade policies fluctuated significantly during four easily discernible phases between 1950-1975. Phase One (1950-1956) synchronized with the First Plan, when agricultural productivity was less than satisfactory and the economy remained stagnant. Measured as a percent of the world, the position of exports actually deteriorated. Imports mainly consisted of foodgrains and agricultural produce and the foreign exchange position remained somewhat comfortable. Phase Two (1956-1962) saw the growing strain of an increasingly unfavorable balance of foreign payment, triggered by a constellation of related forces, a shift in emphasis toward imports of heavy industry, strict industrial licensing and a continued stagnation of export performance. While world trade continued to expand rapidly as new trading countries (West Germany, Japan, Hong Kong, Taiwan, Singapore) assumed importance, India's share of world trade continued to slide. Phase Three (1962-1966) was a period of partial liberalization. Economic performance improved somewhat as industrial growth advanced but the worsening foodgrain position became critical. The Final Phase (1966-1976) was a period of fluctuating policies and economic performance. Foodgrain imports reached new high levels, in the wake of disastrous harvests particularly between 1966 and 1968. Trade at this time was affected by two major changes: the policy of liberalization, and the expansion of India's trading market to include the Soviet bloc and Japan.

GROWTH OF TRADE

In 1947 India ranked among the ten leading trading nations, but by 1976 she ranked below the 40 largest traders, contributing less than 0.5 percent to world trade. This decline in her international trade position corresponded ironically with her period of economic planning and export stimulus. In Asia, her position as a trading nation suffered during the 1950's and 60's as newly developed countries such as Singapore, Hong Kong, Malaysia, Iran and Indonesia emerged as stronger traders.

Statistically, India recorded modest gains in foreign trade following initiation of the Five Year Plans in 1951 (Table 10.1). The total value of foreign trade increased from $3,341 million to $6,576 million (in 1974). Imports rose sharply, from $1,838 million to $2,959 million in 1966 (a year of record foodgrain imports), then fell until 1971, but have been increasing steadily since then. Exports expanded more steadily, as a trend of continued and expanding unfavorable balance of trade was reversed in 1973. The trade gap widened from $335 million in 1951 to $1,268 million in 1966 but gradually narrowed later on.

Clearly, her planning effort, with foreign trade as its integral component, was inadequate and lacked vitality. Export performance, a key element in development planning, had proved particularly unresponsive to government policies. Imports consisted mainly of foodgrains and heavy machines. Imports of capital goods needed for the development of largescale heavy industry rose during the first three Five-Year Plans, but declined in 1966 as the foreign ex-

TABLE 10.1

TRADE BALANCE, 1951 TO 1974

(Selected Years)
(In Millions of Dollars)

	Imports	Exports	Balance	Total Value
1951-52	1,838	1,503	− 335	3,341
1965-66	2,959	1,692	− 1,267	4,651
1970-71	2,179	2,047	− 132	4,226
1971-72	2,416	2,091	− 325	4,507
1972-73	2,311	2.431	+ 120	4,742
1973-74	3,555	3,021	− 534	6,567

change situation deteriorated. Meanwhile, neither the exports of several traditional goods (jute, tea, cashew kernels, mica) nor of non-traditional goods (textiles, cloth, sugar, consumer goods) showed dynamic expansion.

STRUCTURE OF TRADE

In 1973-74 over three-fourths of India's trade was in machinery, transport-equipment, foodgrains, petroleum products, chemicals and manufactured goods. Between 1951-52 and 1973-74, these items accounted for over 80 percent of both imports and exports by value. Machinery and transport equipment led the group among imports (21.5 percent of total value in 1973-74). After 1973-74 oil and petroleum-based products became the second largest category of imports (14.3 percent of all imports in 1972, up from 7.8 percent in 1973-74). Paper and paper-board accounted for over 18 percent of imports and foodgrains a little over 12 percent (down from previous years). Chemicals and fertilizers represented nearly 3.5 percent of import value. Other major imports were raw-cotton, wool and medicines.

The most noticeable shift in import structure since 1966 was the large reduction in foodgrain imports, from 24 percent in value in 1951-52 to 12 percent in 1971-72 (Tables 10.2 and 10.3). Food imports remained substantial, how-

TABLE 10.2

IMPORTS FROM PRINCIPAL SUPPLIERS, 1950-1974

(Selected Years)
(As Per Cent of Total)

	1950-51	1965-66	1970-71	1971-72	1972-73	1973-74
U.S.A.	18.3	37.8	27.7	23.0	12.6	16.9
United Kingdom	20.8	10.6	7.8	12.1	12.7	7.3
Fed. Rep. of Germany	3.3	9.4	6.6	7.0	9.2	6.7
	(1951-52)					
Canada	3.4	2.2	7.2	6.2	5.8	3.6
USSR	0.2	5.9	6.5	4.8	6.1	8.6
East European Countries (Ex. Czech.)	0.4	5.2	7.5	6.6	6.3	4.9
	(1951-52)					
Japan	1.6	5.6	5.1	8.9	9.6	8.6
Iran	5.7	2.4	5.6	6.9	6.3	9.1
Italy	2.5	1.4	1.8	1.3	1.9	1.7
France	1.7	1.3	1.3	2.0	2.1	2.3
Belgium	1.4	0.8	0.7	1.9	2.7	2.2
Switzerland	1.1	1.0	0.7	0.4	0.6	0.6
Saudi Arabia	0.1	0.6	1.5	2.1	2.4	4.5
Czechoslo- vakia	0.4	1.5	1.2	0.6	0.8	0.9
Bangladesh	*	*	*	*	0.2	0.6
Australia	5.1	1.7	2.2	1.6	1.8	1.5
Egypt	5.1	1.4	2.4	1.8	1.5	0.8
Kenya	2.8	0.3	0.6	1.0	0.3	0.5
Sudan	1.1	0.4	1.3	1.4	2.4	0.7
Malaysia	0.1	0.9	0.3	0.2	0.4	1.1
Burma	0.9	0.7	0.6	0.3	0.1	*

*Negligible amount

Source: *India, 1976*, Government of India, New Delhi.

ever, particularly in years of poor monsoons. Imports of basic manufactured goods (iron and steel, copper, paper) essential to development of the industrial sector continued to expand. During and since the Second and Third Plans when the focus of development was on heavy industry, iron and steel imports rose from 2.2 percent to nearly 13 percent in value in 1972 (declining to 8.3 percent in the subsequent year). Singificant increases also occurred in the imports of oil and petroleum products as demand for fertilizers, transport equipment and machinery using petroleum products increased. Their share of import value escalated dramatically after 1973 in face of the steep increase in oil prices by OPEC countries. Oil imports continued to pose a serious fiscal drain (Table 10.3).

Controlled and regulated trade licensing and import substitution between 1956 and 1961, designed to encourage domestic production of consumer goods, affected imports of such items as superior-grade cotton, wool, medicines and fresh fruits, while indigenous supplies increased.

The export trade has always been dominated by three "traditional" commodities: tea, cotton-based goods and jute products. These items represented well over one-half the value of all exports until the late 1960's when increased domestic production and export of such items as cashew kernels, coffee, leather goods and iron ore progessively reduced their share until it reached 27 percent by 1974.

The changing structure of exports is indicated in Table 10.4 which lists major items and their share in the exports of 1950-51 and the selected years between 1965-66 and 1973-74. The three leading exports in 1951-52 (jute manufactures, tea and cotton goods) suffered from competition with synthetic substitutes, as well as from Bangladeshi products. The decline in tea exports stemmed from two basic sources: price-fluctuations in the world market and expansion of tea production in East Africa and Latin America. Labor costs on Indian plantations rose significantly during the 1960's, while African tea prices became competitive. Tariffs imposed on Indian tea imports by Britain rose when Britain entered the Common Market in 1973.

Dramatic decline in the share of cotton-based goods in Indian exports to world markets primarily reflected the emergence in the 1960's of such new producers as Hong

TABLE 10.3

MAJOR IMPORTS, 1950-1974
(Selected Years)
(As Per Cent of Total)

	1950-51	1965-66	1970-71	1971-72	1972-73	1973-74
Iron & Steel	2.2	6.7	9.0	13.0	12.0	8.3
Machinery (Except Elec.)	10.3	22.9	15.8	14.9	15.9	14.3
Petroleum Products	8.3	2.4	1.8	2.4	3.2	4.9
Transport Equipment	5.4	5.0	4.1	5.2	5.4	3.0
Electric Machines	3.4	6.2	4.3	5.8	7.2	4.2
Raw Cotton	15.4	3.3	6.1	6.2	6.9	1.8
Wheat	15.3	18.8	10.6	5.6	2.6	11.9
Petroleum Crude & Refined	*	2.5	5.5	8.1	7.8	14.3
Chemicals	1.4	2.5	4.2	3.9	4.9	3.6
Metal Manufactured	2.1	1.3	0.6	0.7	1.0	0.7
Textile Yarn	2.3	0.4	0.2	0.3	0.2	0.1
Copper	1.3	2.4	3.7	2.8	2.8	2.4
Zinc	1.0	0.9	1.3	1.0	1.2	0.9
Rice	8.2	3.0	1.8	1.0	0.6	0.2
Medicines	1.5	0.6	1.5	1.4	1.2	0.9
Fresh Fruits & Nuts	1.5	1.3	2.2	0.7	2.2	1.2
Raw Wool	0.9	0.4	1.0	0.8	0.6	0.7
Paper & Paperboard	1.6	0.9	1.8	1.9	1.7	1.0
Oil Seeds	0.4	0.6	0.4	0.6	0.7	0.2
Coal, Tar, Dyes	1.8	0.3	0.2	0.2	0.2	0.1
Aluminum	0.4	0.4	0.2	0.5	0.2	0.1
Milk & Cream	0.5	0.5	0.4	1.0	1.0	0.5
Raw Jute	*	0.6	*	*	*	0.4
Vegetables	0.5	0.5	1.4	1.5	0.8	1.9

*Negligible amounts.

Source: *India, 1976, op. cit.*

TABLE 10.4

MAJOR EXPORTS BETWEEN 1950 AND 1974
(As Per Cent of Total)

	1950-51	1965-66	1970-71	1971-72	1972-73	1973-74
Jute Manufactures	18.8	22.5	12.3	16.4	12.5	9.1
Tea	9.9	14.4	9.7	9.7	7.4	5.8
Cotton Manufactures	19.9	7.9	6.3	6.2	6.4	9.5
Textile Fabrics (Ex. Cotton & Jute)	0.8	0.9	0.8	0.8	0.8	1.6
Textile Articles	1.4	0.6	0.5	0.7	0.5	0.4
Textile Yarn	4.3	1.9	2.25	1.7	1.9	1.2
Ore (Non-ferrous)	NA	1.4	1.1	0.9	0.7	0.8
Leather	4.3	3.5	4.7	5.6	8.6	6.7
Raw Cotton	0.8	1.3	0.9	1.0	1.0	1.3
Fresh Fruit & Nuts	1.8	3.3	3.5	3.9	3.7	3.2
Crude Vegetables	2.3	2.1	2.2	3.4	2.0	2.3
Raw Wool	1.3	0.8	0.3	0.2	0.3	0.3
Sugar	*	1.4	1.9	1.9	0.7	1.7
Iron Ore	*	5.3	7.7	6.5	5.6	5.3
Tobacco	2.3	2.4	2.1	2.6	3.1	2.7
Vegetable Oils	4.2	0.5	0.5	0.5	1.3	1.2
Crude Minerals (Ex. coal, Petroleum)	*	1.8	1.4	1.3	1.2	0.9
Woolen Carpets	0.9	0.6	0.6	0.8	1.0	1.0
Iron & Steel	0.5	1.5	5.9	2.5	2.1	2.3
Coffee	0.2	1.6	1.5	1.4	1.7	1.8
Hides & Skins	1.6	1.2	0.2	*	*	*

TABLE 10.4 (continued)

MAJOR EXPORTS BETWEEN 1950 AND 1974

(As Per Cent of Total)

	1950-51	1965-66	1970-71	1971-72	1972-73	1973-74
Petroleum Products	*	0.8	0.6	0.6	0.7	0.5
Coal, Coke	0.6	0.4	*	*	0.2	0.1

*Figures not available

Source: *India, 1976, op. cit.*

Kong, Singapore, Japan and Taiwan. Their product was superior and was in greater demand in international markets. Britain's import policies regarding cotton yarn and woven material, resulting from British commitments to the Common Market, also affected Indian exports. Expansion of the domestic market for cotton textiles did not help the export situation either.

In dollar value, all exports excepting jute goods registered gains, nearly doubling in value during the period between 1950-51 and 1973-74, although their contribution to export trade was drastically reduced. Meanwhile, such non-traditional items as sugar, leather, raw cotton, nuts, vegetables, coffee, engineering goods and petroleum products recorded impressive gains.

In the 1970's engineering goods such as electrical machinery, transmission lines, railroad wagons, and chemical plants, which Indian firms produced more competitively, found their way to markets in Africa, the Middle East and Southeast Asia. The government's policy of import-substitution had one clear effect. It helped reduce the widening trade-deficit by 1966. In 1972-73 India could boast of a modest trade surplus, and since then deficits have been marginal.

A central problem in Indian trade is the heavy reliance of exports on a relatively narrow range of products, particularly the "traditional" items, many of which are being produced more competitively by the developing smaller nations. This trend will continue until India diversifies and intensifies its industrial base so as to produce competitive and quality consumer goods. This was hardly possible during the Second and Third Plans when the emphasis was on creating a base of heavy industry.

TRADE TERRITORY

At the time of Independence Britain supplied most of its imports and absorbed its exports. By 1961 the U.S.A. had passed Britain as India's leading trading partner. During the 1960's the nation's trading orbit had widened to include the Communist world and Japan. In 1976 her trading partners were widely dispersed both spatially and in political persuasion, a situation in keeping with her geographical location, non-aligned foreign policy and developmental needs. Tables 10.2 and 10.5 list India's major trading partners for selected years between 1950-51 and 1973-74.

Nearly one-half of India's international trade is contributed by six countries: the U.S.A., Britain, Japan, the Soviet Union, West Germany and Canada. In 1973-74 these nations absorbed about 55 percent of Indian exports and supplied almost 52 percent of her imports. Despite India's widening trading territory, these countries, as the tables indicate, strengthened their share of trade. The U.S.A. retained its leading position, although her primacy was threatened by the U.S.S.R. and Japan after 1970-71. Since the increase in oil prices in 1973, Iran and Saudi Arabia superceded Canada and West Germany in import value. Since a large part of India's imports were comprised of foodgrains, annual fluctuations in harvest affected the relative position of the main suppliers. By 1970-71 internal production had also increased, markedly reducing foodgrain imports and weakening Canada's position as India's major supplier. Meanwhile Japan, the Soviet Union and West Germany had emerged as the major exporters of a diversified group of technological and manufactured items. Competition from these new exporters also led to a progressive and substantial decline in the value of imports from the U.S.A. (from 37.8 percent of total imports in 1965-66 to 16.7 percent in 1973-74).

TABLE 10.5

EXPORT DESTINATIONS BETWEEN 1950 AND 1974

(As Per Cent of Total)

	1950-51	1965-66	1970-71	1971-72	1972-73	1973-74
U.S.A.	19.3	18.2	13.5	16.4	14.0	13.8
U.K.	23.3	17.0	11.1	10.4	8.7	10.4
USSR	0.2	11.5	13.7	13.0	15.5	11.5
Japan	1.7	7.3	13.2	11.3	11.0	14.3
Australia	4.9	2.2	1.6	1.7	1.3	2.0
Sri Lanka	3.3	1.6	2.1	1.3	0.4	0.4
Fed. Rep. of Germany	*	2.2	2.1	2.3	3.1	3.3
Canada	2.3	2.5	1.8	2.4	1.4	1.2
Burma	4.1	0.4	0.9	0.7	0.2	*
Egypt	1.0	3.4	3.7	1.4	1.6	0.6
France	1.5	1.4	1.2	1.3	2.3	2.0
Argentina	1.8	0.5	0.2	0.4	*	0.3
Sudan	0.7	1.0	2.4	3.2	1.0	0.7
Malaysia	1.0	1.6	0.7	0.7	0.5	1.0
Singapore	5.1	*	1.1	1.0	0.9	1.7
Netherlands	1.7	1.0	0.9	0.9	1.8	0.8
Czechoslo- vakia	1.6	2.0	1.9	1.9	2.34	1.7
Kenya	1.1	0.6	0.5	0.5	0.3	0.4
Italy	2.5	1.2	0.9	1.5	2.5	2.7
Nigeria	1.0	0.5	0.6	0.6	0.5	0.4
New Zealand	0.6	0.8	0.3	0.6	0.4	0.5
Bangladesh	*	0.1	0.3	0.2	0.3	1.1
East European Countries	0.2	7.8	9.9	8.6	8.4	7.8

*Data not available

Source: *op. cit.*

Despite fluctuations and decline, the United States has remained a major supplier of foodgrains, a situation which over the years pushed India into a position of heavily unfavorable trade balance and caused a deterioration in foreign exchange reserves. Most of the foreign exchange needed to cover the import costs was made possible by foreign aid extended by the United States to India. Between 1950 and 1970, India received over $9,517 million from the U.S., 20 percent of which was in the form of outright grants, and 33 percent was refundable over long periods partly in rupees and partly in dollars at low interest rates. The United States also sponsored the Export-Import Bank which oversaw these arrangements. PL 480 Title I agreements enabled India to purchase foodgrains. In addition to foodgrains, India imported metals, machinery, transport equipment, fertilizers and dairy goods from the United States. Increased production of foodgrains at home (the level exceeded 120 million metric tons since 1966) and expansion in industrial production (machinery, farm equipment) during the last decade has substantially narrowed the trade balance deficit.

The United Kingdom, West Germany, France, Belgium, Italy and Switzerland were the principle Western European sources of Indian imports. Britain remained the leading supplier of machinery and industrial plants, although after 1965 West Germany became a serious competitor. Imports from West Germany have included machinery, machine tools, electric goods, chemicals, nitrogenous fertilizers and ships. High-cost, sophisticated, manufactured items, machinery and dairy products have been the chief imports from the West European countries. The trade balance has been normally unfavorable to India. Most imports were financed through long-term aid and loans arranged through agencies like Aid India Consortium, of which most of these countries are members. The comparative decline in India's purchases from Western Europe in recent years stemmed from these countries' strict foreign exchange policies and tariff barriers mandated by their Common Market commitments.

A direct consequence of the increased difficulty experienced by India in her trade with the Common Market countries has been her veering toward East European countries to obtain goods, a position in conformity with her stated neutral stance in foreign relations.

Traditionally Anglo-American and the Western European countries have been important consumers of Indian exports. In 1973-74, 15 percent of India's exports were absorbed by the United States and Canada, a decrease of 6.6 percentage points from the 1950-51 level. India's chief exports to these countries were such traditional items like jute, jute fabrics, fruits, cashew kernels and cotton fabrics. During the last decade India increasingly exported semi- or fully-processed items such as engineering goods, handicrafts, cloth and cotton-piece goods, sugar, leather, woollen carpets and silk fabrics to Anglo-America. The Anglo-American market is quality conscious and future expansion of Indian trade would largely depend on improvement in the quality of her exports.

In 1973-74 about 20 percent of Indian exports found a market in the Western European countries, a substantial decrease since 1965-66. Britain alone absorbed 10.4 percent of all exports, while West Germany accounted for 3.3 percent. France, the Netherlands and Italy were the other customers. Major exports to Britain were jute goods, tea, hides and skins, tanned leather, textiles and carpets. Effective in 1960, Britain imposed a 15 percent duty on all imported manufactured goods and restrictions on the import of textiles from India, resulting in dramatic reductions in her share of India's exports: from 23 percent in 1951-52 to 15 percent in 1965-66 to 10.4 percent in 1973-74. Germany imported tea, jute and iron ore. Tobacco and leather goods were the other items exported to the Western European countries. Like the Anglo-American market, the Western European market is quality conscious. India faced stiff competition from Japan and Hong Kong in promoting her goods in Western Europe.

Extension of Trading
Orbit to the Communist World

As a consequence of mounting imports of foodgrains and machinery needed for her developmental plans during the 50's and 60's, India's foreign exchange position rapidly deteriorated and she was driven into virtual dependence on Anglo-America and Western Europe for her international commerce. In response to growing pressures on her foreign exchange reserves, she sought to widen her trade parameters to include the Soviet Union and the East European countries. In international relations she maintained a posture of nonalignment which was conducive to achieving this aim, and since 1959 has entered into several bilateral trade agreements with these countries. This not only helped India to reduce dependence on her traditional export markets and to obtain capital goods, but the new agreements with the Eastern European countries also allowed transactions in rupee payments which helped alleviate strain on her convertible foreign exchange resources.

That India vigorously pursued this trade policy was evident from the unprecendented growth of India's trade with these countries in the years following 1960. In 1951-52 the Eastern European countries and the Soviet Union absorbed less than 1 percent of India's exports. By 1973-74 the figure rose to 19.3 percent. During the same period, their contribution to India's imports increased from 0.6 to 15.4 percent. Markets for her traditional exports (tea, jute, tobacco, cashew kernels, oil cakes) widened, which in turn promoted a greater degree of price stabilization for these items in international markets. East Europe could also absorb her nontraditional exports (leather, hides, cotton fabrics). In turn, she looked increasingly toward these countries for imports of agricultural and other machinery (harvesters, tractors, etc.) payable through more convenient terms and in rupee currency. Analysts of India's trade have often expressed the view that these arrangements have had a constrictive effect on the pricing of Indian exports and the over-valuation of imports from these countries. While conceding this to be true to some extent, the Indian government maintained that her major objectives of acquiring wider markets and more favorable terms of foreign currency payments were largely fulfilled by these bilateral trade arrangements. India's major Eastern European trading partners in 1973-74 were Poland, East Germany, Yugoslavia and Czechoslovakia, followed by Hungary, Romania and Bulgaria. The Soviet Union's share of India's exports was only 0.5 percent in 1951-52, but has shown a consistent increase since, reaching 8.6 percent in 1973-74.

Indian imports from these countries consisted mainly of industrial plants, construction equipment and machinery for irrigation and power projects, oil prospecting and drillng equipment and agricultural machinery. Imports steadily increased during the Second and Third Plans when the requirements of several industrial projects like Bhilai (set up with Soviet aid) had increased. By 1970, the Soviet Union had advanced over $673 million in grants and loans for various projects in India. Imports from other East European countries included metal-cutting machinery, steam boilers, engineering goods, and plants needed in such industries as sugar-refining and cement-making. Imports from most of these countries increased rapidly and significantly after 1960. Among the items which recorded appreciable increases after 1965 were petroleum and petroleum products, fertilizers, chemicals, dyeing materials, and paper products.

Since 1965-66 this region has also occupied an important position among the markets for India's exports. In 1973-74 it consumed approximately one-fifth of India's total exports; the Soviet Union alone was responsible for absorbing 11.5 percent of Indian exports. Exports to these countries increased more rapidly than imports, however, and India has constantly maintained a favorable balance of trade. Exports to the Soviet Union increased more rapidly than to the rest of Eastern Europe, and the U.S.S.R. even replaced the U.S.A. and the United Kingdom as India's leading customer for certain years since 1970. The main items of export to this region are tea, coffee, cashew kernels, vegetable oils, spices, leather goods, jute, manufactured items, textile materials, live animals, fruits, silks, knitted garments, cigarettes and iron ore.

Although India's traditional exports of raw materials continued to form a major part of her exports to these countries, Indian exports to this region have undergone several compositional changes during the last 15 years. Domestic production of small electric and non-electric machinery increased, including the exports of electric fans, refrigerators, canned fruits, electric transformers, electric water heaters and air conditioners to the Soviet Union. Between 1968 and 1970 the Soviet Union also purchased large quantities of Indian steel and steel products, notably some 1 million tons of steel and 4,000 railroad wagons which were manufactured at the Bhilai plant.

TRADE WITH THE REST OF THE WORLD

India's trade with the rest of the world was very small until 1960, but has increased steadily since. Specifically, trade with Japan has increased dramatically in the recent years. In 1972-73 Japan became the leading supplier of Indian imports, surpassing the United States, the United Kingdom and the Soviet Union.

In the Middle East, Iran and Saudi Arabia were the chief sources of Indian imports in 1973-74, accounting for between 2 to 5 percent each. Major imports from this region were petroleum, fruits and fine-quality cotton, and 1966 imports increased substantially in value after 1966 as a result of greater demand for petroleum by a growing industrial sector, particularly in the manufacture of fertilizers. Trade balance with this region has always remained in deficit for India, and received further severe setbacks in 1972 when the OPEC countries increased oil prices.

In Africa, Egypt, Sudan, Uganda, Tanzania, Zaire and Zambia have been the main sources of India's imports. Raw cotton, cloves, wattle bark, sisal and asbestos were the principle imports from these countries.

In Southeast Asia, Thailand, Burma, Malaysia and Singapore have been the major suppliers. In East Asia, Japan is a principle supplier of such items as machinery, yarn and synthetic fiber. As the Indian industrial sector expanded during the 60's, dependence on Japan decreased.

Imports from neighboring countries (Nepal, Burma, Pakistan, Ceylon, Afghanistan) have always been insignificant because these underdeveloped countries largely duplicated India's own production and could not offer machinery or foodgrains, the items India needed. Trade with Pakistan and China, never substantial, came to a virtual standstill during periods of armed conflict in the 60's. Major imports included tires and hides from Ceylon; fruits from Afghanistan; and *ghee* (clarified butter) from Nepal. India's imports from Latin America have remained insignificant. The major trading partners are Brazil and Argentina, the latter as a principle supplier of foodgrains.

As regards exports, the Middle East consumed 7 to 8 percent of export value in 1973-74. Iran, Saudi Arabia, Iraq,

Kuwait, Qatar and Yemen Democratic Republic were the major customers. Electric and engineering goods were the principle items of export accounting for over 25 percent of total export value. Despite competition from Japan and the United States for manufactured goods and Ceylon and Pakistan for traditional goods, the region remained an important customer for Indian textiles, jute, iron and steel, electric machinery (fans, sewing machines), bicycles, tea, fruits, spices, air conditioners, agricultural implements, sugar, tobacco and footwear.

The countries of East Africa normally consume less than 5 percent of India's exports. The main exports are cotton textiles, jute goods, spices, sugar, vegetable oils and light engineering goods. Egypt, Sudan and Libya are the chief customers. Indian exports to this region have been steadily increasing and the Indian government has been striving to push exports to the large potential markets in Africa for the last two decades.

Exports to Latin America are small, and have been declining in value and relative position since the 60's. The principle customer is Argentina. Major exports are tea, spices, and jute manufactures.

In Asia, Japan has been an important customer since 1950 when she absorbed 1.7 percent of India's exports. In 1973-74 she became the largest buyer of Indian goods, absorbing 14.3 percent of her exports. India's principle exports to Japan include raw cotton, iron ore, iron-ore concentrates, iron and steel scrap, manganese, sugar, deflated groundnuts and cashew kernels. Japan's purchases of India's exports increased rapidly in the 60's, and India's adverse balance of trade with Japan became favorable. In 1970-71 the trade balance surplus with Japan amounted to $160 million. Japan's rapidly growing iron and steel industry and economy afforded incentives for Indian iron-ore production.

In Southeast Asia, Burma, Singapore, Thailand and Hong Kong have been the principle customers; their main items of purchase consist of jute goods, iron and steel products, and engineering goods. There appears to be scope for expansion of markets for such materials as electric and engineering goods and inexpensive semi-manufactured items in this region, especially in Thailand and Malaysia.

India's exports to Australia remained relatively small, amounting to less than 2 percent of the total in 1973-74. Scope for expansion undoubtedly exists, especially for exports of jute products, cashew kernels, hides and skins, woollen carpets and vegetables.

India's current policy aims at export diversification and market expansion in the developing countries. Exportable amounts of fairly high quality manufactured items such as electric fans, bicycles, radios, refined textiles, sewing machines, electric transformers and copper sheets are now being produced. Markets for these items exist in several countries of West Africa, East Africa, the Middle East, Southeast Asia and Latin America. Possibilities for limited expansion of her exports of traditional items (tea, jute, spices and cotton) also exist in Australia and New Zealand. Trade with the Soviet Union and East Europe has stabilized in view of the mutually beneficial trade agreements, while future expansion of exports to the quality conscious markets of the Western European countries would appear to depend on tariff considerations. Exports to the United States may continue to decline to some extent as new markets open up.

CITATIONS AND SELECT BIBLIOGRAPHY

Bhagwati, J. N., et al., *Planning for Industrialization and Trade Policies.* New York, 1966.

Dayal, E., "The Changing Patterns of India's International Trade," *Economic Geography.* Vol. 44, 1968, pp. 240-269.

Draft Five Year Plan 1978-83. Government of India, New Delhi, 1979.

Draft Five Year Plan 1974-1979. Vol. II, New Delhi, 1974.

Dutt, A. K., et al., "Dimensions of India's Foreign Trade," *International Geography, 1972.* Vol. 1, Toronto, 1972.

Epstein, T. S., *Economic Development and Social Change in South India.* Manchester, 1962.

India: Reference Annual 1977 and 1978. New Delhi, 1978.

Malenbaum, Wilfred, *Modern India's Economy.* Columbus, 1971.

Mellor, John W., *The New Economics of Growth*. Ithaca, 1976.

Schwartzberg, J. E., (ed.), *A Historical Atlas of South Asia*. Chicago, 1978.

Stein, A., *India and the Soviet Union*. Chicago, 1960.

Times of India Directory and Yearbook, 1978. Bombay, 1978.

INDEX